# FIELD of GLORY RENAISSANCE

Written by Richard Bodley Scott,
Nik Gaukroger and Charles Masefield

OSPREY PUBLISHING

SLITHERINE

# FIELD of GLORY RENAISSANCE

## WARGAMING RULES FOR RENAISSANCE TABLETOP GAMING

Written by Richard Bodley Scott,
Nik Gaukroger and
Charles Masefield

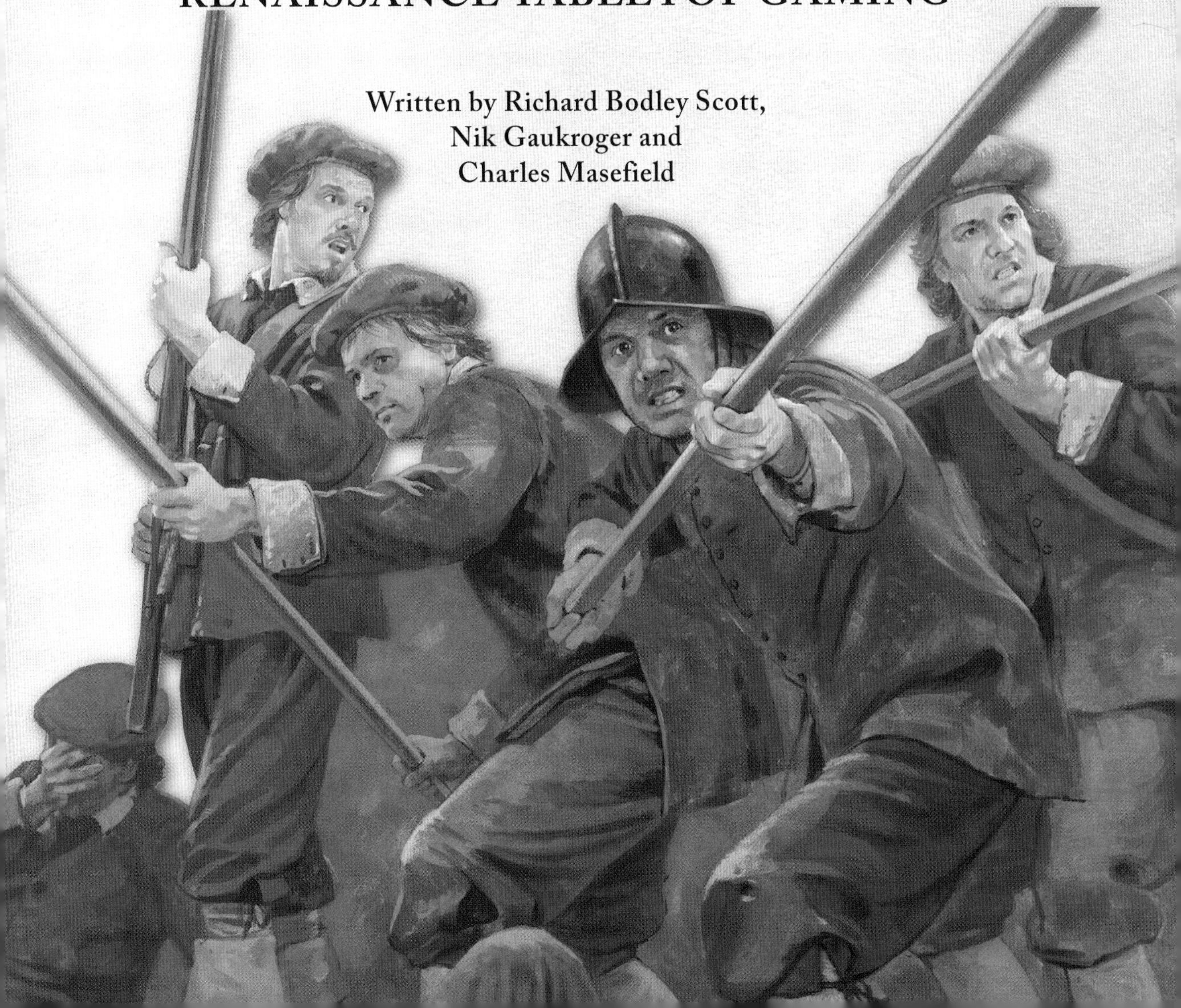

First published in Great Britain in 2010 by Osprey Publishing,
Midland House, West Way, Botley, Oxford, OX2 0PH, UK
44–02 23rd St, Suite 219, Long Island City, NY 11101, USA
E-mail: info@ospreypublishing.com



A CIP catalogue record for this book is available from the British Library

Print ISBN: 978 1 84908 223 5

Cover design and page layout by Myriam Bell Design, France
Index by Timothy Myall and Mike Parkin
Typeset in Adobe Caslon Pro and Snell Roundhand
Cover artwork by Peter Dennis
Photography supplied by Don McHugh, Juergen Mueller, Igwarg, Old Glory UK, Steve Barber Models, Simon Clarke, Richard Ellis, Warlord Games, Legio Heroica & Ancient and Modern Wargame Supplies
Diagrams by Baueda.com

WWW.BAUEDA.COM

Project management by JD McNeil & Osprey Team
Technical management by Iain McNeil
Originated by PDQ Media, Bungay, UK
Printed in China through Worldprint Ltd

10 11 12 13 14 10 9 8 7 6 5 4 3 2 1

FOR A CATALOGUE OF ALL BOOKS PUBLISHED BY OSPREY MILITARY AND AVIATION PLEASE CONTACT:

NORTH AMERICA
Osprey Direct, c/o Random House Distribution Center,
400 Hahn Road, Westminster, MD 21157
E-mail: uscustomerservice@ospreypublishing.com

ALL OTHER REGIONS
Osprey Direct, The Book Service Ltd, Distribution Centre,
Colchester Road, Frating Green, Colchester,
Essex, CO7 7DW
E-mail: customerservice@ospreypublishing.com

FOR DETAILS OF ALL GAMES PUBLISHED BY SLITHERINE SOFTWARE UK LTD
E-mail: info@slitherine.co.uk

Osprey Publishing is supporting the Woodland Trust, the UK's leading woodland conservation charity, by funding the dedication of trees.

www.ospreypublishing.com
www.slitherine.com

# CONTENTS

# INTRODUCTION

*Ottoman assault on the walls of Vienna, 1683, by Peter Dennis © Osprey Publishing Ltd. Taken from Campaign 191:* Vienna 1683.

# RENAISSANCE WARGAMING

*The Renaissance*, the Rebirth, was a time of great change in technology, culture and how nations perceived themselves. Above all it saw rapid advances in the art of warfare! This period, spanning two centuries, saw the descent of the armoured medieval knight into a mere trooper, after a final hurrah best typified by the glory that was the early 16th century French *gendarme*.

It saw the inexorable domination of the battlefield by increasingly disciplined, drilled and uniformed bodies of foot, typified by German *landsknechts*, Spanish *tercios* and the pike and shot of the English Civil War. This domination went hand in hand with increasing sophistication in the use of gunpowder through firearms and battlefield artillery. This was not just a European phenomenon but one that could be observed in different parts of the world, from Panipat in India (1526) to the killing field of Nagashino in Japan (1575) and the streets and temple steps of Tenochtitlan in Mexico (1521).

What makes the Renaissance period so interesting to wargamers is that alongside this revolution in military technology and tactics, weapons and troops that would have been familiar to medieval protagonists still existed and in some areas proliferated – such as the horse archers of the Middle East and the endless steppes beyond.

*French Gendarmes head for the Field of Glory*

*On the Field of Glory*

On top of this, for those with the love of spectacle, a blaze of colour and sheer panache, there are the glorious outfits worn by some of the soldiers of the period. Perhaps the most distinctive are the winged hussars of Poland, who not only dressed with foolhardy indiscretion but were a killer element of the Polish armies of the period. The fanatical *janissaries* of the Ottoman Empire not only reached the apogee of their infamy but also achieved a glorious abandon in their garb – flowing robes and distinctive tall headgear. Some will even find beauty in the clumsy, armoured functionality of Haselrigge's Lobsters of the early days of the English Civil War.

But of course the reason why you'll be using these rules is to command armies and, dare we say, emulate the great commanders of the era. Most will be familiar with the exploits of the famous English Civil War commanders. Have you the discipline and willpower of Oliver Cromwell, infamous (or righteous, depending on your viewpoint) creator of the Ironsides? Or perhaps you wish to emulate Prince Rupert in leading the dashing Cavaliers, accompanied by his dog, Boy. Indeed, be ye for King or Parliament?

Maybe you feel you should look at a broader field to display your skills. The Thirty Years' War and the battles of the brilliant Gustavus Adolphus, the Lion of the North, may therefore beckon. Beware lest you meet his fate leading from the front at Lützen (1632). This war also saw other generals worthy of your attention, for example

The Count of Tilly and Pappenheim. If the generals of Europe are not sufficiently inspiring, then the world really is your oyster. As Suleiman the Magnificent, you can lead the Ottoman hordes on the march to Vienna. You can be Manco Inca, leading the Incas in their doomed fight against the Conquistadors, or Babur the Great in his struggles to establish the Moghul dynasty. You can lead the forces of sixteenth century Japan and, taking your cue from the Daimyos Oda Nobunaga and Tokugawa Ieyasu, combine the cutting power of the *naginata* and *katana* with the firepower of the arquebus (*teppo*)!

However, to achieve the glories of these generals you will have to master the basics of the infantry and cavalry tactics of the time! But beware, in such a time of military innovation and change no tactic or formation is guaranteed to succeed. Do your cavalry charge with cold steel, be that the lance or the sword? Will they adopt the *caracole* and the discharge of pistols at range, or will they hold their fire until the moment before contact or even push the barrel of their pistol under the rim of their foeman's armour before firing? Do you rely on a push of pike to settle the brutal, bloody struggle of the infantry? Or do you embrace new technology, exploiting the firepower provided by the matchlock? Perhaps the mighty Spanish *tercio*, combining the steadiness of large bodies of pikemen with the ranged effect of the arquebus, is the compromise you seek. Perhaps you prefer the more streamlined pike and shot formations pioneered by Maurice of Nassau, or the maximised firepower of later 17th century infantry formations, with only a smattering of pikemen or just bayonets to hold off enemy cavalry. Maybe you should rely on the tried and trusted weapons of the horse archer and light armoured lancer in the armies of the Ottomans, Safavids and Moghuls. The choice is yours!

However, before you decide, perhaps consider the lessons of history and then choose wisely, for these decisions will decide your fate on the **Field of Glory**!

# THE DEVELOPMENT OF EUROPEAN WARFARE IN THE 16TH AND 17TH CENTURIES

*At the beginning* of our period, in 1494, the French King Charles VIII decided to resurrect the old French dynastic claim to the throne of Naples and attempt to conquer an empire in Italy. He thus began the Italian Wars, a futile struggle between France and the Imperialists (Spain and the Holy Roman Empire). This confrontation continued on and off until 1559.

The French army relied for heavy cavalry on fully armoured *gendarmes* – the successors of medieval knights, charging fiercely with lances. Swiss and German mercenaries formed the core of the infantry. They advanced in huge deep blocks of pikemen, armed with pikes up to 6 metres (20 foot) long. Native French infantry were not highly regarded. At the start of the wars the crossbow was still their main missile weapon, gunpowder firearms (arquebuses) not yet having caught on in France. They did, however, have an excellent train of gunpowder artillery. Their Imperialist opponents also relied on massed pikemen, mostly German *landsknechts*. They also had good Spanish and rather less effective Italian infantry. Their armies included substantial numbers of arquebusiers, who proved increasingly effective. Their mounted arm was usually outmatched by the French in numbers and quality.

The massed attack by huge blocks of pikemen had proved very successful for the Swiss in the 15th century, and had been copied as a military system by the *landsknechts* of Germany. However, the early years of the Italian Wars were to reveal its deficiencies. At Cerignola (1503) and Bicocca (1522) the previously invincible Swiss foot were defeated by field fortifications manned by artillery and arquebusiers, with pikemen in support. Suffering severe losses from artillery fire in the approach, the Swiss formations were then subjected to a hail of arquebus shot before finally being repelled by pikemen at the fortifications. At Marignano (1515) the Swiss advance was halted by repeated French cavalry charges, until the Swiss losses from the French artillery became too much to bear and they began to retreat.

As the wars proceeded, both sides, particularly the Spanish, began to experiment with different mixed infantry formations of pike and shot in close cooperation. At first (from 1505) the Spanish fielded mixed units (*colunelas*) of approximately 1,000 pikemen, arquebusiers and sword-and-bucklermen. Later, in the 1530s, they developed the mighty *tercio*, a huge unit of 3,000+ men, forming up with a central block of pikemen, surrounded by arquebusiers, with large clumps of arquebusiers at each corner. Each *tercio* was in effect a mobile fortress that could advance inexorably across the battlefield yet was able to repel attacks from any direction.

Cavalry warfare also developed. While the French and Spanish stuck with the lance as the weapon of choice of their heavy cavalry, the Germans changed over to pistols. These *reiters* (or *schwartzreiters* because of their habit of wearing black armour) became the usual sort of mercenary German horse hired by the various combatants in the wars. They developed the *caracole*, a system whereby a deep formation of pistoleers could deliver a continuous barrage of pistol fire against a stationary target (usually a pike block) – each rank firing in turn then moving off to the rear to reload. Each man carried up to three pistols, two in holsters and one in the right boot.

Soon after the Italian Wars ended in 1559 with the Treaty of Cateau-Cambrésis, France dissolved into anarchy in the Wars of Religion between the Catholics and the Protestants (Huguenots), which lasted from 1562 until 1598. In the second half of these wars, the Huguenots replaced their lance-armed gendarmes with pistol-armed cuirassiers. Unlike the now-traditional German *reiters*, these did not attempt to shoot the enemy at a distance, but saved their pistols for the moment of impact. These tactics proved superior both against lance-armed *gendarmes* and traditional *reiters*. Despite

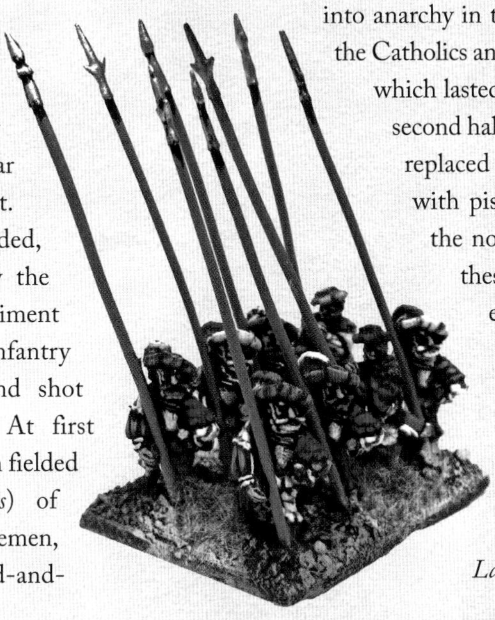

*Landsknecht Pikemen*

this, for three-quarters of a century there continued to be proponents of the lance and the use of pistol or carbine at a distance. Towards the end of the wars, Henri of Navarre (later Henri IV of France) pioneered the use of commanded shot – detached bodies of arquebusiers, placed between the blocks of horse to offset enemy cavalry superiority.

Infantry developments in the later 16th century included a reduction in the proportion of pike to shot, and the gradual replacement of the arquebus with the longer-ranged musket. Despite their advantages, large *tercio*-style units had a major disadvantage. This was that the depth of their formation meant that it was impossible to bring all their firepower to bear frontally. In 1590 Prince Maurice of Nassau became commander-in-chief of the Dutch armies, which had been fighting a war of independence against the Spanish since 1568. He reorganised the army into smaller battalions of 500 to 600 men. These formed up in shallower formations, so were able to bring a much higher proportion of their firepower to bear. This proved a decisive advantage at the Battle of Nieuwpoort (1600).

Over the following decades, Maurice's smaller battalions became the standard organisation of most European armies, though reduced tercios remained in use until the early 1630s, during the Thirty Years' War (1618–1648). Further developments were made by the Swedish army under Gustavus Adolphus, who entered the Thirty Years' War in 1630. Firepower was increased by the

*English Civil War Lobsters*

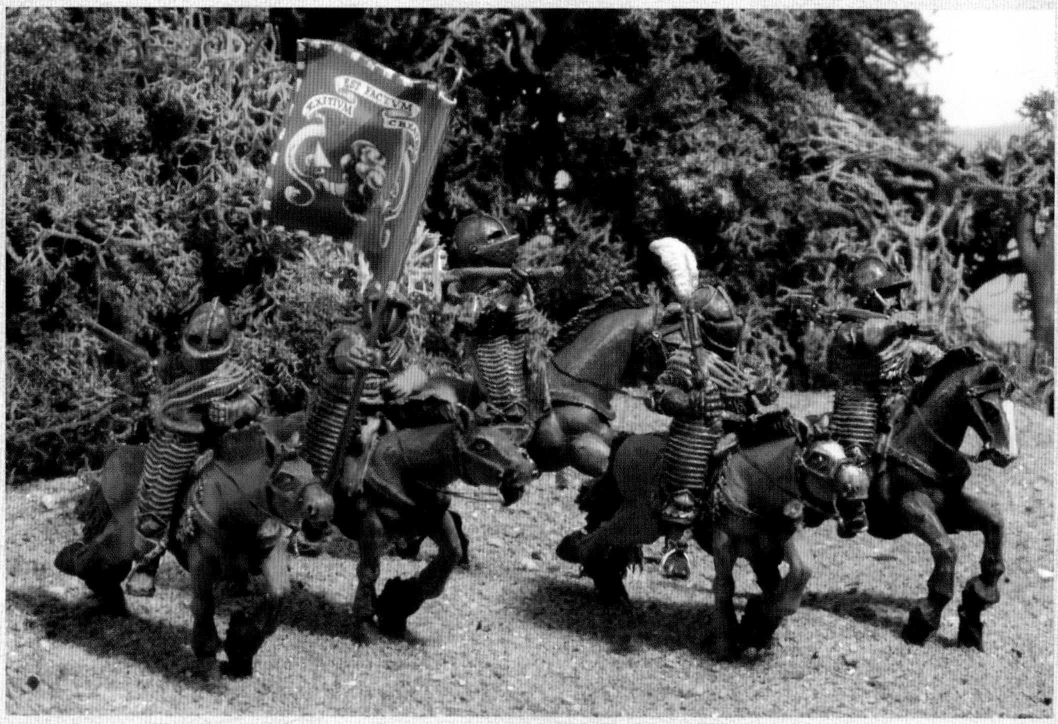

attachment of 12 fast-loading 3-pounder guns to each infantry brigade. Swedish musketeers, normally deployed six ranks deep, were trained not only to fire by counter-march like other European armies, but also, when required, to double the files to form a three deep formation and all fire simultaneously (the famous Swedish salvo), front rank kneeling, second rank crouching and third rank standing. The pikes would then immediately charge the enemy before they could recover from the salvo. However, salvo tactics were replaced by simpler drills after the Swedish army's veterans were nearly wiped out at Nördlingen (1634).

The proportion of shot steadily increased through the 17th century, and pikemen steadily lost their armour – even when it was supplied by the state, the soldiers often discarded it on campaign. In the last quarter of the century, the bayonet started to come into use, giving musketeer-only units better protection against cavalry. However, early bayonets were of the plug type, which fitted into the barrel of the musket, thus preventing it from being fired. Most European armies retained a small proportion of pikemen in each battalion right up until the end of our period, when both pike and plug bayonet were definitively replaced by the socket bayonet. This, though it somewhat hindered reloading, allowed the musket to be fired with the bayonet in place.

Cavalry tactics also developed through the 17th century, with the use of shallower formations, more aggressive charges and a further reduction in armour. By the end of the 17th century, most European cavalry were unarmoured.

These were the developments in continental Europe. On the fringes, and elsewhere in the world, developments were often slower and obsolete systems sometimes persisted. English armies continued to be based on the traditional longbow and bill until late in the 16th century, and only really caught up with European developments during the English Civil War (1642–1651). Ottoman infantry made the transition from bow to firearms, but, lacking pikemen, could not stand against cavalry in the open. Their cavalry persevered with the bow until the 17th century. Nevertheless, the Turks remained a serious threat to Christian Europe.

*Ottoman Sultan leads the charge*

The period covered by these rules was one of continuous military evolution, beginning with the medieval forces of the start of the Italian Wars, and ending with the stabilisation of the Western military system into the triad of horse, bayonet-armed musketeers and artillery, which then persisted, largely unchanged, for over a century.

# INTRODUCTION TO THE RULES

*This book is designed* both to explain the game and be a reference guide when playing. To make the rules easier to follow we have added examples, detailed descriptions and explanations of unusual cases in an appendix at the end of the book.

Throughout the rules ***bold italicized*** text indicates that there is more information to be found later. You will also find numerous diagrams that will assist your understanding together with a number of useful **TIPS** or hints to assist your game-play.

# DESIGN PHILOSOPHY

*This section explains* the rationale behind the different terms used and outlines the design concepts and approach that we have adopted.

The design team are passionate about history. We are dedicated to historical realism, but, without compromising on that, our aim is to create a game that is easy and fun to play. We have used the same basic mechanisms that will be familiar to players of the original *Field of Glory* rules for ancient and medieval warfare, but have given them new twists to bring out the unique flavour of Renaissance warfare.

In *Field of Glory Renaissance*, you take the role of the army commander and his senior generals, giving the rules a top-down style and feel. Historical accounts describe battles as a series of events and phases rather than unremitting action. We have tried to reflect this ebb and flow of events rather than get locked into a fixed timeframe.

Armies of this era had a common theme, whatever their organisation at the micro level.

*French Regiment La Mark prepare to volley*

*The Battle of Roundway Down*

Each had a commander-in-chief and a few senior commanders who would usually take charge of a wing or the centre. Subordinate to these was another layer of commanders who would control the various tactical "formations" which often consisted of a number of "units" or regiments brigaded together. In *Field of Glory Renaissance* we call these formations ***battle groups***.

In *Field of Glory Renaissance*, you will take command of an army consisting of typically 10–15 battle groups led by the C-in-C and his senior commanders. The game has been designed to ensure that, just as in reality, the commanders (you) are fully occupied from the outset. Your objective is to outmanoeuvre the enemy army and concentrate your forces at the critical points in the battle. If executed well this should destroy the enemy's will to fight and deal a devastating blow to the morale of their commanders (your opponent).

Our companion army list books contain details and organisation for a wealth of accurately researched armies, ensuring that your battles will have a realistic and historical feel. In reality, some of the armies would be relatively small, consisting of as few as several hundred men, whilst others would number in the tens of thousands. *Field of Glory Renaissance* allows you to see what might have been had these forces been equally matched, as each army can be scaled up or down whilst retaining its individual mix and balance of troops to allow "what if" encounters.

This rule set is built on the popular *Field of Glory* rules for ancient and medieval warfare and retains their concepts, structure and design philosophy. These have enabled us to model the formations and manner of fighting unique to this period with greater accuracy than before. Gamers who have played *Field of Glory* will find much that is familiar, but the new features we have introduced give *Field of Glory Renaissance* a period flavour all its own.

*Samurai on the killing field*

Throughout we have attempted to adhere to the style and layout of *Field of Glory* as far as possible, so that players familiar with that ruleset will readily adapt to this period. Occasionally we have taken the opportunity to clarify some areas.

Our most important objective is to make the game fun to play whilst retaining a strong historical feel. If we achieve this we have met our goal. So whether you fancy being Gustavus Adolphus or Henri IV it's up to you, happy gaming and may your dice roll high!

# THE BASICS

*Night attack on the Honmachi bridge, 1615, by Richard Hook © Osprey Publishing Ltd. Taken from Campaign 170:* Osaka 1615.

# WHAT YOU NEED TO PLAY *FIELD OF GLORY RENAISSANCE*

- An opponent is ideal: games can be played with one player on each side, solo, or with multiple players on each side.
- A tabletop/board – the game is designed to be played on an area of 180cm x 120cm (or 72" x 48"), but smaller or larger spaces can be used.
- Two opposing armies of miniature figurines suitably painted and mounted on bases of the same width. These figurines can be of any scale. Those which work best are 15mm or 25/28mm tall. These can be easily obtained either painted or unpainted from a wide range of suppliers.
- Terrain for your battlefield, such as hills, rivers, marshes and so on. These are all commercially available and described in more detail later. In particular we recommend the range of terrain specially designed for *Field of Glory* from Miniature Worldmaker.
- Dice: normal cubes numbered 1 to 6 (d6). Ideally, each player should have about 10 of one colour and 5 each of two other colours.
- A means of measuring distances: a tape measure or a set of measuring sticks marked off in inches or mm.

### TIP!

Which figure scale you choose is unimportant in *Field of Glory Renaissance* as the rules are designed to suit any scale. Try to find out what other local players are using and plan accordingly.

# MEASUREMENT

*Measurement in Field of Glory Renaissance* is by **movement units**. One movement unit, or MU for short, is usually either 25mm or 1 inch, as agreed by the players or decided by tournament organisers, regardless of figure scale. Alternatively, if using 25/28mm or larger figures on a table larger than 6 x 4 feet, a scale of 1MU = 1.5 inches or 40mm may be preferred.

*The capture of the fortress of Pusan, 1592, by Peter Dennis © Osprey Publishing Ltd. Taken from Campaign 198:* The Samurai Invasion of Korea 1592–98.

# BASES

*A base is a rectangle* on which model figurines are mounted. The number and type of figurines gives a visual representation of the troops involved. Each base represents a certain number of actual men, and this is explained in further detail in ***Appendix 1***. Our companion army list books specify the number and type of bases which make up a battle group. These are the playing pieces in *Field of Glory Renaissance*.

All the figurines used in *Field of Glory Renaissance* are mounted on bases of the same width. When using 15mm or smaller scale figures, a base is 40mm wide, for 25/28mm figures it is 60mm wide. The depth of bases and the number of figures mounted on each base are listed in *Appendix 1*.

*French Royal Hussars*

# TROOPS

*Mercenaries at the siege of Haddington, 1548–49, by Graham Turner © Osprey Publishing Ltd. Taken from Elite 167:* Scottish Renaissance Armies 1513–1550.

*Field of Glory Renaissance* features a wide range of different troop types. These reflect the huge variety that existed in armies of the period. Bases of different troop types are represented in a number of ways. Fast moving, lightly-equipped troops will usually have fewer figurines on a base than slower moving soldiers who fight in close order.

The photograph below shows several different types of troops. These are defined by four parameters: ***troop type***, ***armour***, ***quality*** (skill) and ***combat capabilities***. It is this mix of parameters that allows *Field of Glory Renaissance* accurately to portray the wide variety of troop types that existed in the early modern world.

# TROOP TYPE

*Troop types are divided* into three categories, and then several sub-categories, according to how they moved and fought on the battlefield. Different troop types are based in different ways. The two main categories are foot and mounted, and they are sub-divided as follows (see *Appendix 1* for further information).

## FOOT

They can be: ***determined foot***, ***heavy foot***, ***medium foot***, ***warriors***, ***light foot***, ***dragoons***, ***mob***, ***battle wagons***, ***light artillery***, ***medium artillery*** or ***heavy artillery***.

*Armoured Ottoman Sipahi*

## MOUNTED

They can be: ***gendarmes***, ***cavaliers***, ***horse***, ***determined horse***, ***light horse***, ***cavalry*** or ***camelry***.

## ELEPHANTS

They can only be elephants.

## ARMOUR

Some troops benefit from wearing armour. For others, factors such as their mounts or vehicles make these less relevant. There are four levels of armour used in *Field of Glory Renaissance*. These are, in order of decreasing protection: ***fully armoured***, ***heavily armoured***, ***armoured*** and ***unarmoured***.

All troop types have one of these armour qualifiers, except for the following: battle wagons, elephants, and artillery of all types.

## QUALITY

Some troops were better fighters because of their training, experience, morale and/or weapon skills. There are four categories of troop quality: ***elite***, ***superior***, ***average*** and ***poor***.

Only exceptional troops with the highest morale are classified as elite. Some of history's finest armies contained a high proportion of superior combatants, whilst others consisted of average or poorer quality troops. Generally, an army of inexperienced troops will be weaker than a veteran force. To compensate for this, in *Field of Glory Renaissance*, it costs fewer points per base (see our companion army list books for more information on troop point values) so the inexperienced army can be much larger.

## TIP!

A small force of high quality troops applied at the right time and place can often shatter poorer quality forces, leading to a breakthrough that can be exploited.

## CAPABILITIES

The weapons and tactical abilities that influence combat effectiveness are called **capabilities.** The names of some capabilities are well known terms, others less so and have been created to give memorable names to particular behaviour or weapons training. In *Field of Glory Renaissance* it is not enough simply to possess a weapon to be regarded as capable: troops are only classified as having a capability if use of such a weapon and fighting technique was a major part of their tactical methods or doctrine, e.g. Ottoman cavalry often carried a lance but their main fighting method was as mounted bowmen armed with sabre or mace, and it is therefore only these latter capabilities that we recognise.

The capabilities are: *light artillery, medium artillery, heavy artillery, musket, musket*, salvo, arquebus, carbine, bombs, pistol, bow, bow*, crossbow, sling, javelins, heavy lancers, light lancers, impact mounted, impact foot, pike, heavy weapon, spearmen, bayonet, light spear and swordsmen.*

## IN SUMMARY

The four qualifiers **quality, armour, type,** and **capabilities** are used together to describe a base of figurines. Although at first glance this appears a little complicated, you will soon get used to it and our companion army list books describe the troop types in detail. A little knowledge of history can help e.g. Hastily raised raw troops with little training or esprit de corps (poor quality), may be supplied with

## TIP!

Pick an army that interests and enthuses you. You will find this much easier to paint and there are no super armies in *Field of Glory Renaissance*. Each has its strengths and weaknesses: e.g. an early English Civil War Royalist army consists mainly of cavalry (cavaliers with impact pistol and melee sword or pistol capability) and pike and shot foot (1/3 heavy foot with pike and 2/3 medium foot with musket*). The cavalry, usually deployed on the wings, are especially aggressive, capable of sweeping away less determined opponents by their fierce onslaught but hard to rally after pursuit; while the foot are solid but lacking in firepower against most contemporaries. Compare this with an early Swiss army with lots of the most feared soldiers of their day (elite or superior armoured determined foot with pike or halberd). They are highly manoeuvrable, aiming to disconcert opponents by advancing at speed and attacking with overwhelming force. Both quite different armies with completely contrasting fighting doctrines, both have the potential to win if used well. The choice is yours.

*Milanese Elmeti arrayed for battle*

obsolete weapons (arquebus capability) or short of firearms (musket* capability) and lacking in armour (unarmoured). Contrast these with Cromwell's Ironsides who are well disciplined, of high morale and accustomed to winning (superior armoured determined horse); they are equipped with pistols used for shooting at point blank range (impact and melee pistol capability). The relative strengths and weaknesses of each troop type will become easier to understand and master as you play.

# TROOP FUNCTION CATEGORIES

*The troop types* noted above are grouped into the following categories to describe the function they performed on the battlefield. These terms are used throughout the rules to avoid the need for repetition:

### LIGHT TROOPS:

- battle groups entirely of light foot
- light horse
- dragoons

## BATTLE TROOPS:

- any troops other than light troops
- mixed battle groups partly of light foot

## SHOCK TROOPS:

- any battle group including mounted with heavy lancers, light lancers or impact mounted capability, except light horse
- gendarmes
- cavaliers
- determined horse
- any battle group including foot with impact foot or salvo capability
- *keils* (see ***Battle Group Formations*** below)

## SHOT

- any foot with arquebus, musket, musket* or salvo capability

### TIP!

Knowing how to utilise your troops the way a commander of this era would do is a great benefit when playing – e.g. use your light troops to chase off enemy light troops or soften up enemy battle troops. They are not close combat troops.

# CAMPS

*Each army has* a **supply camp**. If an enemy battle group ends a move with any part of its front edge in contact with an unfortified supply camp, the camp is immediately sacked and lost.

*German nobility in the safety of their Camp*

A fortified supply camp is assumed to be defended by camp guards, who must be defeated before the camp can be sacked.

(See ***Sacking Camps*** in the ***Melee Phase*** section.)

## TIP!

Place your camp somewhere relatively safe and protect it. Armies who lost their supply camp were generally in serious trouble. In *Field of Glory Renaissance* this will weaken your army, possibly contributing to your defeat.

*Bavarians counter-attack*

# BATTLE GROUPS

*Attack of the Strathbogie Regiment, 1645, by Gerry Embleton © Osprey Publishing Ltd. Taken from Campaign 123:* Auldearn 1645.

*Now that you understand* bases and troop types, we will explain how these are grouped together into battle groups.

A typical army has ten to fifteen battle groups. Each battle group consists of from two to sixteen bases of figurines. The arrangement of the bases in a battle group can change, but they always move together as a group. The bases of a battle group cannot be separated, except where this is specifically allowed by the rules.

Each battle group is assumed to comprise one or more individual regiments or tribal contingents under the command of a junior commander, who is not represented in the game.

All of the bases of a battle group must be of the same quality. Similarly, all troops in the battle group with the same troop type and combat capabilities must be of the same armour class. Where an army list in our companion army list books permits a choice of quality class or armour, this allows battle groups to differ from each other. It does not override the above rules for each battle group.

Each battle group must initially have an **even number of bases,** unless specified otherwise by our companion army list books. The army's supply camp is not a battle group.

# BATTLE GROUP FORMATIONS

*In general, troops must* be in an approximately **rectangular formation** with all bases facing in the same direction, in edge and corner contact with each other. In an unmixed battle group, only the rearmost rank is allowed to have fewer bases (subject to the exceptions specified below). So, for example, a battle group of 8 bases could be deployed 1 wide and 8 deep, 2 wide and 4 deep, 3 wide with only 2 bases in the third rank, 4 wide and 2 deep and so on.

Subject to the exceptions specified below, mixed battle groups must have the bases of each troop type in rectangular formations (and not intermingled) with all bases facing in the same direction and with only the rearmost rank of each rectangle allowed to have fewer bases; and each rectangle of the same troop type within a battle group must have the same number of bases as far as possible.

The rearmost rank of a battle group or rectangle within a mixed battle group can have any number of bases provided these are fewer or equal in number to the other ranks.

Many of the infantry formations of this period included a mix of pikemen and men bearing firearms. Early on the pikemen formed the greater proportion of the whole and were regarded as the dominant force on the battlefield; the missile troops were intended to harass the enemy and retire on the pikemen if threatened. As time went on, and firepower techniques improved, the proportion of shot to pike increased; but pikemen remained important to protect the shot against cavalry until the widespread adoption of the socket bayonet at the end of our period rendered the pikeman substantially obsolete.

# KEILS

*In the early part of* the period, the main close-fighting infantry formations consisted of deep formations of pikemen (often including integral halberdiers and/or swordsmen).

To count as a "keil" for the purpose of the rules, a battle group must include at least two files each including at least 4 bases. At least 2 of these 4 bases must have pike capability, and the rest either pike, heavy weapon or swordsmen capability.

Some later deep pike formations also had shot wings. These only count as keils if they do not qualify as tercios.

*Swiss keil prepares to attack*

# TERCIOS

*Circa 1534, the Spanish* reorganised their infantry into tercios. The theoretical strength of a tercio exceeded 3,000 men. These formidable bodies were intended to act like human fortresses: combining a central core of pikemen with arquebusiers at the four corners (horns) giving all-round fire protection. We term such formations "early tercios".

Although the official strength was 3,000+, a tercio was as much an administrative body as a fighting unit, and the full strength was not always deployed for battle. Alternative flatter and/or narrower formations were used when fewer soldiers were fielded. By the early 17th century smaller, shallower, formations without "horns" were the normal deployment. We term such formations "later tercios". Additionally some very large pike and shot formations lacking horns, such as those used by late 16th century Germans, are treated as later tercios.

Battle groups only count as early or later tercios if so specified in their army list in our companion army list books. Note that even some Spanish units historically termed tercios do not qualify as early or later tercios for the purpose of the rules – some earlier ones had too high a ratio of pike to shot (so are treated as keils) and later in the period, though still called tercios, they were much smaller and fought in much the same way as contemporary Dutch-style pike and shot units.

EXAMPLES OF TERCIOS

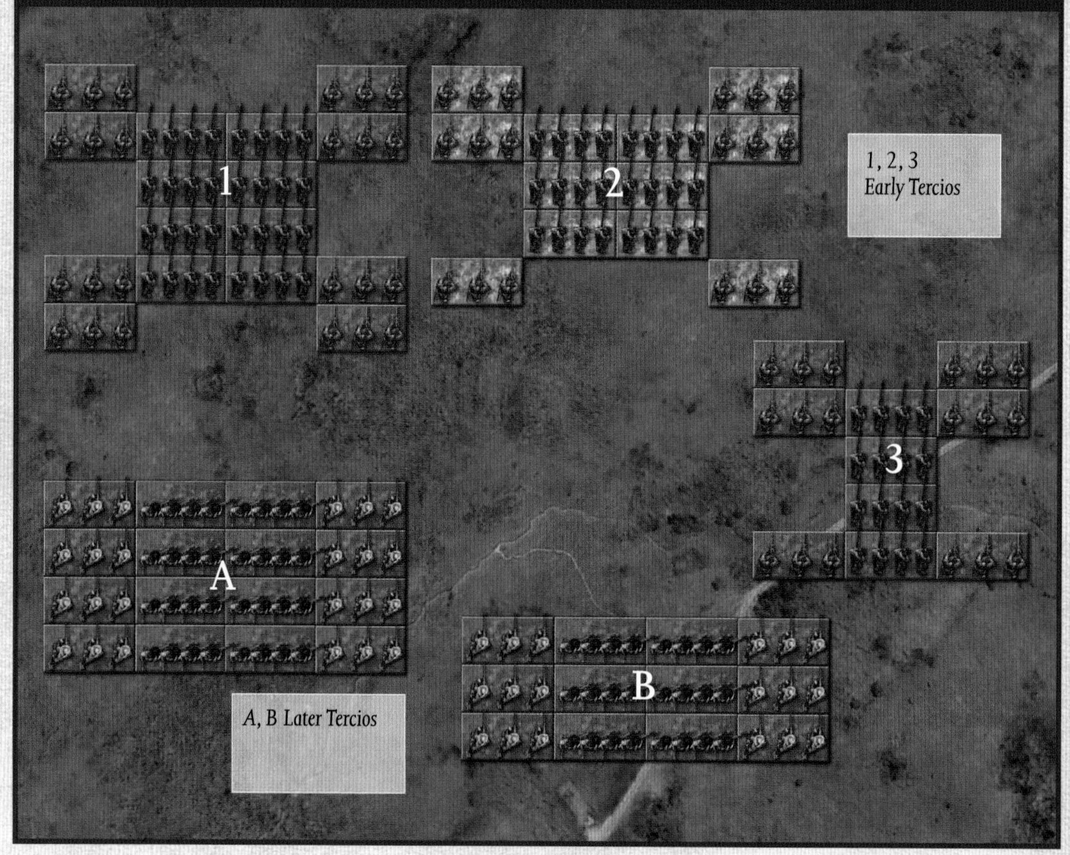


Diagram 1 shows examples of some tercio formations.

Early tercios must comply as far as possible with all of the following:

- Pike bases must be positioned together in 1 or 2 files, 3-4 ranks deep.
- The shot must be positioned in four horns, each consisting of 1 or 2 shot bases. The

front base of each front shot horn is placed in rear corner contact with the front corner of the front base of the adjacent pike file. The front base of each rear shot horn is placed four base depths behind the front of the front shot horn.
- Shot bases cannot normally be in the same file as pike bases and vice versa.
- All bases must be facing the same direction, and (apart from shot bases in corner to corner contact with pike bases) in edge and corner contact with another base of the battle group.

Later tercios must comply as far as possible with all of the following:

- Pike bases must be positioned together in 1 or 2 files, 2–4 ranks deep.
- Half the shot bases must be positioned in single file on one flank of the pike bases and the other shot bases in single file on the other flank of the pike bases.
- Shot bases cannot normally be in the same file as pike bases and vice versa.
- All bases must be facing the same direction and in edge and corner contact with another base of the battle group.

**EXAMPLES OF TERCIOS WHICH HAVE SUFFERED CASUALTIES**

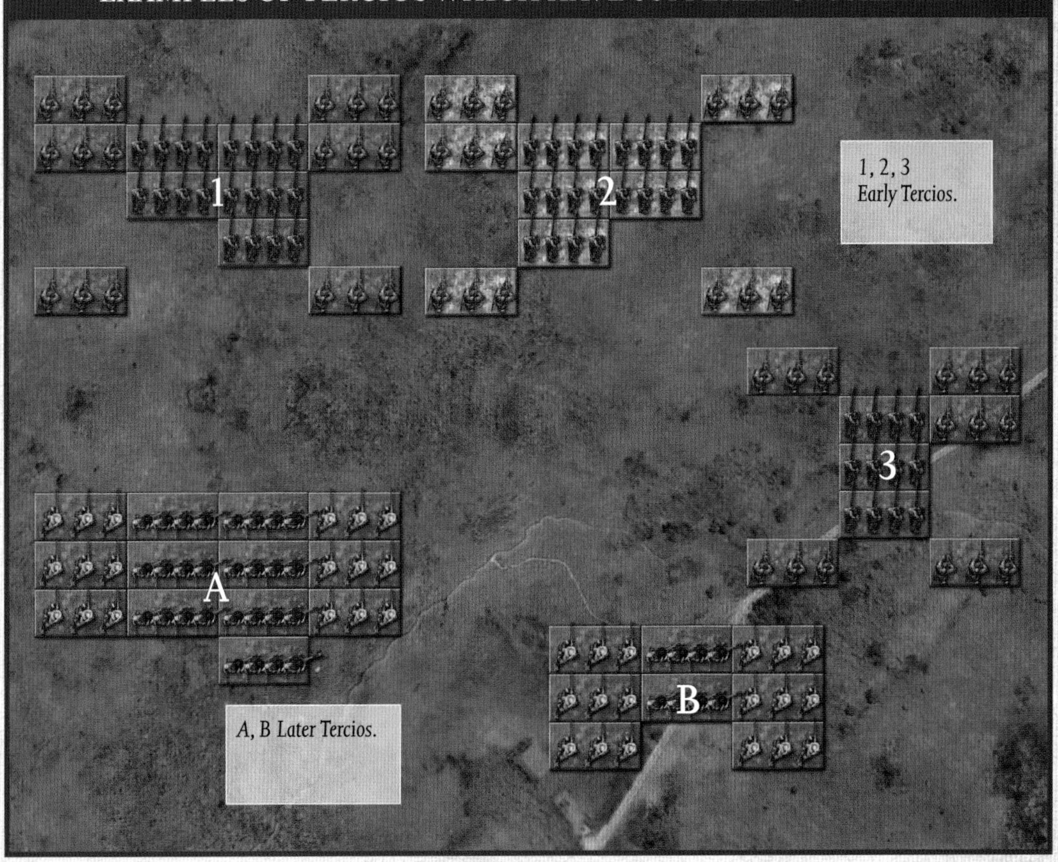

Bases lost as casualties may require some of the pike or shot files to have an uneven number of ranks. All bases must be in edge or corner contact with another base of the battle group except that early tercio shot always remain in the appropriate horn positions relative to the pike even though this will mean bases will be separated.

> **EXAMPLE:**
>
> The top left hand early tercio, which initially comprised 8 pike and 8 shot bases, has lost 3 pike and 2 shot bases as casualties. This leaves it with 1 file of 2 pike bases and 1 of 3, and 4 horns of shot, two of which only have 1 base.

If a tercio which started with two files of pike is reduced to 4 pike bases or fewer, the player can choose to keep 2 shallow files of pike or contract to 1 deeper file and adjust the horn positions accordingly. This can only be performed at the time a pike base is lost, and does not require a "contraction" or "formation change" (see the *General Movement* section). It cannot be performed if it removes the tercio from an enemy restricted area. Subject to that, the tercio's owner decides which front corner shifts.

If an early tercio ceases to have a shot base in each of the 4 horn positions at any time:

- It immediately assumes a formation that would be legal for a later tercio (bases are shifted by the minimum necessary to achieve this). This is automatic and does not require a "formation change".
- It functions thereafter for the remainder of the game as a later tercio. However, if it was initially deployed as a ***grand battle group*** (see *glossary*), it still counts as such if BROKEN, routed off table or destroyed.

Note: it was usual for tercios to have some shot deployed in front of the central pike block but these are not represented by separate bases. In 6mm or smaller scales the front rank pike bases could include a rank or two of shot in front of the pikemen figurines to represent these. Similarly, tercio formations would usually have musketeers who would initially deploy on each face of the core of pikemen.

> **EXAMPLE:**
>
> An early tercio with 6 bases of pike and 6 bases of shot was initially deployed with 2 shot bases in each of the front horns and 1 shot base in each of the rear shot horns. When it loses a shot base, the player can choose whether to replace the lost base from one of the rear horns, in which case frontal firepower will be maintained but the battle group will immediately become a later tercio as above, or leave one of the front shot horns with only 1 base, so as to retain the benefits of an early tercio while losing some frontal firepower.

# OTHER PIKE AND SHOT FORMATIONS

*Pike and shot battle groups* which are not tercios must comply as far as possible with the following:

- The pike bases must be together in a single rectangle in edge contact with one another, at least 2 ranks deep if there is more than one pike base.
- Later battle groups starting with only 1 pike base and 5 shot bases must have the pike base in the centre (if possible) of the rearmost rank.
- Other battle groups must have their shot bases as equally divided as possible between two single files, one on either side of the pike rectangle. Exception – if the battle group includes no more than 2 shot bases, these can be deployed in one single file on either side of the pike rectangle.
- With the exception of Swedish brigades (see below) the front edge of all files must be level.
- Pike and shot bases cannot be in the same file.

Infantry specified by our companion army list books as using the Gustavan **Swedish brigade formation** have a file of 2 pike bases flanked by a file of 2 shot bases on each side and an extra pike base in front of the front rank pike base in **point position** so that the formation shape simulates a flattened arrowhead. Except as specified below, the formation is maintained while the battle group has at least 2 pike bases, with no pike base in the 3rd rank if necessary. The pike base in point position is ignored for all purposes when measuring distances to and from the battle group, and for line of sight. The pike file is shifted back level with the shot files if it obstructs movement (of its own or other battle groups) in any way, or when the battle group is in close combat or defending field fortifications, an obstacle or the edge of a terrain feature, or providing rear support to artillery. In such cases the battle group still receives the normal benefits of Swedish brigade formation.

**PIKE AND SHOT FORMATIONS**

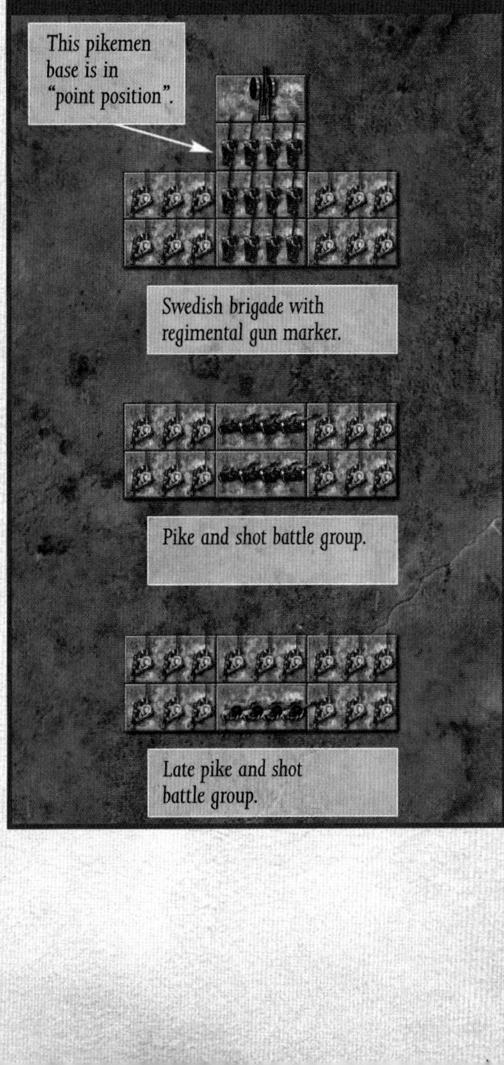

# OTHER MIXED FORMATIONS

*Unless specified otherwise* in our companion army list books, battle groups having a mix of bases with missile capability and bases with close combat capability are subject to the same constraints as pike and shot battle groups. Treat the close combat capability bases as if pike bases and the other bases as if shot bases.

Battle groups having a mix of pike and bases with swordsmen or heavy weapon capability, with or without shot bases, can have files of pike (which must always be the centre files, if more than 2); and files of other troop types which may have a different number of ranks. Such battle groups that include shot must adhere to the formation rules that apply to pike and shot units. Heavy weapon or swordsmen bases can be in a file with pike or shot. As per the normal rules for replacing front rank base losses (see the ***Battle Group Deterioration*** section), base losses amongst the pike can be replaced from the rear ranks of pike.

**PIKE AND HALBERD AND EARLY SPANISH FORMATIONS**

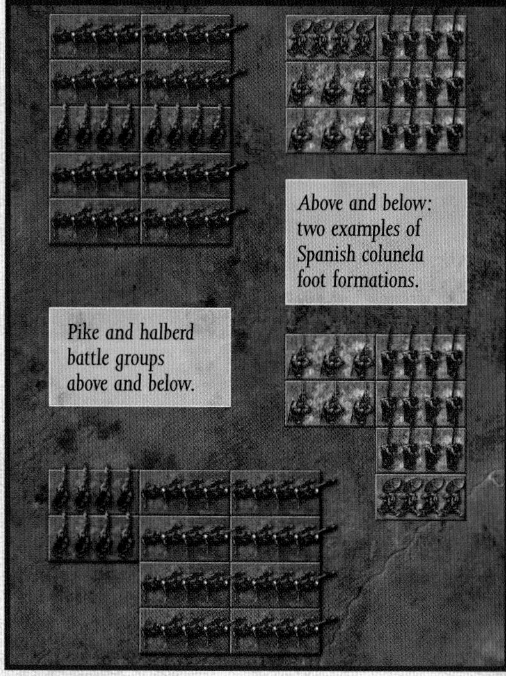


# EXCEPTIONS

*There are four exceptions* to the general rules for permitted formations set out above:

1 ***Columns*** – subject to the exception below, any battle group can form a one base wide column of march which must be "kinked" at points where it has wheeled (e.g. to follow a road) until the whole column has passed that point. Exception: Any battle group which could never expand into a legal formation from a one base wide column in one move cannot be deployed in or form a column during the game.

2 A battle group that is, or has been, ***fighting enemy in two directions*** may have bases facing in different directions until it reforms.

3 A compulsory move specified by the rules or one ending in contact can temporarily force a battle group out of formation until it reforms.

4 Some battle groups can form *square*, which results in bases facing outwards.

# BATTLE GROUP QUALITY – QUALITY RE-ROLLS

*The effect of the quality* difference of troop types is determined by re-rolling dice. Where a section of the rules states 'quality re-rolls apply' the following rules are used:

- Elite troops can re-roll 1's and 2's.
- Superior troops can re-roll 1's.
- Poor troops must re-roll 6's.
- A dice is only re-rolled once.

A commander fighting in the front rank of a battle group in close combat allows the close combat 'to hit' dice (but not any other dice rolls) of that battle group to be one re-roll level higher: Elite troops re-roll 1's, 2's and 3's; superior 1's and 2's; average '1's and poor troops need not re-roll their 6's.

For any re-roll of 1's, 2's and 3's the re-rolled dice is never taken as less than the original roll. This is rare but possible, e.g. an elite battle group rolling two 2's for a score of four gets two re-rolls. If these come up say 6 and 1, the score is counted as eight, 6 and 2. The re-rolled 2 cannot go down to a 1.

### TIP!

Make good use of your quality troops. You will not win battles by relying entirely on your weaker troops. Choose carefully whether to put a commander into combat to inspire the troops to fight harder. Once committed to a close combat he is there to the finish and risks being lost. The loss of command and control could be catastrophic.

# REGIMENTAL GUNS

*Battalion or regimental guns* significantly increased the firepower of units to which they were attached in this period. Where a battle group has regimental gun capability, when shooting, or fighting in the impact phase, it receives one extra combat dice. Such battle groups are identified by having a single regimental gun marker, normally positioned immediately in front of the centre front rank base.

Regimental gun markers do not count as bases, but must have appropriate models fixed to them. They are moved out of the way if they would obstruct movement (of their own or other battle groups) or their battle group is in close combat to its front, or defending field fortifications or an obstacle, or providing rear support to artillery. In such cases they still count as if in their normal position. They are ignored for all purposes when measuring

*Regimental guns positioned to the fore*

distances to and from the battle group, and for line of sight. They are not counted for purposes of HPxB (see ***glossary***) or Autobreak (see the ***Battle Group Deterioration*** section). Any rules applying to "artillery" do not apply to regimental guns.

Regimental guns are lost if their battle group breaks. Their marker is permanently removed from play.

# BATTLE GROUP COHESION LEVELS

*All battle groups begin* the game in good order – we refer to this as *steady*. As they suffer battle damage their current willingness and effectiveness in battle is reduced, resulting in changes to their *cohesion level*. These changes can occur gradually or suddenly and represent a mixture of morale effects and loss of formation.

There are four levels of cohesion:

- *Steady*: the battle group is in good order and ready to fight
- *Disrupted*: reduced in effectiveness, but still in the fight (DISR)
- *Fragmented*: in a critical state, unable to fight effectively (FRAG or FRG)
- *Broken*: no longer able to fight, fleeing, or about to flee

Cohesion states are usually indicated by appropriate counters. These can be simple coloured counters or more elaborate ones depicting casualties in 2- or 3-D. When a battle group is broken, its bases are turned around and it will then flee at the time specified in the turn sequence.

### TIP!

Battle group cohesion is an accurate indicator of how the battle is going. To be victorious in *Field of Glory Renaissance*, it is necessary to break the opposing army's will to fight on, by forcing their battle groups down the cohesion "ladder" until they break. When enough of them become fragmented or broken, the enemy army will collapse and rout.

# BATTLE GROUP DISORDER

*Bases of a battle group* positioned in certain types of ***terrain*** can be disordered, making them function less effectively, especially if they are of a type that depends on keeping formation to be fully effective. E.g. a block of pike relies on keeping close order and is therefore badly affected by anything other than open terrain, whilst light foot never suffer such problems as their loose formation permits them to operate effectively in almost any type of terrain. Disordered or Severely Disordered bases are not STEADY.

Terrain can also affect movement distances – see the ***General Movement Rules*** section.

Individual bases that are in more than one type of terrain are affected by the terrain that reduces their movement most or causes them the most disorder.

Only bases that are at least partially in the terrain are affected. For example, if a battle group has 8 bases of Landsknecht pike, 4 fully in open terrain and 4 in a forest, only the 4 in the forest are affected (severely disordered) by terrain for

*Disordered troops fight through village*

combat purposes. However, movement distance will be affected for the entire battle group, as will complex move tests (see the ***General Movement Rules*** section) and cohesion tests (see the ***Battle Group Deterioration*** section).

If the battle group has mixed troop types, only those bases which are in the terrain and of a type affected by the terrain are disordered for combat purposes. The battle group will only count as disordered or severely disordered for complex move tests and cohesion tests if any bases of a type affected by the terrain are in the terrain. However, it will have its movement distance reduced to the speed that its slowest type would have in the terrain even if there are no bases of that type in the terrain. For Example: A pike and shot battle group of 2 heavy foot pike flanked on each side by 2 medium foot shot has 2 of the shot bases only in an enclosed field and the other bases are entirely in open ground. No part of the battle group is disordered because medium foot are not disordered by rough going. This battle group does not count as disordered for complex move tests. If the pike bases were also in the field, the pike would be disordered for combat purposes but the shot would not. However, the whole battle group would count as disordered when taking complex move tests. In both cases, the battle group's move distance would be reduced to 2 MUs – the heavy foot move in rough terrain – even though in the first case no heavy foot bases are in the terrain.

Good order recovers automatically when a base leaves the terrain that caused the disorder.

**ROYALIST CAVALIERS AND FOOT STRADDLING ROUGH TERRAIN**

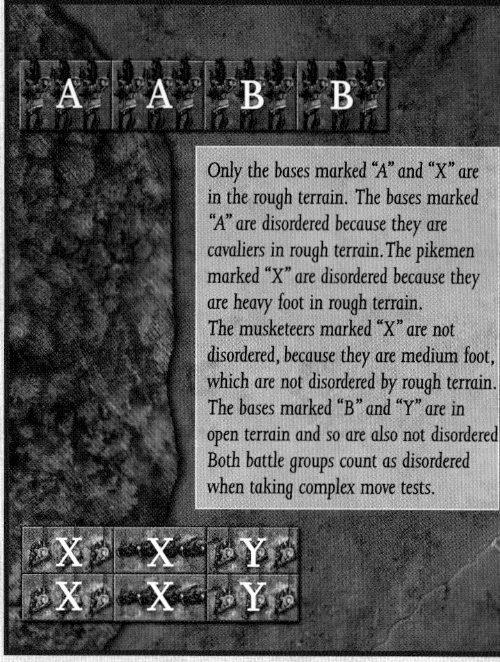


Only the bases marked "A" and "X" are in the rough terrain. The bases marked "A" are disordered because they are cavaliers in rough terrain. The pikemen marked "X" are disordered because they are heavy foot in rough terrain.
The musketeers marked "X" are not disordered, because they are medium foot, which are not disordered by rough terrain.
The bases marked "B" and "Y" are in open terrain and so are also not disordered.
Both battle groups count as disordered when taking complex move tests.

## TIP!

Before playing a game study the troop types that are available to the enemy (see the companion army list books). Try to place or arrange terrain that will create a tactical advantage for your army. E.g. If you have a lot of mounted troops you need open spaces; if you have lots of foot light troops you might select steep hills. Once the battle field is laid out, deploy your troops to take best advantage of the available terrain and try to dominate areas where you have an advantage. It is seldom wise to contest areas where you are at a disadvantage or disperse your "bad terrain" troops too thinly to contest a tactically important terrain piece.

# COMMAND AND CONTROL

*Francis I and his Gendarmes, 1525, by Graham Turner © Osprey Publishing Ltd. Taken from Campaign 44:* Pavia 1525.

# COMMANDERS

*With the exception* of *commanders,* all bases must be part of a battle group. Commanders are represented by individual bases and can move independently or with a battle group they have temporarily joined.

Each army must have a *commander-in-chief* and 1 to 3 *subordinate* or *ally commanders.*

A commander is an individual of high rank, responsible for influencing one or more battle groups. A base representing a commander must be easily distinguishable from other bases in the army. All commanders have a *command range*: i.e. the distance within which they can influence battle groups. There are three levels of commander and those available are set out in the companion army list books:

- *Great commander* (GC), command range 12 MU:
  Gonsalvo de Cordova, Babur, Alexander of Parma, Gustavus Adolphus and Turenne would all fit this category.
- *Field commander* (FC), command range 8 MU:
  A competent commander, able to command an army, or a reliable subordinate.
- *Troop commander* (TC), command range 4 MU:
  A junior commander, able to command a small part of the army, or a very weak commander of a large army, such as Hatzfeldt, Charles I or James II.

A commander can only be with one battle group at a time. When that battle group is in close combat, he can elect either to fight in the front rank, or to encourage the battle group from the rear. Unless he is fighting in the front rank in close combat, he can influence other battle groups that are in his command range and not in close combat.

To count as **with** a battle group, a commander's base must be in edge to edge and corner to corner contact with a base of this one battle group. To count as **not with** a battle group his base must

*Prince Rupert and Boy*

*The Earl of Essex*

not be thus touching any battle group. To move a division, he must be **with** one of the battle groups comprising the division and his base must be within command range of all battle groups comprising the division.

## LINE OF COMMAND

Commanders can only affect battle groups for which they are **in line of command**.

The C-in-C and subordinate commanders are in line of command for all battle groups in the main army, but not for any in allied contingents.

Some armies can have one or more **allied contingents**. Ally commanders are only in line of command for battle groups of their own contingent.

### TIP!

Deciding which commanders to select and how to use them is important. Do you commit them to lead the attack at a crucial moment, by fighting in the front rank to inspire the troops, or do you keep them behind your lines for command and control? Making this decision wisely can often be the key to success in *Field of Glory Renaissance*.

*Divisions advance to contact*

# DIVISIONS

A *division is a collection* of battle groups where all of the following apply:

- Each battle group in the division is within 4MUs of another battle group in the division.
- At the start of a divisional move, each battle group in the division is separated by at least a base width from any other friendly battle group, unless that battle group is any of the following:
  - a keil.
  - light foot.
  - commanded shot and all friends within a base width are mounted troops.
  - artillery.
- Every battle group in the division must be within the command range of one particular commander (in line of command), who must be with one of the battle groups comprising the division.
- The battle groups in the division are specified to the opposing player before any of them are moved.

The following restrictions apply:

- Mounted troops cannot be in a division with foot troops other than ***commanded shot*** (see ***Glossary***) or dragoons.
- Warriors, artillery or battle wagons cannot be part of a division.
- Severely disordered, fragmented or broken troops cannot be part of a division.
- Battle groups that are part of an allied contingent can only be part of a division with other battle groups of the same allied contingent.

A division allows multiple battle groups to move together, with the following restrictions:

- They can only do so as an *advance* – i.e. a forward move with no more than a single wheel. No 90° or 180° turns are permitted.
- Apart from shifts (see the ***General Movement Rules*** section below) they must either all move the same distance straight forward, or the division must wheel as a whole. The move can, however, be partly straight forward and partly wheeling. When wheeling, measure the distance using the outside front corner of whichever battle group moves the furthest.

## TIP!

It was common practice in the seventeenth century for commanders to have pre-prepared deployment plans which would be used as a guide to the army deployment before battle. Wallenstein's deployment at Lutzen and Rupert's at Naseby were largely worked out well in advance of those battles and adapted on the day to reflect the terrain and troops available. In *Field of Glory Renaissance*, you will do well to emulate them.

## MOVEMENT BY DIVISION

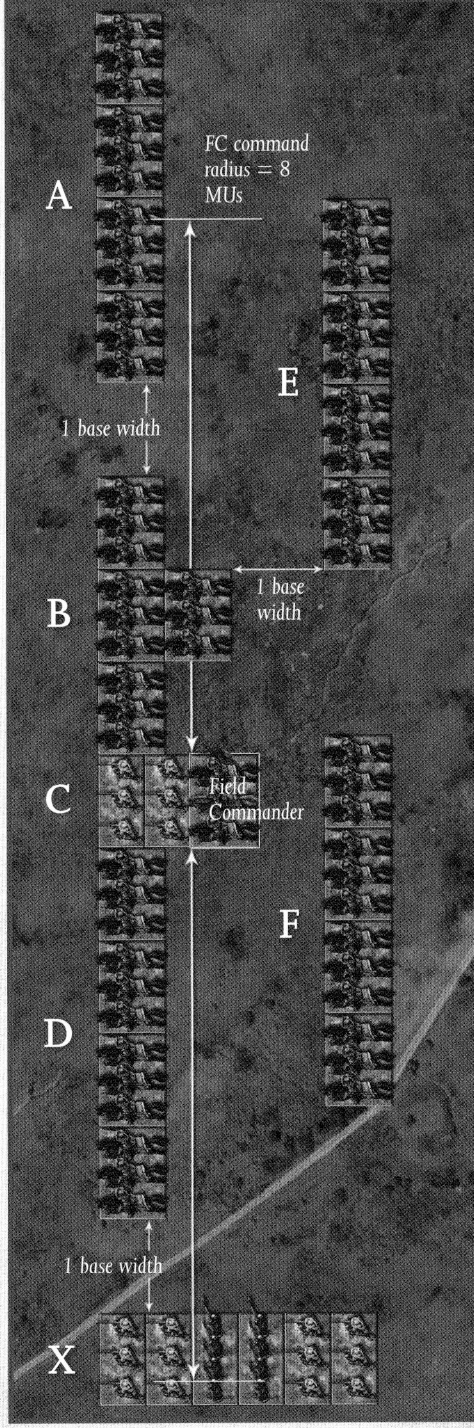


Battle groups "A" to "F" inclusive intend to move by division and can do so because they are all within the 8 MUs command radius of the Field Commander (who is with battle group "C"), and (with the exception of "C") are all separated from each other by at least one base width.
Because "C" is commanded shot, it is allowed to move as part of the division even though it is within one base width of the other BGs constituting the division.
All these BGs can only move at the speed of the slowest constituent of the divison, which is battle group "C" as they are all in open terrain.
If the division conducts a wheel to the right, the furthest out front corner on that side remains stationary (in this case the right front corner of "A"), and the move is measured from whichever battle group's front corner move the furthest (in this case the left front corner of "D").
All the BGs must move as if they were joined to the other BGs in the division and maintain their positions relative to each other exactly.

Note that:

The front corner of "D" cannot move further than the maximum permitted move of "C" even though "C" might not exceed its move if "D" did so.

The front corners used as pivoting point and measuring point will not always be those of the furthest forward BGs.

Although the FC is within 40mm of other BGs forming part of the division, his presence does not breach the 40mm rule because his base is only a marker.

Battle group "X" is within the command radius of the Field Commander, but as it is foot other than commanded shot it cannot move as part of a division including mounted troops. If it was mounted, it could but is not required to move with the division. Note that if battle group "X" were less than 40mm away from battle group "D", then battle group "D" would not be able to move as part of the division.

- If one battle group forming part of a division conducts a shift, all the battle groups in the division must shift to the same extent.
- All of the battle groups comprising the division, and its commander, must be in exactly the same positions relative to each other after the move as they were before.
- Divisions have the move distance of their slowest battle group.

*English Civil War armies clash*

# STARTER ARMIES

*Haselrigge's Lobsters at Roundway Down, 1643, by Angus McBride © Osprey Publishing Ltd. Taken from Elite 27:* Soldiers of the English Civil War (2): Cavalry.

*Now that you understand* how an army operates it is time to look at some typical armies. The following are "starter" armies from the middle phase of the Italian Wars, and from the later part of the English Civil War.

| FRENCH ARMY | |
|---|---|
| C-in-C: King Francis | Troop Commander |
| Sub-Commander: La Palice | Troop Commander |
| Sub-Commander: Montmorency | Troop Commander |
| 4 x Gendarmes | Superior, fully armoured gendarmes, heavy lancers, swordsmen |
| 4 x Gendarmes | Superior, fully armoured gendarmes, heavy lancers, swordsmen |
| 4 x Argoulets | Average, armoured light horse, crossbow, swordsmen |
| 10 x Swiss | 8 x superior armoured determined foot, pike and 2 x superior armoured determined foot, heavy weapon |
| 12 x Lansquenets | 10 x average armoured heavy foot, pike and 2 x average armoured heavy foot, heavy weapon |
| 4 x Swiss arquebusiers | Average unarmoured light foot, arquebus |
| 4 x Lansquenet arquebusiers | Average unarmoured light foot, arquebus |
| 8 x Aventuriers | Average unarmoured light foot, crossbow |
| 2 x Artillery | Average medium artillery |
| Unfortified camp | |

| IMPERIALIST ARMY | |
|---|---|
| C-in-C: De Lannoy | Field Commander |
| Sub-Commander: Del Vasto | Troop Commander |
| Sub-Commander: Pescara | Troop Commander |
| 4 x Spanish men-at-arms | Superior heavily armoured gendarmes, light lancers, swordsmen |
| 4 x Jinetes | Average armoured light horse, javelins, swordsmen |
| 4 x Mounted arquebusiers | Average unarmoured light horse, carbine |
| 6 x Colunela foot | 3 x superior armoured heavy foot, pike; 2 x superior unarmoured medium foot, arquebus and 1 x superior armoured heavy foot, swordsmen |
| 6 x Colunela foot | 3 x superior armoured heavy foot, pike; 2 x superior unarmoured medium foot, arquebus and 1 x superior armoured heavy foot, swordsmen |
| 6 x Colunela foot | 3 x average armoured heavy foot, pike; 2 x average unarmoured medium foot, arquebus and 1 x average armoured heavy foot, swordsmen |
| 8 x Arquebusier companies | Average unarmoured medium foot, arquebus |
| 12 x Landsknechts | 10 x average armoured heavy foot, pike and 2 x average armoured heavy foot, heavy weapon |
| 4 x Landsknecht arquebusiers | Average unarmoured light foot, arquebus |
| 2 x Artillery | Average medium artillery |
| Unfortified camp | |

| ROYALIST ARMY | |
|---|---|
| C-in-C: Prince Rupert | Field Commander |
| Sub-Commander: Lord Astley | Field Commander |
| Sub-Commander: Langdale | Troop Commander |
| 4 x Cavaliers | Superior armoured cavaliers, impact pistol, melee pistol |
| 4 x Cavaliers | Superior armoured cavaliers, impact pistol, melee pistol |
| 4 x Cavaliers | Superior unarmoured cavaliers, impact pistol, melee pistol |
| 4 x Cavaliers | Superior unarmoured cavaliers, impact pistol, melee pistol |
| 6 x Foot | 2 x superior unarmoured heavy foot, pike and 4 x superior unarmoured medium foot, musket |
| 6 x Foot | 2 x superior unarmoured heavy foot, pike and 4 x superior unarmoured medium foot, musket |
| 6 x Foot | 2 x average unarmoured heavy foot, pike and 4 x average unarmoured medium foot, musket |
| 6 x Foot | 2 x average unarmoured heavy foot, pike and 4 x average unarmoured medium foot, musket |
| Unfortified camp | |

*New Model Army assaults Royalist position*

| NEW MODEL ARMY | |
|---|---|
| C-in-C: Fairfax | Field Commander |
| Sub-Commander: Cromwell | Field Commander |
| Sub-Commander: Ireton | Troop Commander |
| 4 x Horse | Superior armoured determined horse, impact pistol, melee pistol |
| 4 x Horse | Average armoured determined horse, impact pistol, melee pistol |
| 4 x Horse | Average armoured determined horse, impact pistol, melee pistol |
| 4 x Horse | Average armoured determined horse, impact pistol, melee pistol |
| 3 x Dragoons | Average unarmoured dragoons, musket |
| 6 x Foot | 2 x average unarmoured heavy foot, pike and 4 x average unarmoured medium foot, musket |
| 6 x Foot | 2 x average unarmoured heavy foot, pike and 4 x average unarmoured medium foot, musket |
| 6 x Foot | 2 x average unarmoured heavy foot, pike and 4 x average unarmoured medium foot, musket |
| 6 x Foot | 2 x poor unarmoured heavy foot, pike and 4 x poor unarmoured medium foot, musket |
| 2 x Artillery | 2 x average medium artillery |
| Unfortified camp | |

# PLAYING THE GAME

*Swedish cavalry at Lützen, 1632, by Richard Hook © Osprey Publishing Ltd. Taken from Men-at-Arms 262:* The Army of Gustavus Adolphus (2): Cavalry.

# SETTING UP A GAME

*The first task is* to position the terrain on the battlefield and then deploy the armies. You can do this in a number of ways depending on the type of game to be played. If you are re-fighting an historical battle or campaign it is likely that you will have researched the terrain and battlefield deployments. This will therefore dictate your layout. However, if this information is not available or you simply want an 'equal points' battle you can follow the system described in ***Appendix 4*** at the back of this book.

# PLAYING THE GAME

*The game is played* over a number of turns with players alternating who is 'active' in each successive turn until the scenario is complete, one army routs or time runs out. We consider that three hours should be sufficient time for two players of average experience to complete a game. During his turn the active player can declare charges and manoeuvre his troops. His opponent can make only those response moves permitted by the rules. Both players' troops can shoot and fight, and both players can move their commanders in the final phase of the turn. The following turn the active player is changed and the process is repeated till the game ends.

The game ends either when time runs out or at the end of the current phase if one army (or both) has suffered an *army rout*.

Total up the number of battle groups in the army at the start of the game. This is the **break point** of the army. Any battle group initially comprising more than 12 bases is a ***grand battle group*** and counts as two battle groups for this purpose.

An *army rout* occurs when an army's attrition points, calculated as per the table below, equal or exceed its break point. It is possible for both armies to break at the same time.

| ATTRITION POINTS | |
|---|---|
| Each grand battle group currently BROKEN, routed off table or destroyed | 4 |
| Each grand battle group currently FRAGMENTED | 2 |
| Each grand battle group straggling off table | 2 |
| Each other battle group currently BROKEN, captured, routed off table or destroyed | 2 |
| Each other battle group currently FRAGMENTED | 1 |
| Each other battle group straggling or evaded off table | 1 |
| Camp sacked by enemy | 2 |

## EXAMPLE:

An army with 2 grand battle groups and 9 other battle groups has a break point of 13 attrition points. One of its grand battle groups has routed off the table, the other is FRAGMENTED, three of its other battle groups have been destroyed or are currently routing, and one has evaded off table. The army has therefore accumulated 13 attrition points and is routed.

# TURNS AND PHASES

A *turn is divided into* five phases. These are played strictly in the following order:

1 **The Impact Phase:** The impact phase covers ***charges*** and any combats resulting from these. The active player can initiate charges intended to result in close combat. The opposing player can respond with ***evades*** or ***interception charges*** where permitted. Impact combat is then resolved. Historically a ferocious charge by certain troop types could break the enemy on contact or cause serious disruption or worse. Gendarmes or cavaliers should do well here.

**The Manoeuvre Phase:** The active player can move any of his unbroken troops that are not already committed to close combat or still pursuing routers, provided that they did not charge, pursue or evade (unlikely but possible) in the impact phase.

2 **The Shooting Phase:** Both sides **must** shoot with any troops able to shoot at enemy bases in this phase.

3 **The Melee Phase:** All troops still in close combat now fight again. Melee combat is separate and distinctly different from impact combat. This allows us accurately to model historical differences in troop behaviour. Some troops depended on sweeping all before them in a ferocious charge whilst others were more steadfast in the push and grind of hand to hand combat that we model in melee. Armour and capabilities such as *swordsmen* are now important.

4 **The Joint Action Phase:** Occurs at the end of each player's turn, but does not 'belong' to either player. In this phase both players can move their commanders. This is an important

## TIP!

You will often have crucial decisions to take in the Joint Action Phase. Do you use your commanders to bolster the morale of your main attack or attempt to rally the battle group that has got into trouble? Just be careful not to chase a lost cause. The choices you make here will often decide the battle.

feature of *Field of Glory Renaissance*. Players need to make effective use of their commanders, by positioning them carefully to influence troops in the coming turn or by joining any battle group needing assistance e.g. to bolster its cohesion or rally it from rout. If the game is being played to a time limit, the last turn ends just before the Joint Action Phase, so there is no opportunity to bolster or rally troops in that turn.

The sequence must be played in strict order. The full and detailed sequence of play is shown in ***Appendix 9*** at the back of the book.

*Polish General joins Pancerni*

# GENERAL MOVEMENT RULES

*The Foot Guards crossing the Nebel stream, 1704, by Graham Turner © Osprey Publishing Ltd. Taken from Campaign 141:* Blenheim 1704.

*This chapter covers* all of the movement rules that are not phase specific. Note that some move types are unavailable to certain troop types and others are not available in all the phases. The restrictions are detailed in the relevant sections.

# MOVEMENT RULES

- A permitted move of any battle group or commander can be taken back and redone, but only if its initial position was marked or can be unambiguously referenced. Otherwise its move is over.
- A battle group or commander's move is over if the player moves another battle group or commander, or makes a dice roll for another battle group.
- Movement is made by an individual battle group, by multiple battle groups moving together as a division, or by commanders' bases moving independently.

# MOVE DISTANCES AND DISORDER

*The following table* cross references troop type with terrain to show the effect on order and maximum move distances in MUs. For movement purposes, a *terrain* type is assigned one of four difficulty levels: *open, uneven, rough* or *difficult*. The effect of terrain types is covered in *Appendix 2*.

| MOVE DISTANCES (MU) & TERRAIN DISORDER | | | | |
|---|---|---|---|---|
| Troop type | Open | Uneven | Rough | Difficult |
| Light foot | 4 | 4 | 4 | 3 |
| Warriors | 4 | 4 | 4 | 3 |
| Medium foot, mob | 3 | 3 | 3 | 2 |
| Determined foot | 4 | 4 | 3 | 2 |
| Heavy foot | 3 | 2 | 2 | 1 |
| Light horse and commanders | 6 | 6 | 5 | 3 |
| Gendarmes (if not fully armoured), cavaliers, horse, determined horse, cavalry and camelry | 5 | 4 | 3 | 1 |
| Fully armoured gendarmes | 4 | 3 | 2 | 1 |
| Elephants | 4 | 4 | 3 | 1 |
| Dragoons | 5 | 5 | 4 | 3 |
| Battle wagons | 3 | 2 | 1 | N/A |
| Light artillery | 2 | 1 | 1 | 1* |
| Limbered artillery | 2 | 1 | 1 | N/A |
| Unlimbered medium artillery | 1* | 1* | 1* | N/A |
| Unlimbered heavy artillery | 1* | N/A | N/A | N/A |
| * Pivot only on either front corner of battle group | | | | |
| NO EFFECT | DISORDER | SEVERE DISORDER | | |

- The lower move distance applies *to the whole move* if any part of any base of the battle group is in distance-reducing terrain at any stage of its move. As a result, sometimes battle groups can reach the edge of a piece of terrain but not enter it. e.g. if cavaliers have moved at least 3 MU in the open and meet rough terrain, they have already moved their maximum rough terrain distance, so cannot enter it.
- Troops in a 1 base wide ***column*** (throughout the move) move at :
  - +1 MU through any terrain if the indicated move distance is less than their move distance in ***open terrain***.
  - Open terrain move distance +3 MU along roads (unless any part of the move is within a village).
- Battle groups with mixed troop types have the move distance of the slower type.
- Divisions have the move distance of their slowest battle group.
- Battle groups moving through more than one type of terrain are limited to the shortest move distance shown for any of those terrain types. Battle groups with mixed troop types use the shortest move distance that would apply to any base in the battle group, even if that base is clear of the terrain. e.g. a mixed battle group of pike (Heavy Foot) and shot (Medium Foot) move at 2 MU in rough terrain, even if only the shot is in the rough terrain.
- Roads always count as open ground. If a battle group is astride a road, whichever file is most on the road always counts as in open ground (even if its bases are partly in other terrain) as long as all of its bases are at least partly on the road.
- A battle group only gains the extra move distance for moving along a road if it is in a single base wide column and all of its bases are at least partly on the road throughout the move.

# SIMPLE AND COMPLEX MOVES

*Moves fall into three categories*, simple, complex or impossible. The table below cross references move types against troop types and shows the category of move. A move must be from a single section of the table (e.g. charges, advances or expansions). Moves by lone commanders are always simple.

A complex move requires a test to be passed before it can be made. All types of move can be constrained by other restrictions, described later in this chapter, or by limitations imposed in specific phases.

Divisions are limited to the "Advances" section of the table.

| SIMPLE AND COMPLEX MOVES | | *Troop Type* | |
|---|---|---|---|
| *Type of move* | **Move to be made** (*advance* means a move from the Advance section below) | **Light Troops** | **Others** |
| *Charge* | Any charge move | simple | simple |
| *Advance* | Any other forward move with no more than a single wheel | simple | simple |
| *Double Wheel* | A forward move including 2 wheels | simple | impossible* |
| *Pivot light or medium artillery* | Pivot forwards up to 1 MU on one front corner of the battle group | n/a | simple |
| *Pivot heavy artillery* | Pivot forwards up to 1 MU on one front corner of the battle group | n/a | complex |
| *Unlimber* | Unlimber medium or heavy artillery | n/a | complex |
| *2nd move* | *Advance* by a single battle group or division if all requirements for a 2nd move are met. | simple | simple |
| *3rd move* | *Advance* by a single battle group of mounted troops or dragoons or a division entirely of mounted troops and/or dragoons if all requirements for a 3rd move are met. | simple | simple |
| *Expansion* | Expand frontage by 1 or 2 bases while stationary | simple | complex |
| | Expand frontage by 1 or 2 bases followed by an *advance* | simple | impossible |
| *Contraction* | Contract frontage by 1 or 2 bases with an *advance* of at least 3 MUs before or after | simple | simple |
| | Contract frontage by 1 or 2 bases while stationary or with an *advance* of less than 3 MUs before or after | simple | complex |
| *Formation change* | Any of the following (singly or in combination): Turn a tercio or keil 90 degrees. Form **square**. Move bases around in the battle group, without changing its facing or the position of its front corners (except to turn a tercio or keil 90 degrees or form square). | n/a | complex** |
| *90 degree turns (not tercios or keils)* | Turn 90 degrees while stationary | simple | simple |
| | Turn 90 degrees with an *advance* before or after – only possible for light troops and mounted troops | simple | complex |
| *180 degree turns* | Turn 180 degrees while stationary | simple | simple*** |
| | Turn 180 degrees with an *advance* before or after – only possible for light troops | simple | impossible |
| | Turn 180 degrees, move up to 3 MUs in an *advance* and turn back again – only possible for light troops | complex | impossible |

** Simple for a 1 base wide column moving entirely along a road*
*** Formation changes permitted or required in the impact phase do not require a CMT.*
**** Complex if turning captured or recaptured artillery 180 degrees.*

# ADVANCES

*An advance is a move* from the 'Advances' section of the table. Some moves from other sections are permitted to include an *advance*.

# THE COMPLEX MOVE TEST (CMT)

*The following procedure* must be followed if a complex move test is required:

| COMPLEX MOVE TEST | |
|---|---|
| **Roll two dice, apply quality re-rolls, and add the scores. Apply the following modifiers.** | |
| +1 if a commander in *line of command* is in *command range* | |
| +1 if this same commander is with the battle group testing | |
| +1 if this same commander is a great commander | |
| -1 if testing to stop pursuing or looting | |
| -1 if any of the bases are DISRUPTED or DISORDERED, or are warriors | Count the worst of these two, but never both. |
| -2 if any of the bases are FRAGMENTED or SEVERELY DISORDERED | |
| Score to pass | 8 |

## POINTS TO NOTE ON THE CMT

- Battle wagons must pass a CMT to carry out any move, whether simple or complex.
- If an artillery battle group fails its CMT it cannot move at all. Any other battle group which fails its CMT can make a simple move.
- Once the dice have been rolled, that battle group must make its move, if any, before others are moved or tested. It is **not** permitted to arrange to make or change a move conditionally depending on the result of a subsequent battle group's test.
- Only one commander can influence the test.
- To be able to influence a CMT a commander must be with the testers from the start of the phase to count as with them, in command range from the start of the phase to count as in command range.
- If a commander is with a battle group when it takes a CMT, he must remain with the same battle group for the rest of the phase.
- Quality re-rolls apply to the CMT – unless specified otherwise in the rules.

### TIP!

Think ahead. Wherever possible avoid complex moves, or make them early so you get time for a second chance.

# MOVING ARTILLERY

*Light artillery is deployed* unlimbered, and can move normally in any terrain except Difficult.

Medium and heavy artillery can only move normally while limbered. They can be deployed limbered or unlimbered. If deployed limbered, limber markers must be used. These are positioned in front of the artillery bases. The latter are deployed facing away from the limber markers to the rear of the battle group, to indicate that the artillery are limbered.

Limber markers are not bases, but obstruct the movement of other battle groups as if they were. They must have models of limbers and draught animals fixed to them.

When artillery unlimbers (for which they must pass a CMT), the limber markers are removed and the artillery bases repositioned on the spaces occupied by the markers, facing forward. Once artillery has unlimbered, it remains unlimbered for the rest of the game.

Unlimbered medium or heavy artillery (and light artillery in Difficult terrain) can normally only move by a single pivot on any one corner of the battle group's formation. This is performed in exactly the same way as a wheel. Artillery

*Artillery position under close assault*

defending fortifications, an obstacle or a river bank cannot pivot.

When pivoting artillery has friendly foot battle troops providing ***rear support*** (see the ***Combat Resolution*** section), it can still pivot forwards as normal and the friends providing rear support can be shifted as necessary so that they maintain the same formation and position relative to the artillery battle group as before. If the supporting battle group overlaps the artillery, this may result in part of it being shifted backwards. If the shift is obstructed by other troops, impassable terrain or a table edge, it cannot be made. Supporting battle group(s) which shift in this way cannot make any other move in the same phase.

In addition, if any artillery has been captured or recaptured (by a battle group of pike and/or shot) the new owner can turn it 180 degrees as a complex move.

## MOVING AND UNLIMBERING ARTILLERY

*While limbered, the artillery are positioned behind the limber markers with the artillery bases rear edges in contact with the rear edges of the markers.*

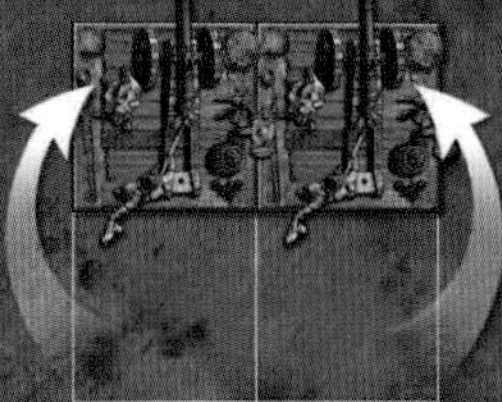

*As the artillery unlimbers the limber markers are permanently removed, and the artillery bases are repositioned in their place, facing forward.*

# WHEELING

*Wheeling is a change* of direction by rotating around one front corner of the battle group or division. One corner of the front edge remains in the same position. For ease of measuring, the distance moved during the wheel is taken as the straight line from the starting position to the ending position of the moving front corner.

No single or double wheel can exceed a total of 90 degrees. A move cannot include more than two wheels, except by a 1 base wide column moving entirely along a road. If wheeling a division, no battle group can exceed the full move distance of the slowest battle group in the division.

When a battle group wheels out of a solid line, adjacent battle groups do not obstruct the wheel because the men in the rear ranks of the wheeling battle group do not start wheeling until they reach the initial position of the front rank. At the end of its move, however, all bases of the wheeling battle group must have moved sufficiently to clear the adjacent battle group, or the move is not possible.

**WHEELING A DIVISION**

## TIP!

When wheeling, be careful not to slide the corner on which the battle group is pivoting as this is not permitted by the rules.

# TURNING 90 DEGREES

*Tercios and keils cannot make* a simple 90 degree turn but must use a Formation Change (see below) instead.

Other troops turn 90 degrees as follows: The old side edge of the battle group becomes the new front edge. The old front edge becomes the new side edge. The corner does not move. (The projecting pike base of a Swedish brigade is ignored for the purpose of determining the position of the stationary corner.)

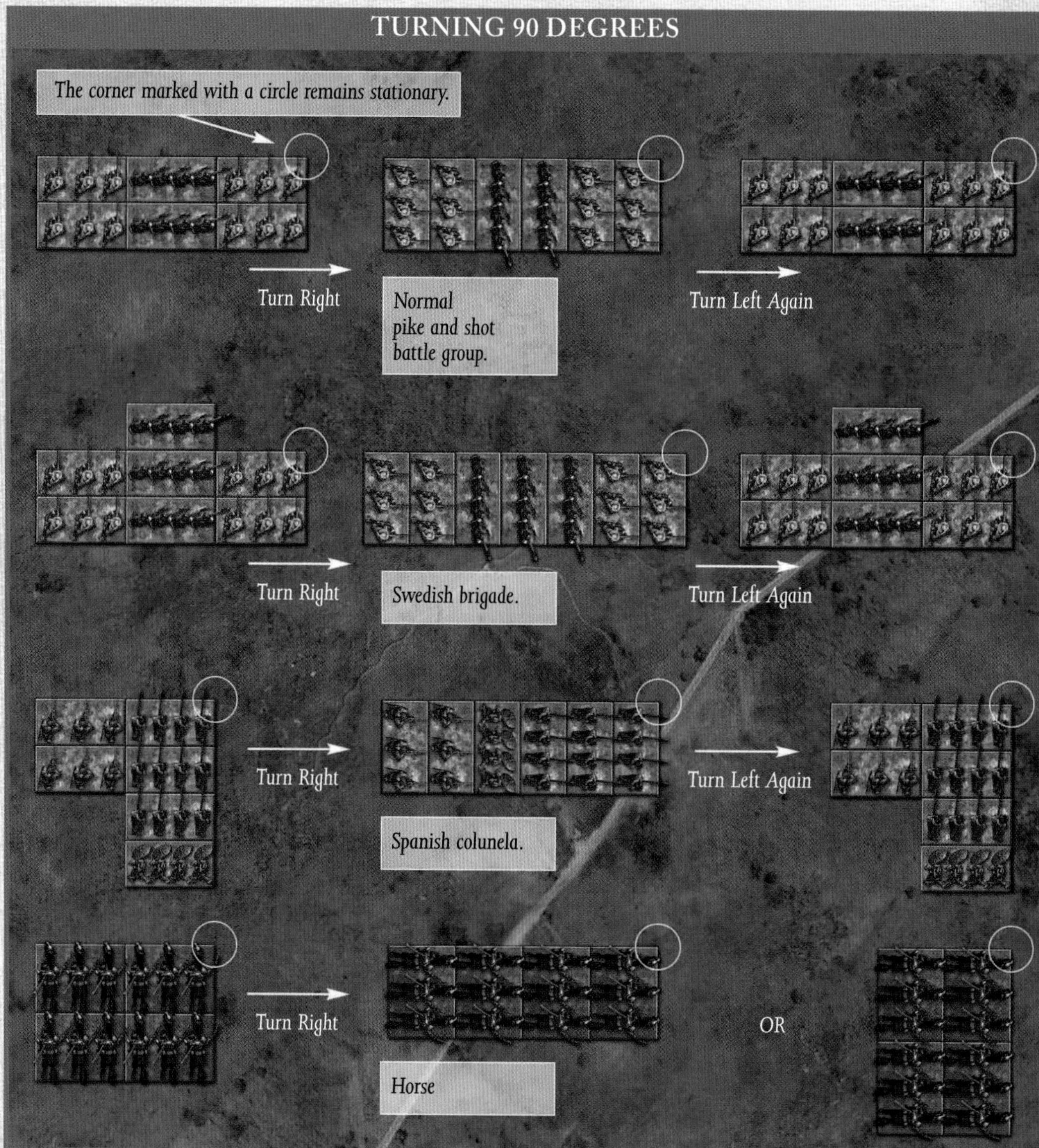

Foot battle troops normally turn 90 degrees by forming a single base wide column. If, however, foot battle troops are already in a single base wide column, mixed foot battle groups turn into their normal formation, unmixed foot battle groups turn as specified for mounted troops below.

Mounted troops, elephants and light troops turn as follows: If the depth of the battle group prior to turning corresponds to an exact number of base widths, the new front edge must consist of that number of bases. If not, it can be wider or narrower than the former depth, provided that the new width is less than one base width more or less than the depth prior to turning and that, of course, it is a least one base wide. For example, in 15mm scale, a battle group of 6 reiters in 3 ranks will have a depth of 90mm. When it turns, it can have a new frontage of 2 bases – 80mm wide or 3 bases – 120mm wide. If the battle group does not contain sufficient bases to match the required new frontage as above, it cannot turn if it is battle wagons, otherwise it forms a single rank.

Other bases are repositioned behind to make the new formation legal. If the above is not possible due to obstructing troops, impassable terrain or a table edge, the turn cannot be made (but see the section below on ***Turns Blocked by Enemy***).

When a battle group, with a front rank having one troop type only and another rank or ranks having a different troop type, turns, its new front edge must, if possible, consist of the same base types as the old front edge. Bases are simply relocated to achieve this.

# TURNING 180 DEGREES

*When turning 180 degrees*, the battle group ends in exactly the same formation as before, but facing in the opposite direction, with its new front edge on the line of its old rearmost edge. The bases comprising the old front rank become the new front rank, and so forth.

# SHIFTING

***An advance can include*** a 'free' sideways shift of up to half a base width sideways:

- If this is necessary to avoid "clipping" terrain or friendly troops, and at least one front corner of the battle group moves at least 1 MU (excluding the shift). The shift cannot be greater than is necessary to avoid the obstacle.
- To move into an ***overlap position*** (see the ***Manoeuvre Phase*** section) against an enemy battle group that is already in close combat to its front.
- To move foot into a position to give ***rear support*** to friendly artillery (see ***glossary***).
- To place the flank edge or corner of foot battle troops touching difficult terrain, an obstacle or the rear edge of field fortifications.

Shifts are not permitted when charging, nor in second or third moves, nor in the same phase as double wheels, expansions, contractions or turns (except as specified under the rules for evading and routing troops).

SHIFTING

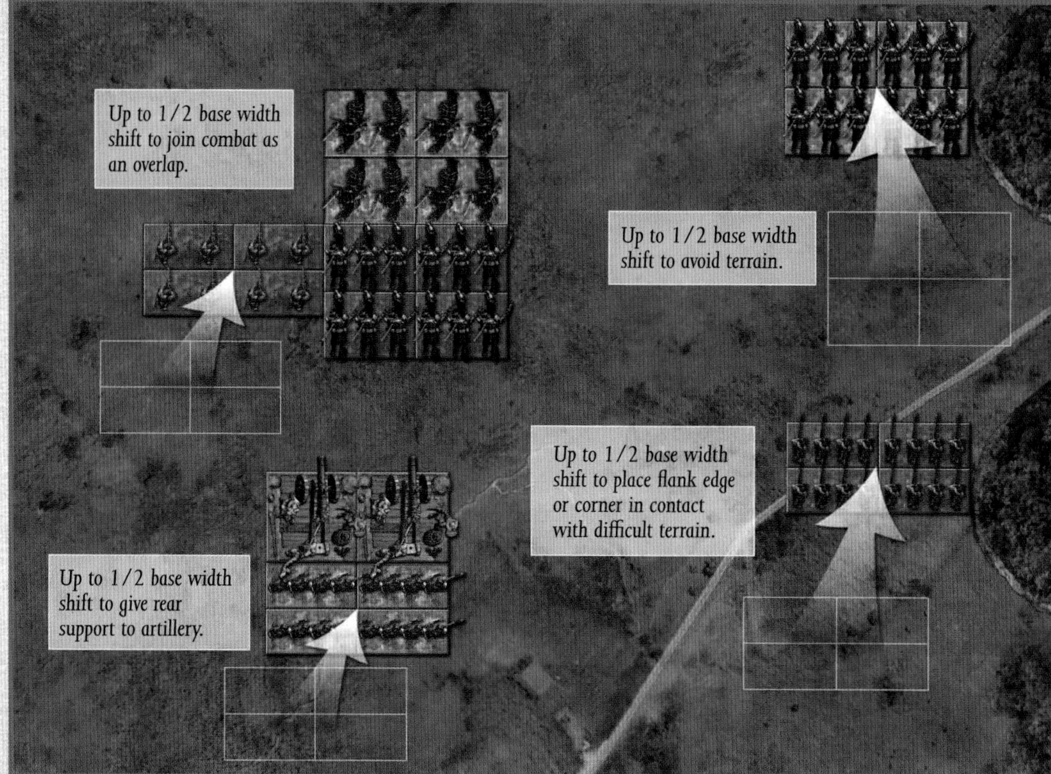


# EXPANSIONS

*Expansion by a battle group* that is not in close combat is carried out as follows: Increase the width of the front rank by adding one or two bases taken from other ranks. If two bases are expanded, they can either be added to the same side, or one to each side. Then move bases not in the front rank to make the formation legal. Expansions **cannot** be used to create an illegal formation.

EXPANSIONS

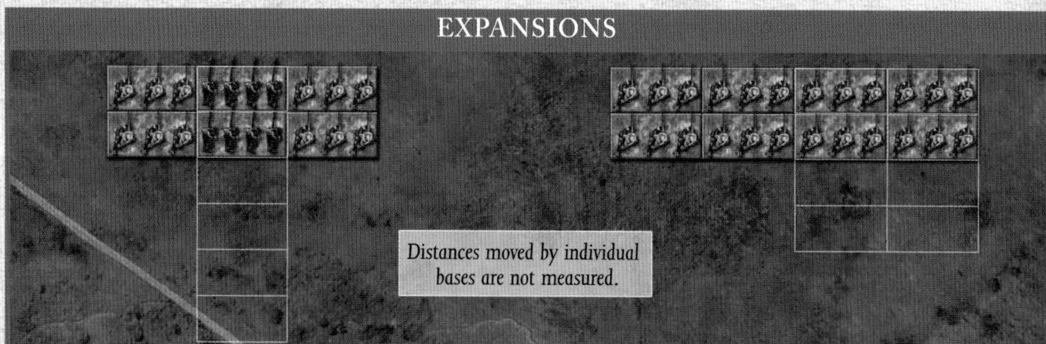

# CONTRACTIONS

*Contraction by a battle group* that is not in close combat is carried out as follows: Remove one or two bases from the same or opposite ends of the front rank and place them in any other rank. Move bases not in the front rank to make the formation legal. To qualify as having advanced at least 3 MUs when contracting, both front corners of the final formation must have moved at least 3 MUs. Contractions **cannot** be used to create an illegal formation.

CONTRACTIONS

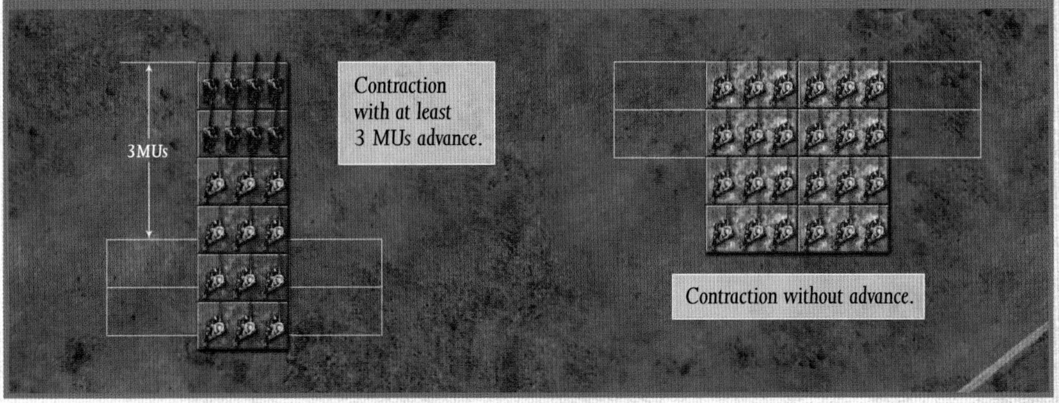


# FORMATION CHANGES

*A formation change is used* to accomplish manoeuvres that cannot be completed by expansions, contractions and turns. It can be used to perform any of the following (singly or in combination):

- Turn a tercio or keil 90 degrees. The frontmost base corner on the side to which it is turning remains stationary. The whole battle group reforms on this point in its previous formation facing the new direction.
- Form *square*. (See the *Special Features* section.)
- Move any number of bases to a different position in the battle group, without changing the battle group's facing or the position of its front corners (except to turn a tercio or keil 90 degrees or form square). The final formation must be legal.

## FRONTING TO FLANK

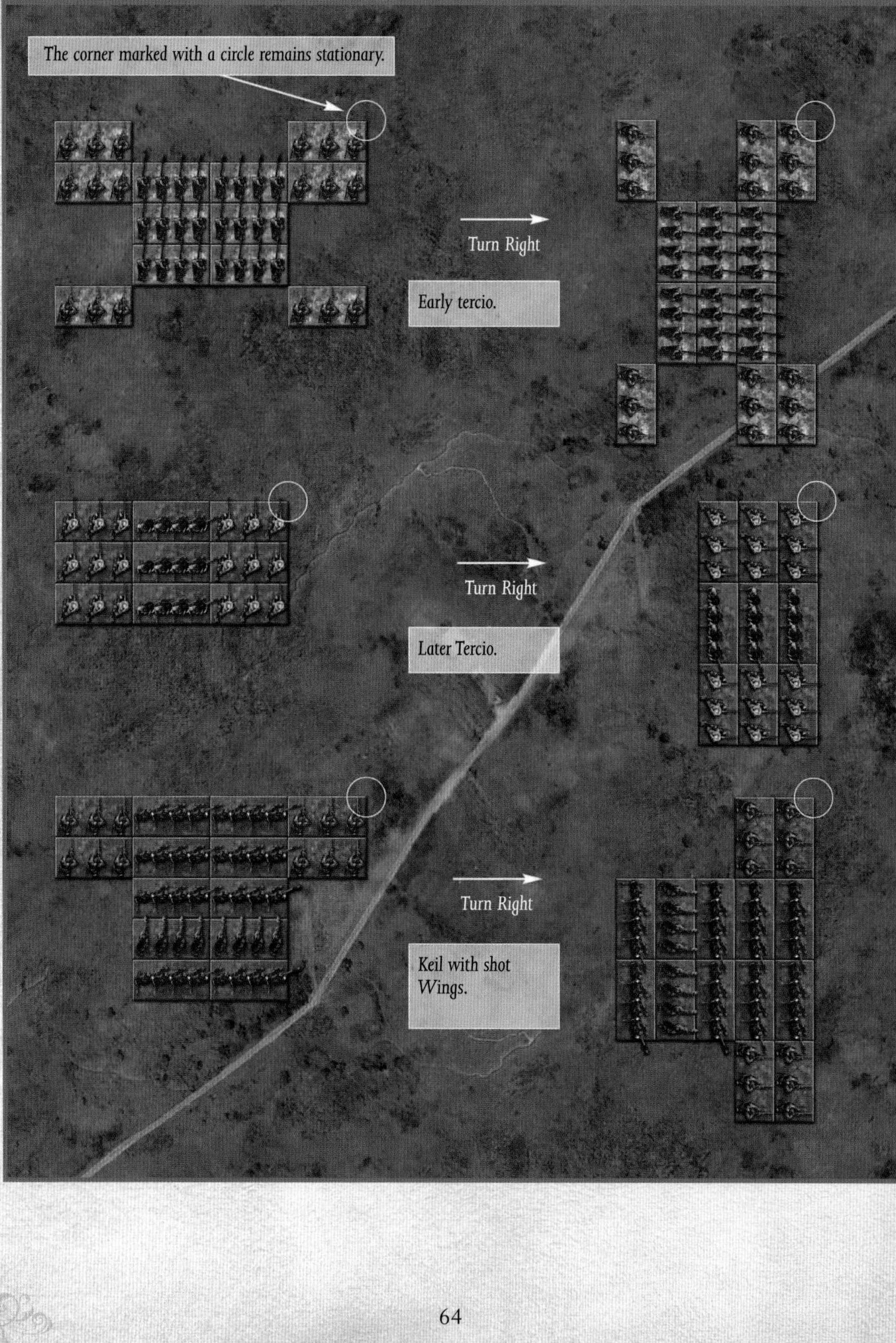

# TURNS BLOCKED BY ENEMY

*Owing to the requirement* for many battle groups to maintain specific historical formations, it may occur that a turn is physically blocked by the presence of enemy troops. In reality, of course, troops were not on rigid bases, and would still be able to turn even if space was limited.

Consequently, when a battle group that is neither evading nor routing wishes to make a 90 or 180 degree turn (normal or by formation change) at the start of its move:

- If any **enemy** troops physically block the turn, they are shifted out of the way sufficiently to make room, provided that they are not currently in contact with it or any of its friendly battle groups. Further enemy battle groups blocking the shift are

TURNS BLOCKED BY ENEMY

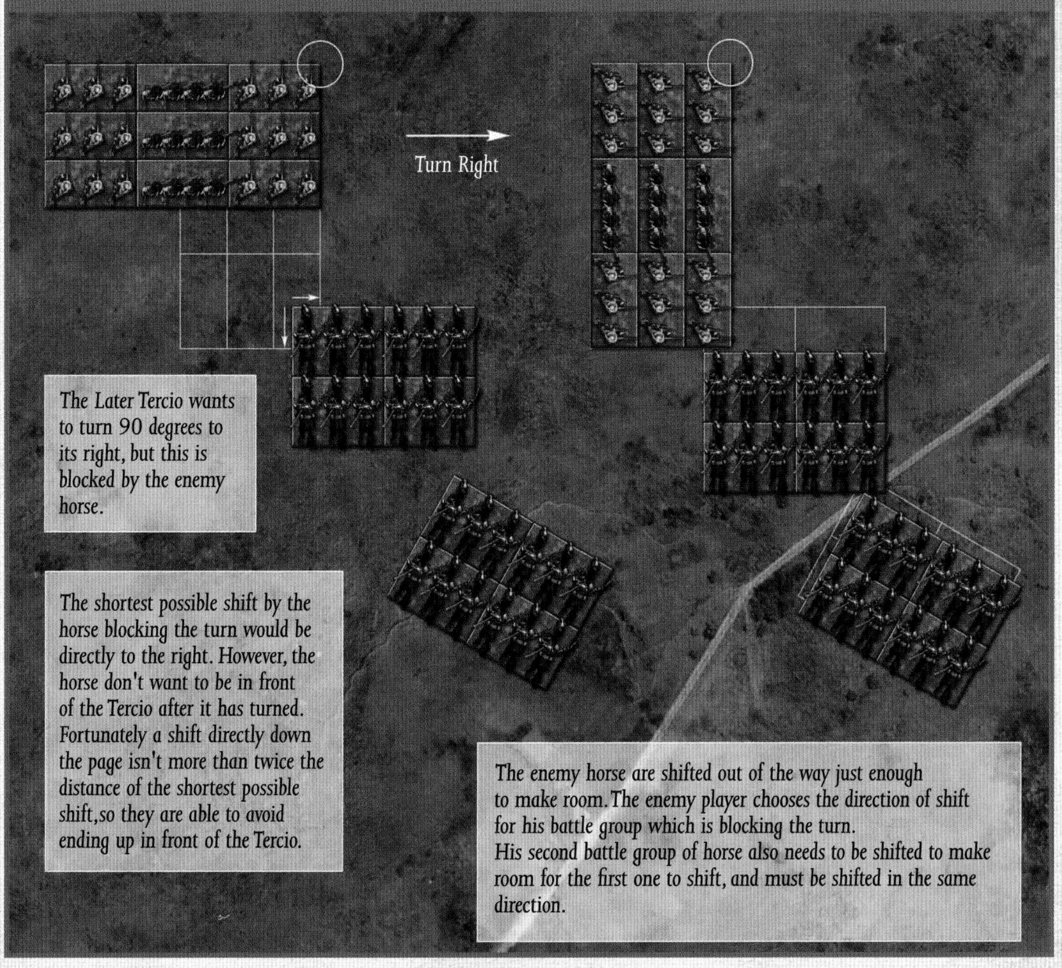

in turn shifted to make room, subject to the same proviso.

- Friends of the turning battle group are **not** shifted.
- The player whose troops are being shifted chooses the direction of shift, but cannot choose a direction that will prevent the shift if it is possible in another direction, nor one which requires a shift of over 1 MU that is more than twice the shortest possible distance.
- The shifted troops are shifted just enough that they are not in contact with the turning battle group after it has turned.
- Each battle group that itself blocks the turn can be shifted in a different direction. Any battle groups friendly to it and blocking its shift are shifted in the same direction.
- Battle groups do not change facing when they shift.
- If it is impossible to complete all shifts because these are blocked by friends who cannot be shifted, enemy, impassable terrain or a camp, or because any bases would cross the table edge, then the turn is cancelled.

# VARIABLE MOVES

*In some situations* move distances are not fixed. If the rules state that a variable move must be made, roll one dice and consult the table below to determine any change to the distance to be moved. This is generally the case when making ***evades*** or ***charges on an evading target*** or ***routs/pursuits***, and will sometimes result in the troops being caught or outdistancing the enemy.

| VARIABLE MOVEMENT DISTANCE (VMD) | |
|---|---|
| Roll 1d6 | |
| 1 | -2 MUs |
| 2 | -1 MU |
| 3 or 4 | Normal distance |
| 5 | +1 MU |
| 6 | +2 MUs |
| **Quality re-rolls do not apply** | |

## TIP!

Keep variable move distances in mind when approaching enemy troops with light troops, as troops that normally move less may still catch you due to the VMD.

# MOVING THROUGH FRIENDLY TROOPS

*In certain circumstances* your battle groups can move voluntarily through other friendly troops, but at other times this may happen involuntarily and may cause deterioration in the cohesion of the battle group being passed through.

## INTERPENETRATIONS

Interpenetrations are situations where you can choose to move through friendly troops and where there is no penalty for doing so. No interpenetrations are permitted when charging.

The following interpenetrations of friendly troops are permitted:

- Commanders can pass through and be passed through by any troops in any direction.
- Light foot can pass through any troops in any direction.
- Cavalry, dragoons, light horse, and elephants can pass through light foot in any direction.
- Foot can pass through artillery perpendicularly from back to front or front to back only.
- If a battle group does not have sufficient move distance to pass fully through another battle group it cannot pass through at all unless there is room beyond and any of the following apply, in which case it can pass completely through, maintaining its prior formation:
  - It starts its move already in front edge contact with the front or rear edge of the battle group being interpenetrated, it passes through perpendicularly to that edge, and it has sufficient move for its front edge to reach the far side of the

### INTERPENETRATIONS

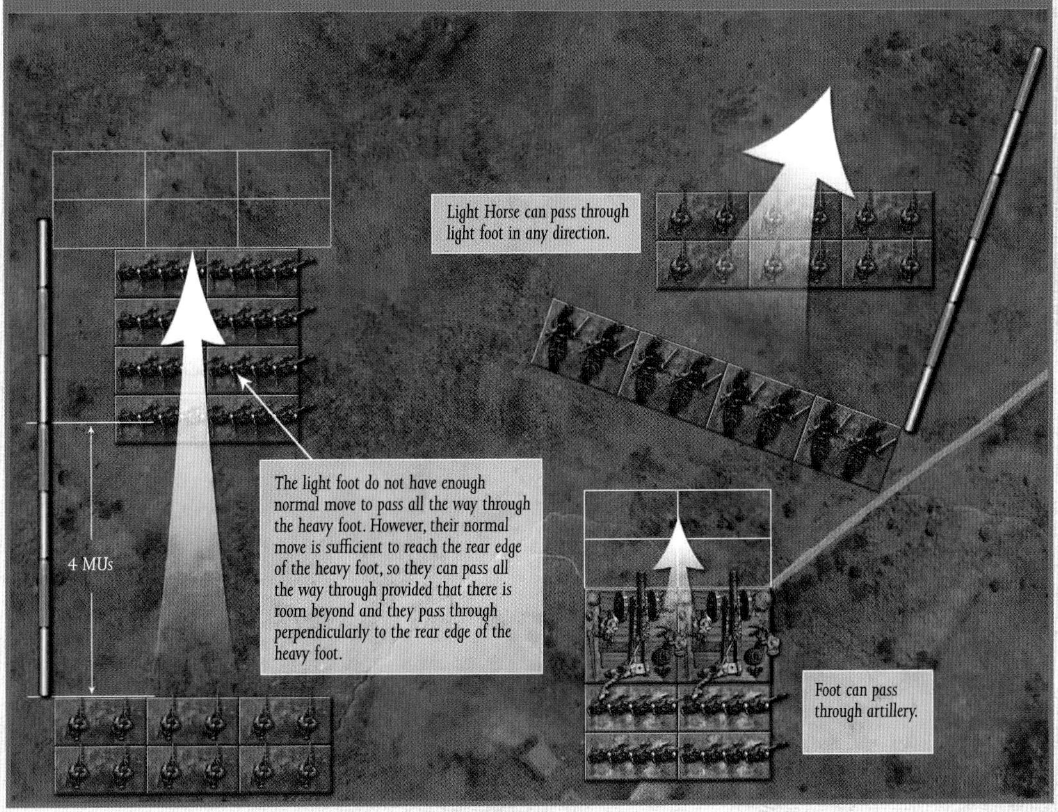


MOVEMENT RULES
MOVE DISTANCES AND DISORDER
SIMPLE AND COMPLEX MOVES
ADVANCES
THE COMPLEX MOVE TEST (CMT)
MOVING ARTILLERY
WHEELING
TURNING 90 DEGREES
TURNING 180 DEGREES
SHIFTING
EXPANSIONS
CONTRACTIONS
FORMATION CHANGES
TURNS BLOCKED BY ENEMY
VARIABLE MOVES
MOVING THROUGH FRIENDLY TROOPS
MOVEMENT OF COMMANDERS
MOVING FROM AN OVERLAP POSITION
TROOPS LEAVING THE TABLE

battle group being passed through.
- It is light foot which has sufficient move for all of its front rank bases that will pass though to reach whichever is nearer of the front or rear edge of the battle group being interpenetrated, and it passes through perpendicularly to that edge. It cannot then shoot this turn.
- It is evading or routing light foot which has sufficient move for all of its front rank bases that will pass through to reach the battle group being interpenetrated.
- It is other evading or routing troops and has sufficient move for all of its rear rank bases that will pass through to reach the battle group being interpenetrated. [Note that this only applies to permitted interpenetrations – burst throughs are dealt with as below.]

- No battle group can pass through a battle group that already passed through it this phase.
- No battle group can make any turns, expansions or contractions before or after passing though another battle group this phase.

### TIP!

Be careful not to let battle groups become trapped in front of your main battle line with no escape route. If you delay too long you might get trapped. Light horse and dragoons can evade enemy charges, but need gaps to pass through.

### BURSTING THROUGH FRIENDS

A battle group burst through by friendly evaders or routers drops one cohesion level. Move the evading or routing battle group to the full extent of its move. If its move does not completely clear all friends, it is placed beyond any battle group(s) it is **currently** bursting through if there is room for it beyond; otherwise it is destroyed and removed from the table. No cohesion test is taken for friends seeing this.

A battle group that is burst through by more than one friendly battle group in the same phase only drops one cohesion level.

## MOVEMENT OF COMMANDERS

- A commander who is with a battle group at the start of a phase can move with the battle group as it moves. A commander not with a battle group, or who wishes to leave a battle group (and is not fighting in the front rank), can move in the manoeuvre phase of his own side's turn and **again** in every joint action phase.
- Commanders, however depicted, have the move distance of light horse when not with a battle group.
- Commanders can move in any direction without any CMTs and without having to wheel or turn the base to face the direction of movement.

- Commanders' bases represent only the commander and a few aides. Therefore they do not obstruct the movement of other troops. Commanders can interpenetrate any friendly troops in any direction and vice versa.
- When a commander joins a battle-group:
  - His base must be placed in edge to edge and corner to corner contact with a base of the battle group. He must be able to reach this position within his normal move distance.
  - His base can be moved at any time the minimum necessary to a new such position **if this is necessary** to avoid obstructions or make way for friendly or enemy troops. (This is not permitted if he is fighting in the front rank – see below.) If there is no room left for him to be so placed, a marker must be placed on top of one of the bases of the battle group to represent his position.
  - He can only be with one battle group at a time. If possible, he must be placed in a position that makes it clear which battle group he is with. If not, the player must declare which battle group he is with.
  - He can only leave the battle group, or voluntarily move to a different position in contact with it, during the manoeuvre or joint action phases. If he moves with the battle group, he must remain in exactly the same position relative to it, unless its formation changes. In that case he moves the minimum necessary to a new permitted position.
- The base of a commander fighting in the front rank is placed anywhere in the front rank (player's choice) to show that he is fighting. The base(s) he displaces is (are) placed behind him, but still count as being in their original position, and fight accordingly. Once there, the commander cannot leave the front rank of that battle group until it is no longer in close combat and no longer pursuing enemy routers.
- If a battle group's move would take it into contact with an enemy commander who is not with a battle group, he must immediately move (in any phase or turn) to join a friendly battle group, if there is one within his normal move distance. If not, he does not move and is immediately lost. It is not necessary for the enemy to declare a charge on him, nor to halt their move at the point of contact.

# MOVING FROM AN OVERLAP POSITION

A *battle group* which fought in melee in a previous turn as an *overlap* only, can choose to charge a different enemy or evade in the impact phase, move normally in the manoeuvre phase, or continue to fight against its existing opponents in the next melee phase.

# TROOPS LEAVING THE TABLE

- If any part of any base of a battle group leaves the table, that battle group is removed from play and cannot return during the game. If it routed off the table it counts as 2 attrition points towards its side's defeat (4 if it was initially deployed as a grand battle group), if it evaded off the table it counts as 1 attrition point.
- Except by evading, battle groups cannot voluntarily leave the table except in campaign games or in scenario games where this is allowed by the scenario.
- A charging or pursuing battle group whose move would take any part of it off the table edge instead halts its move at the table edge.
- In situations where battle groups are shifted to make room for others, they cannot be shifted if this would take any part of any base off the table.
- If a commander is routing or evading with a battle group that leaves the table, he is removed from play for the remainder of the game. It is not necessary to take a cohesion test for battle groups seeing this.

# IMPACT PHASE

*The charge of the Polish Winged Hussars, 1683, by Peter Dennis © Osprey Publishing Ltd. Taken from Campaign 191:* Vienna 1683.

T*he impact phase is* divided into four stages:

- Declaring charges.
- Troops responding to charges by intercepting or evading the chargers.
- Moving the chargers into contact.
- Resolving combats for battle groups that have come into contact.

All activity in the impact phase is resolved by battle groups. Divisions are not used in the impact phase at all. We start by describing a straightforward sequence of events showing what happens in a charge when there is no special reaction possible by the opponent. We then consider battle groups that are unable or unwilling to charge. Finally we consider what happens when troops intercept or evade the chargers.

# DECLARATION OF CHARGES

T*he active player* declares which of his battle groups are to charge and by convention places a dice behind each to note this. To be allowed to declare a charge, there must be a visible enemy base that can be "legally"' contacted by the charging battle group within its normal move distance through the terrain to be crossed. A battle group can declare charges on as many enemy battle groups as can be "legally" contacted within this move distance. When the charge declaration stage is over, no charge declarations can be rescinded, nor additional voluntary charges declared.

Any enemy battle group in the path of a charge counts as being charged if it can be "legally" contacted, even if it was not one of the originally declared targets of the charge. This applies even if it can only be contacted by bases stepping forward (see below). It does not apply if, due to intervening friends, it could not be contacted even by stepping forward bases – unless the situation changes, as follows: If a battle group is revealed and can now be contacted due to friends evading or breaking and routing, it becomes a target of the charge and will therefore take any required tests once the evade or rout move has occurred.

If a CMT is required to make a charge against certain troops, it must be taken if required for any of the battle groups that can be "legally" contacted in the chosen direction of charge, including by stepping forward bases. It need not and cannot be taken for those not visible to it or that can only be contacted if another battle group evades or routs.

# LEGAL CHARGE CONTACT

A *battle group makes a "legal"* charge contact if at least one of its bases contacts an enemy base either with its front edge, or with its front corner only against the enemy base's edge. Other bases of the charging battle group may contact the enemy in other ways (e.g. only corner to corner), but will not be eligible to fight in the impact phase combat.

*Imperialist Horse charge French Foot*

# CHARGING WITH YOUR BATTLE GROUPS

A *charging battle group* moves up to the full extent of its move (plus any variable move distance to contact evaders) to "legally" contact any part of the target battle group(s).

A charge move can include a single wheel of up to 90 degrees. The following restrictions apply:

Any wheel must be specified (using a measuring stick or tape to indicate the final direction of the charge) before any charge responses are declared. (The exception to this is that the charge direction can later be changed if all the charge targets evade out of the original path of the charge – see "Evade moves" below.)

The wheel must be made at the start of the charge move. Any straight ahead movement must be after the wheel is completed.

Unless required to avoid friends, a wheel cannot be made if it would result in fewer bases being eligible to fight in the impact phase combat than would occur if the battle group charged straight ahead. (This is determined from the positions prior to interception charges or evades, but takes into account automatic formation changes that will occur when a battle group is contacted – see below.)

If charging enemy who could evade, the charging battle group cannot wheel beyond the position at which the enemy would be contacted if they did not evade.

A charge cannot be declared if it would contact only the flank or rear edge of the 1st or 2nd rank base in a file which is already in melee to its front, except by a "legal" flank or rear charge (or a charge that would count as such if the target were not a tercio or keil – see below). A battle group unable to charge in such a case may be able to move into an overlap position in the manoeuvre phase.

**TIP!**

If your troops are best at impact, make sure your charges arrive with as many bases in contact as possible. Don't waste valuable shock troops such as heavy lancers in small scale contacts where only a few will fight at impact.

# FORMATION CHANGES WHEN CHARGING OR BEING CHARGED

*When an early tercio charges* or is charged, the pike are automatically moved forward to make a level fighting front with the shot. This does not count as stepping forward. (The same thing occurs when an early tercio in close combat to its flank or rear *reforms* – see the *Manoeuvre Phase* section – facing that way.)

When a battle group using Swedish brigade formation charges or is charged, the pike are automatically moved back to make a level fighting front with the shot. If the early tercio or Swedish brigade also steps forward, the distance is measured from the first point of contact by the new level fighting front.

**TRYING TO CHARGE**

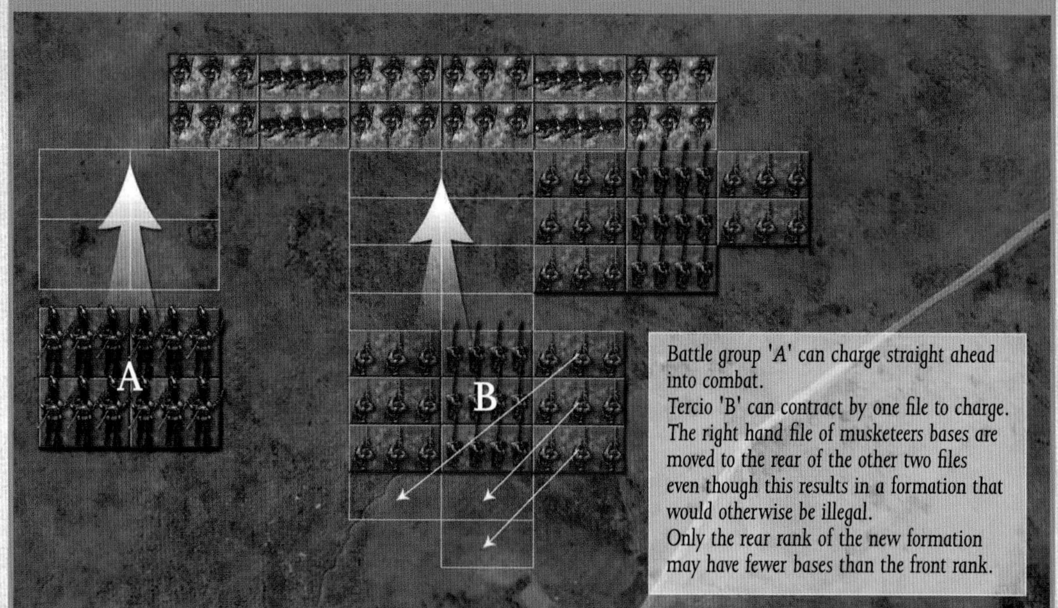


Battle group 'A' can charge straight ahead into combat.
Tercio 'B' can contract by one file to charge. The right hand file of musketeers bases are moved to the rear of the other two files even though this results in a formation that would otherwise be illegal.
Only the rear rank of the new formation may have fewer bases than the front rank.

When a battle group which started the game with one pike base and five musketeer bases has its pike base in the rearmost rank and charges or is charged, the owner can exchange the pike base with the musketeer base at the front of its file. (If preferred, this can simply be assumed to have been done without physically moving the bases.) When such a battle group ceases to be in close combat, it immediately reforms automatically with the pike base swapped to the rearmost rank.

Except as specified above, the **only** change in formation that is allowed during a charge move is to contract the battle group's frontage by one base only, at any point during the charge move, **if necessary** to pass friendly troops. This does not require a CMT. The frontage is reduced and bases fall back behind those in front even if this results in an illegal formation. A charging battle group cannot be contracted to avoid hitting enemy who would otherwise be in the path of its charge. No shifts, turns or expansions are permitted. If, owing to these restrictions, contact is not possible, the charge cannot be made and is cancelled.

# CHARGING TO CONTACT AND STEPPING FORWARDS

*To charge, move* your battle group forward making any wheels or formation changes allowed, until a "legal" contact is made. If it is now possible to get more bases into contact with the same or different enemy battle groups you MUST step them forward to make further contacts, unless exempted by the following rules:

To step forward after initial contact, slide any files of your battle group not yet in contact straight forward until the front base makes contact with enemy bases, subject to the following conditions:

- No file can be stepped forward more than 2 MUs from the original line of contact.
- Every stepped forward file must end in contact with an enemy.
- Every base in a file must step forward the same distance as the front rank base. This includes the rear shot horns of an early tercio.
- Each file must remain in at least corner to corner contact with an adjacent file of the battle group. (Exception: Rear shot horns of an early tercio that has suffered base losses may not be in corner to corner contact with any other base – see *Tercios* in the ***Battle Groups*** section.)
- The stepped forward distance is additional to the normal move distance plus any variable move distance already added.
- Light troops need not step forward into contact with an enemy battle group of battle troops that they otherwise would not contact.

Stepping forward therefore results in a battle group having an uneven line.

## CHARGE TO CONTACT

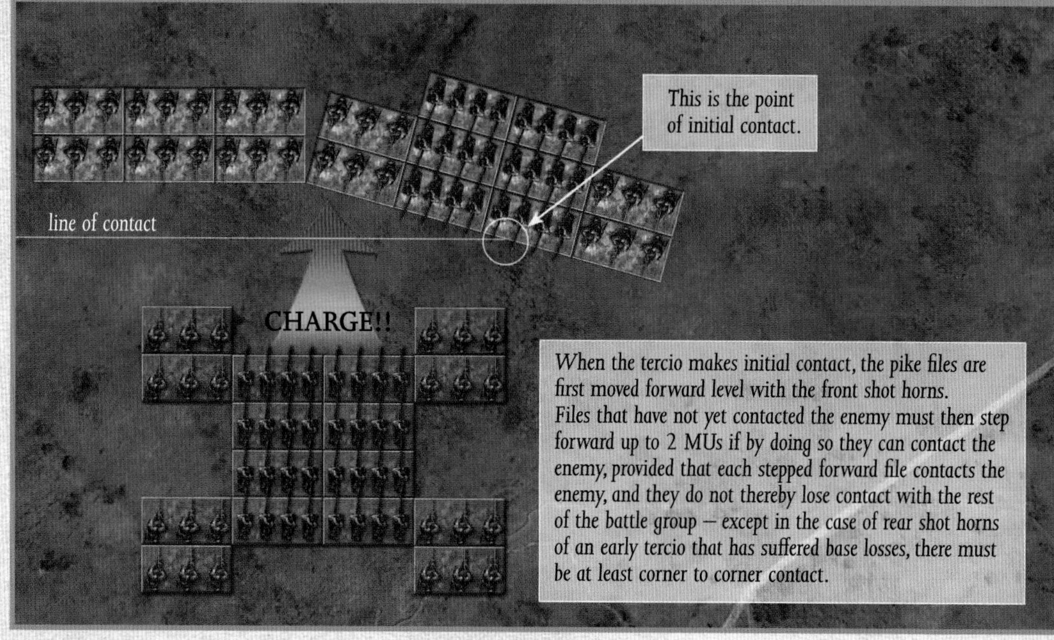


## STEPPING FORWARDS INTO CONTACT

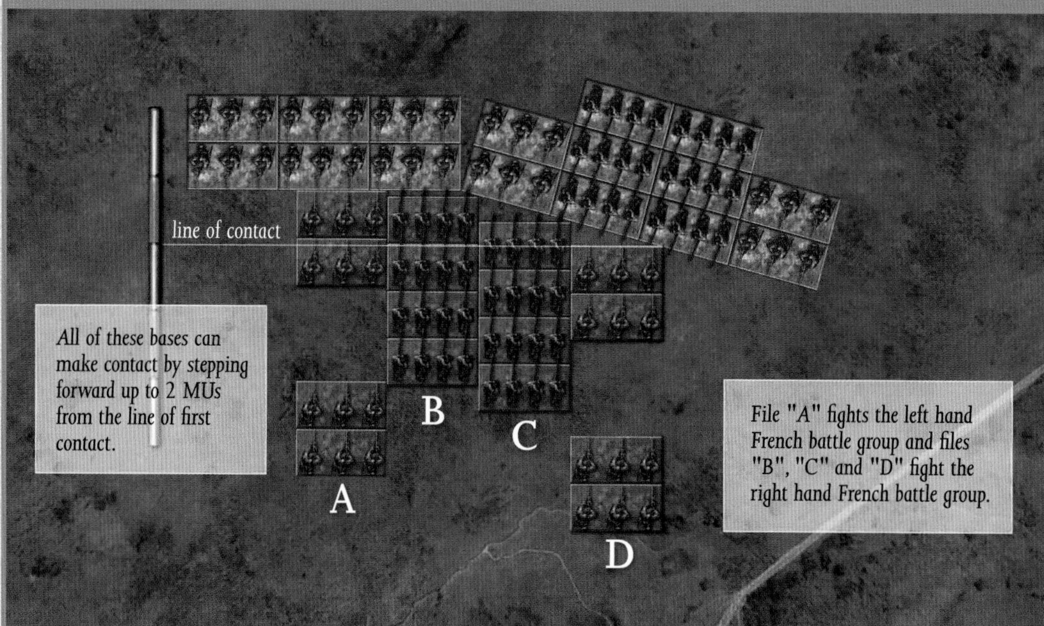

# CHARGING A FLANK OR REAR

*Flank and rear charges* can be devastating in effect but are more difficult to engineer. Subject to the exceptions below for tercios and keils, a battle group charged in the flank or rear may suffer an immediate drop in cohesion and always fights at a major disadvantage in the impact phase. The following rules apply to flank and rear charges:

- A battle group can only charge an enemy battle group in the flank or rear if it starts its charge in a position where both of the following apply (see diagram):
  - The charging battle group starts with no part of any of its bases directly in front of any part of any base of the target battle group.
  - The charging battle group starts with at least one base entirely behind a straight line extending the front edge of the enemy battle group. If the enemy battle group is in Swedish brigade formation and/or has regimental guns, its front edge is taken as the front edge ignoring the pike base in point position and the regimental gun marker. If the enemy battle group has some files stepped forward, its front edge is taken as the front edge of the file on the flank charged. If the enemy battle group is facing in more than one direction, it has more than one front edge for this purpose – the above requirement must be satisfied for all of them.
- For a charge to qualify as a flank charge both of the following must apply:
  - The first part of the enemy battle group contacted must be the side edge or rear corner of one of its bases.
  - The charge cannot include a wheel unless the charging battle group starts its move with its nearest point at least 1 MU away from the battle group being charged.
- For a charge to qualify as a rear charge, the first part of the enemy battle group contacted must be the rear edge of one of its bases.
- Battle wagons, early tercios, troops in ***square*** and troops attacked across fortifications (or an obstacle) they are defending (see the ***Special Features*** section) never count as being charged in flank or rear. Later tercios and keils never count as charged in flank. Battle wagons and troops in square do not turn if contacted on their side or rear base edge.
- Battle groups which are contacted by a flank or rear charge immediately drop one cohesion level unless they are battle troops contacted by light troops. (If contacted in flank or rear by more than one enemy battle group in the same turn, they only drop one level.)
- Bases contacted on a side or rear edge, or a rear corner, by an enemy flank or rear charge are immediately turned 90 degrees to face a flank charge, 180 degrees to face a rear charge, using the normal rules for turning, provided that they are not in the first two ranks of a file already in contact with enemy to its front. However, a second rank base that does not turn when contacted in flank will fight to the flank, and is treated as if it was facing the flank for the purpose of ***protection*** (see the ***Combat Mechanism*** section). The following special cases may occur:
  - If only one base of a file is contacted in flank, two bases are turned if eligible as



DECLARATION OF CHARGES
LEGAL CHARGE CONTACT
CHARGING WITH YOUR BATTLE GROUPS
FORMATION CHANGES WHEN CHARGING OR BEING CHARGED
CHARGING TO CONTACT AND STEPPING FORWARDS
CHARGING A FLANK OR REAR
CHARGING THE FLANK OR REAR OF A TERCIO
CHARGING THE FLANK OF A KEIL
TROOPS WHO CANNOT CHARGE
ATTEMPTS TO CHARGE MOUNTED BATTLE TROOPS OR ELEPHANTS WITH FOOT BATTLE TROOPS
ATTEMPTS TO CHARGE OR RECEIVE A CHARGE WITH LIGHT TROOPS
ATTEMPTS TO CHARGE WHEN DISRUPTED OR FRAGMENTED
ATTEMPTS TO CHARGE WHEN COUNTING THREATENED FLANK
BEING CHARGED WHILE FRAGMENTED
BEING CHARGED WHILE ROUTING
POSSIBLE RESPONSES TO CHARGES
SEQUENCE OF CHARGES AND RESPONSES
RESOLVING IMPACT PHASE COMBAT

TROOPS ABLE TO CHARGE A FLANK OR REAR

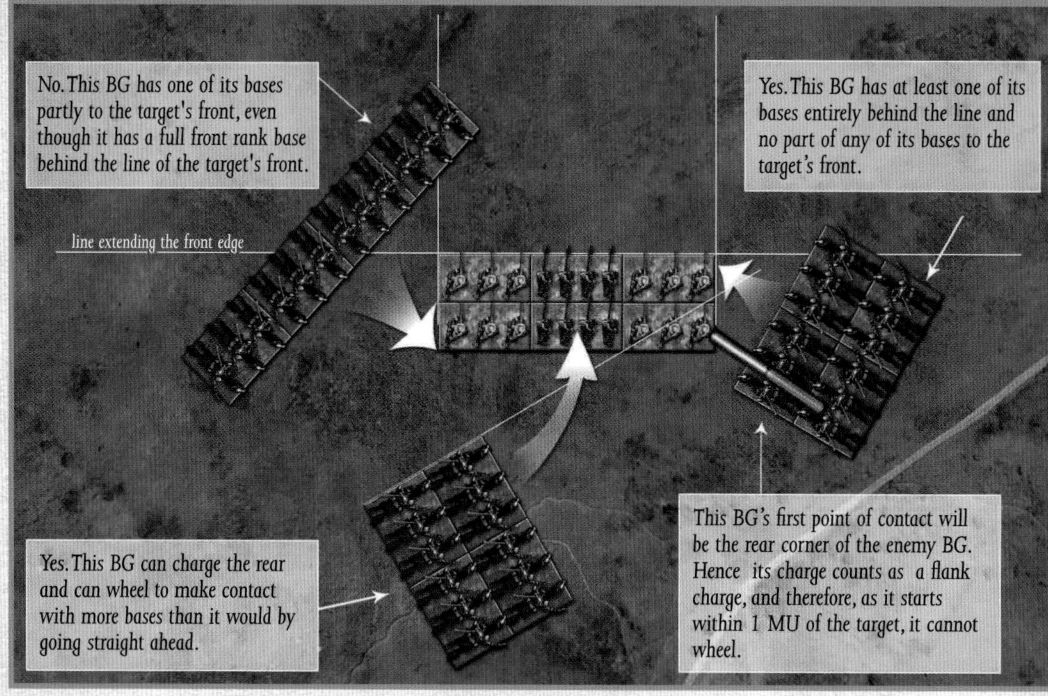


above (see the diagram *Tercio Responding to Two Flank Charges*).

- If none of the contacted bases are eligible to turn, one of them is nevertheless turned if the contact counted as a flank or rear charge, to indicate that this was so.
- If chargers block the turn, they are shifted back the minimum necessary to make room.
- If turning creates a gap between the bases that have been turned and the other bases of the battle group, the turned bases are shifted so as to remain in contact. The flank charging battle group then moves forward to maintain contact even if normal movement distance is exceeded.

- Flank/rear chargers always fight on a final overall ++ *Points of Advantage* (POA) (see the *Combat Mechanism* section) in the impact phase. Bases fighting against a flank or rear charge in the impact phase always fight on a final overall - - POA. No other POAs apply. (This means that flank/rear chargers always need 3s to hit whilst those being charged need 5s.)
- A charge which does not qualify as a flank or rear charge can still contact the flank or rear edge of enemy bases. Such a charge does not count as a flank or rear charge, and is treated as a normal charge on the enemy front:
  - Tercios and keils can always be so contacted, and turn bases as specified below.
  - Other battle groups can only be so contacted on bases which are not the 1st or 2nd rank of a file that is already in melee to its front. The contacted bases do

not turn. The normal POAs are used as if the charge had contacted the front of the enemy file. Thus, for example, if the 3rd rank base of a 4 rank deep pikemen battle group is contacted, the pikemen get their normal POA for 4 ranks deep pikemen. The chargers must, if possible, align with the enemy front in the manoeuvre phase. Even if it is not possible to align, troops charged in this way do not suffer a - POA in the subsequent melee phase(s) for "fighting enemy in two directions".

**TIP!**

Be careful to protect your flanks. It can be disastrous to get hit in the flank or rear by enemy.

# CHARGING THE FLANK OR REAR OF A TERCIO

*Early tercios never count* as being charged in flank or rear. Later tercios never count as being charged in flank. Bases of a tercio contacted in circumstances which would otherwise qualify as a flank or rear charge, are turned as if it was a flank or rear charge. All contacted bases fight the same enemy they would if it was a flank or rear charge.

In addition, when any base of an early tercio is contacted to its flank or rear, pike belonging to the battle group, who are not the front rank of a pike file or already in front edge contact with enemy, are automatically moved into position, in up to 2 ranks, level with the shot on that edge and facing the enemy. (This will give ***protection*** to both – see the ***Combat Mechanism*** *section.*) These pike bases will then fight in the impact phase with any enemy bases in contact (who must, if necessary, be moved back to make room). The new position occupied by the automatically moving pike bases must be within the "footprint" (see ***glossary***) of the tercio.

Similarly, if any base of a later tercio is contacted to its flank, shot in the 3rd or 4th rank (if any) are moved to any other part of the battle group, and pike belonging to the battle group, who are not the front rank of a pike file or already in front edge contact with enemy, are automatically moved into position, in up to 2 ranks, level with the remaining shot on that edge and facing the enemy. 1st and 2nd rank shot, even if not contacted, are also turned to face the flank unless the front rank base is already in close combat to its front.

## TERCIO RESPONDING TO TWO FLANK CHARGES

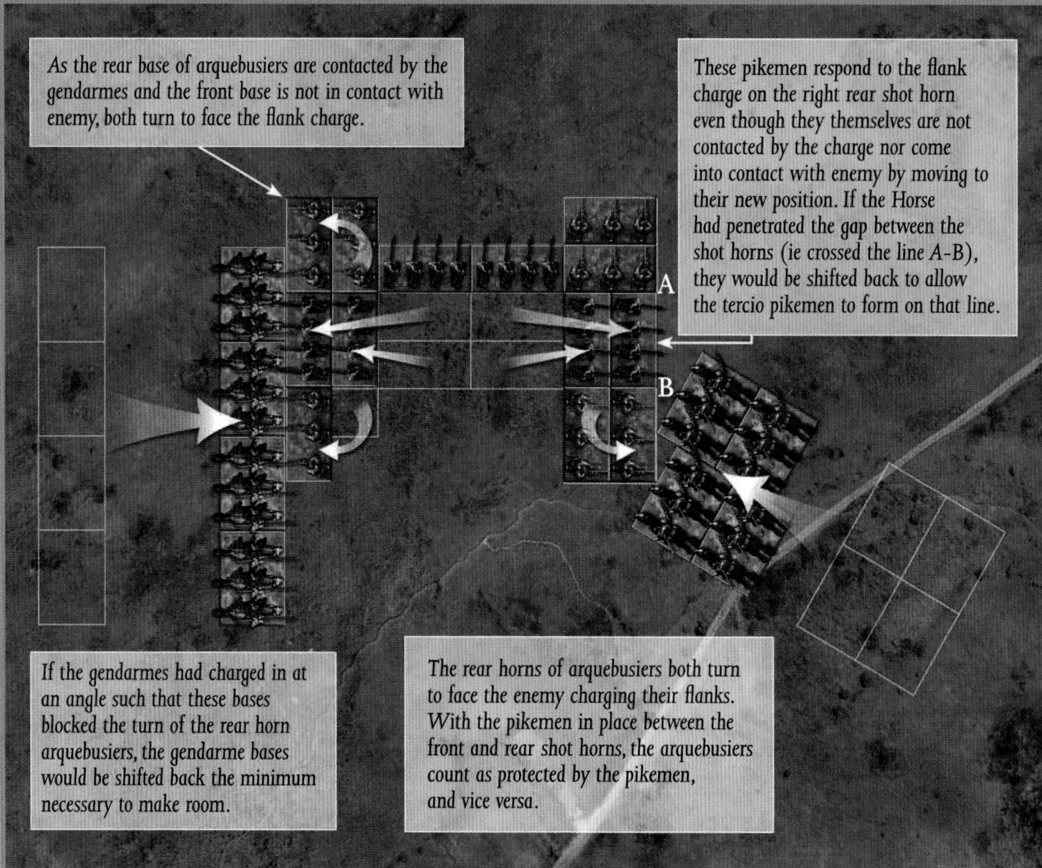


# CHARGING THE FLANK OF A KEIL

*Keils never count* as being charged in flank. If any bases of a keil not in a file with pikes are contacted in flank, all the bases in their file are moved to the rear of the pike files and the enemy is moved into contact with the nearest pike file. If any halberdier or swordsmen bases in a pike file are contacted in flank, they are moved to any other part of the battle group and replaced by pike bases. Pike bases are turned to face the enemy as if it was a flank or rear charge, in up to 2 ranks. All bases then in contact fight the same enemy they would if it was a flank or rear charge.

## SWISS CHARGED FROM FRONT AND FLANK (1)

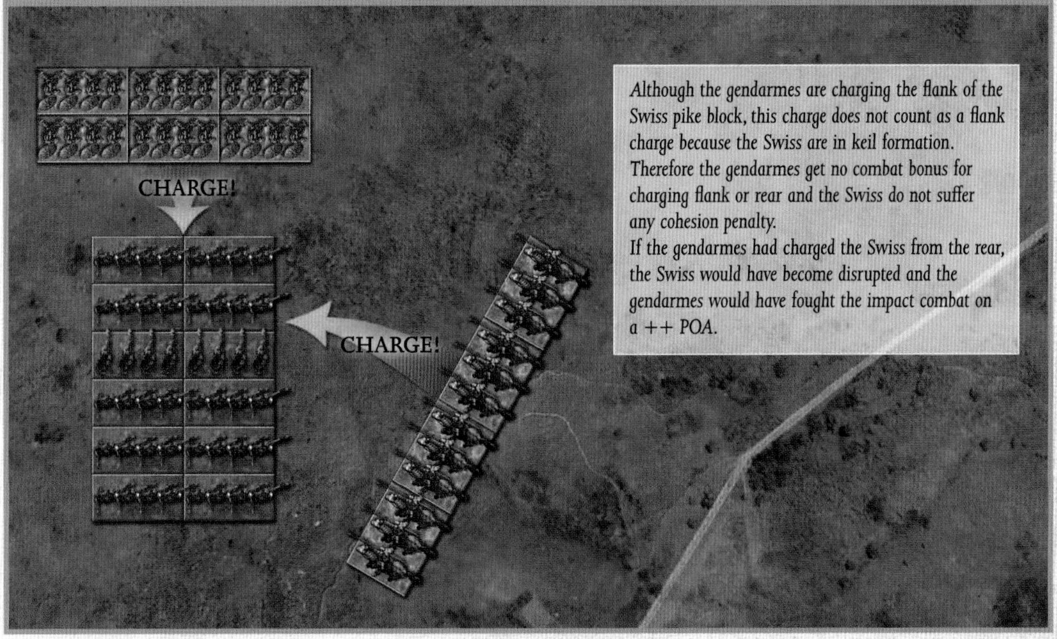


*Although the gendarmes are charging the flank of the Swiss pike block, this charge does not count as a flank charge because the Swiss are in keil formation. Therefore the gendarmes get no combat bonus for charging flank or rear and the Swiss do not suffer any cohesion penalty.*
*If the gendarmes had charged the Swiss from the rear, the Swiss would have become disrupted and the gendarmes would have fought the impact combat on a ++ POA.*

## SWISS CHARGED FROM FRONT AND FLANK (2)

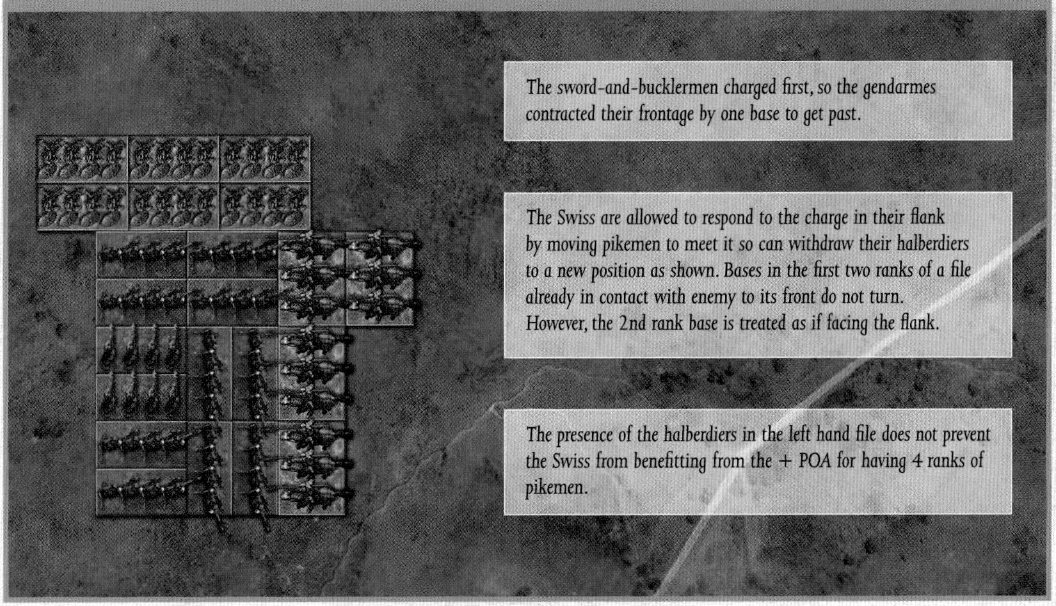

The sword-and-bucklermen charged first, so the gendarmes contracted their frontage by one base to get past.

The Swiss are allowed to respond to the charge in their flank by moving pikemen to meet it so can withdraw their halberdiers to a new position as shown. Bases in the first two ranks of a file already in contact with enemy to its front do not turn. However, the 2nd rank base is treated as if facing the flank.

The presence of the halberdiers in the left hand file does not prevent the Swiss from benefitting from the + POA for having 4 ranks of pikemen.

# TROOPS WHO CANNOT CHARGE

*Battle wagons and artillery* cannot move in the impact phase. They cannot charge and cannot intercept.

# ATTEMPTS TO CHARGE MOUNTED BATTLE TROOPS OR ELEPHANTS WITH FOOT BATTLE TROOPS

*Unless charging their flank* or rear, foot battle troops must pass a CMT to charge unbroken mounted battle troops or elephants.

Foot battle troops cannot intercept mounted battle troops in any circumstances.

# ATTEMPTS TO CHARGE OR RECEIVE A CHARGE WITH LIGHT TROOPS

*Light troops are understandably* reluctant to engage in close combat with more heavily equipped troops. As a result:

- Light foot, dragoons and light horse can charge artillery unless it is unlimbered and has ***rear support*** (See the ***Combat Mechanism*** section).
- Otherwise:
  - Light foot cannot charge unbroken battle troops in ***open terrain*** (see ***glossary***), even in the flank or rear. They cannot intercept in any circumstances.
  - Dragoons cannot charge unbroken battle troops in open terrain, even in the flank or rear, unless the enemy are FRAGMENTED. They cannot intercept in any circumstances.
  - Light horse must pass a CMT to charge unbroken battle troops unless charging their flank or rear. They cannot intercept battle troops in any circumstances.
- If any of their charge targets evade, light troops must halt their charge 1 MU away from enemy to their front whom they would not normally be allowed to charge without a CMT (unless the enemy was an eligible charge target at the time of charge declaration and they passed a CMT to charge them).

- Light troops must pass a CMT to receive a charge by enemy battle troops (and must evade if they fail the CMT) unless either of the following applies:
  - They are already in close combat other than only as an overlap – in which situation evading is never possible.
  - They are light foot or dragoons entirely in uneven, rough or difficult terrain or defending fortifications, an obstacle or a riverbank.

# ATTEMPTS TO CHARGE WHEN DISRUPTED OR FRAGMENTED

*Troops who are disrupted* or fragmented are less keen to charge. As a result:

- DISRUPTED non-shock battle groups must pass a CMT to charge.
- FRAGMENTED battle groups cannot charge.

# ATTEMPTS TO CHARGE WHEN COUNTING THREATENED FLANK

*Foot battle troops counting* as having ***threatened flank*** (see ***glossary***) must pass a CMT to charge.

# BEING CHARGED WHILE FRAGMENTED

*A fragmented battle group* is very vulnerable and is quite likely to turn and flee if charged. As a result:

- FRAGMENTED battle groups must take a cohesion test if being charged by any troops other than light foot.
- If they BREAK as a result of the test, they cause immediate cohesion tests on friendly battle groups in range, and then make an initial rout move before the chargers are moved.

Where a friendly battle group initially blocks them from being contacted by an enemy charge, they need not take a cohesion test unless the friendly battle group moves to clear the path by evading or routing.

# BEING CHARGED WHILE ROUTING

*If routing troops of any type* are charged they make no response of any kind. The chargers are moved into contact with them, but nothing else happens until the Joint Action Phase (see the ***Joint Action Phase*** section). In the JAP the chargers are treated as normal pursuers, and will inflict base losses if they remain in contact at the end of a pursuit move.

Note that pursuers who have lost contact with routers cannot charge them again until they have stopped pursuing.

# POSSIBLE RESPONSES TO CHARGES

*Prior to moving chargers*, there are three possible responses by the enemy: receiving the charge, interception charges and evade moves. We cover each in turn.

## RECEIVING THE CHARGE

Troops receiving a charge **never** count as "charging" when determining combat factors. However, the combat factors are designed to take account of any appropriate response, e.g. Royalist cavaliers being charged by Cromwell's Ironsides can be assumed to countercharge. We do not depict this minor movement on the tabletop, but the combat factors take account of the full interaction.

*Musketeers receive charge*

## INTERCEPTION CHARGES

Each battle group has a zone to its front where it can interfere with the charge of an opposing battle group. This mechanism allows you to cover flanks and protect nearby friendly troops. We call this the **Zone of Interception (ZOI)**:

- The ZOI is 2 MUs for foot and 4 MUs for mounted troops and elephants. It extends only directly to the intercepting battle group's front and only through terrain that does not disorder or severely disorder it. A battle group cannot intercept an enemy battle group if, due to intervening terrain, no part of the enemy battle group is visible to it before either battle group moves.
- If an enemy battle group attempts to charge through the ZOI of a battle group that is not itself a target of any charge this turn, that battle group has the option of making an interception charge on the chargers.
- DISRUPTED non-shock troops must pass a CMT to intercept.
- FRAGMENTED troops, light foot, dragoons, artillery, battle wagons, troops in square and troops defending field fortifications or an obstacle cannot intercept.
- Light horse cannot intercept battle troops.
- Foot battle troops cannot intercept mounted battle troops.
- A battle group that is itself charged cannot intercept. This applies even if a charge was

### CATHOLIC LEAGUE CUIRASSIERS INTERCEPT A PROTESTANT CHARGE TOWARDS CATHOLIC LEAGUE FOOT

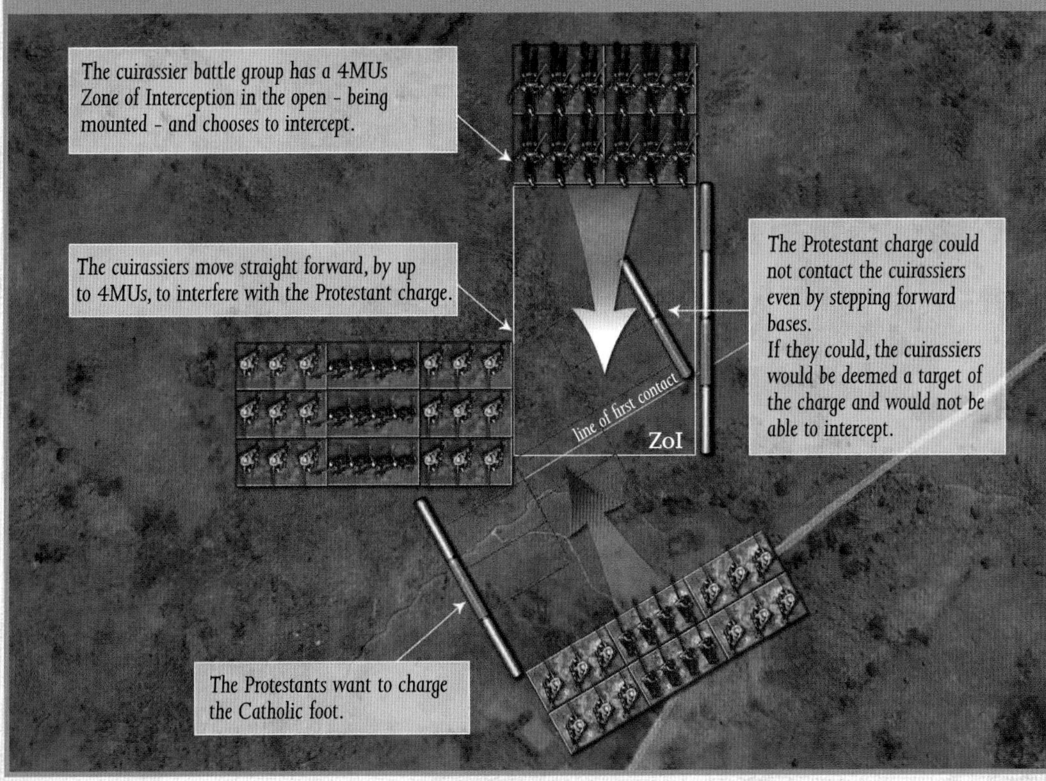

## BLOCKING MOVE BY INTERCEPTING MOUNTED

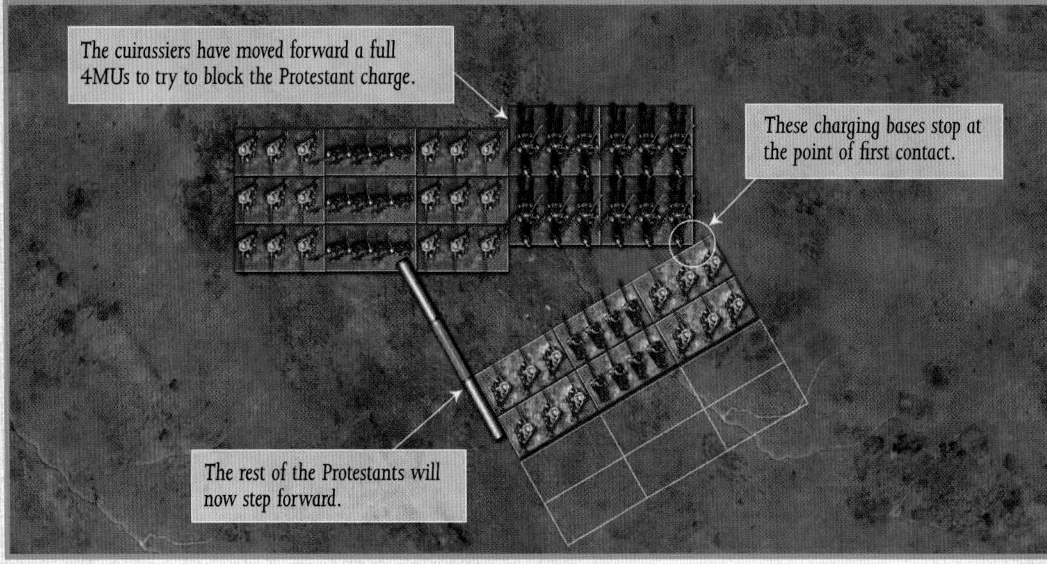


not declared on it, if it is in the path of a charge and would be contacted (including by bases stepping forward) if no friendly battle group evaded.

- An interception charge must be straight forward (except in the special circumstances specified in the first bullet below) and can be up to the limit of the battle group's ZOI. It cannot include any shifts, changes of formation or interpenetrations. It must either:
  - Cross the path of the charging enemy battle group, stopping short of contacting it. Interceptors move before chargers. If this would result in the enemy chargers contacting its flank, the intercepting battle group can and must wheel towards them to avoid this, its total move distance including the wheel not exceeding 4 MUs if mounted troops or elephants, 2 MUs if foot. If it cannot avoid being contacted in the flank, the interception is cancelled.
  - Contact the flank or rear of the charging enemy battle group only. This is only permitted if the intercepting battle group started in a position to charge the flank or rear of the enemy battle group as previously described (or would be in such a position if the enemy battle group was not a tercio or keil). It cancels the enemy battle group's charge completely. Despite the fact that it happens in the enemy's turn, it is treated as a normal charge, counting as a flank/rear charge if the intercepted battle group is not immune to such. The intercepting battle group steps forward as it would in a normal charge.
- Unless its charge is cancelled as above, the original charging battle group must now complete its charge move. This may partly or wholly contact the intercepting battle group, and may or may not contact the original target of the charge at all. Under no circumstances can chargers evade or halt to avoid contacting interceptors.
- An intercepting battle group cannot itself be intercepted.

FINAL POSITION AFTER STEPPING FORWARDS

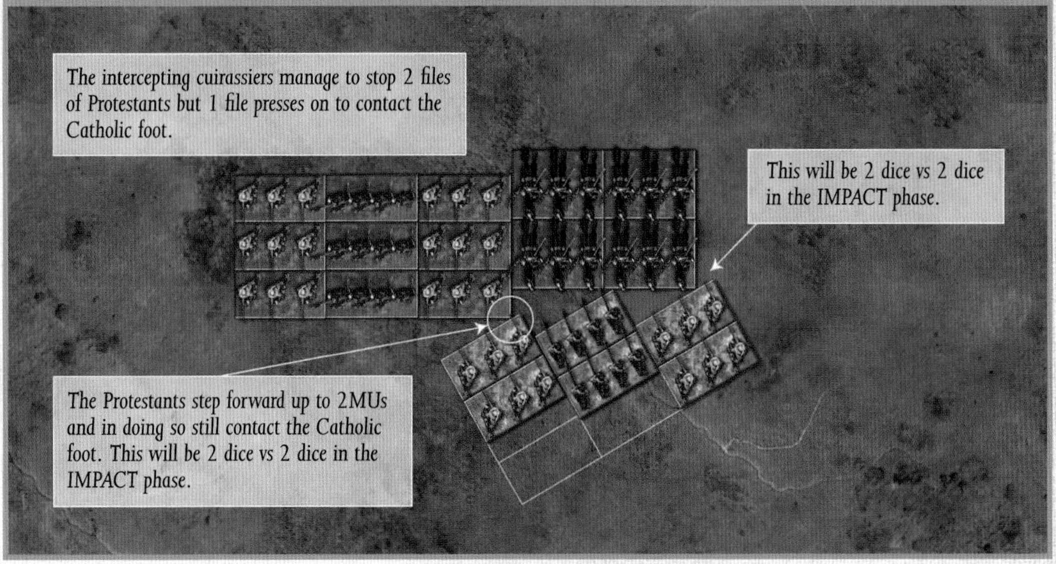


- Interceptors are treated as charging for the purpose of determining Impact Phase combat POAs (see the ***Combat Resolution*** section).

## TIP!

Position some of your battle groups so that they can cover your flanks by intercepting enemy chargers. Watch for enemy who could intercept your own planned charges – especially in flank or rear.

## EVADE MOVES

Some troops are able to harass the enemy then retreat out of the way if charged. We call this evading. The distance moved by both evaders and chargers is variable so there is a risk that evaders may get caught.

Light troops can evade whatever their formation. Cavalry and camelry who are not shock troops can evade if they are formed up *entirely 1 base deep*. This represents a looser, more flexible formation than when they are deployed 2 or more bases deep, often in reality consisting of small clumps of men separated by gaps.

The procedure is as follows:

- Non-shock cavalry or camelry entirely 1 base deep or light troops can choose to evade an enemy battle group's charge unless they are already in close combat other than only as an overlap or are routing. A commander with a battle group that evades must evade with it.
- Light troops must pass a CMT not to evade from charging enemy battle troops unless either of the following apply:
  - They are already in close combat other than only as an overlap – in which situation evading is never possible.
  - They are light foot or dragoons entirely in uneven, rough or difficult terrain or defending fortifications, an obstacle or a riverbank.
- When troops who can evade are charged, their player must decide whether or not they will evade.

- The evading troops then have two choices:
  - They can evade in the direction of the charge. If charged by two or more enemy battle groups, bisect the angle between the enemy charge directions.
  - Unless charged in flank or rear they can evade directly to their own rear.
- After choosing which of the above two options to adopt, the evader makes a variable move distance roll.
- If evading to its own rear, the battle group turns 180 degrees, and makes its evade move directly forwards (which is to its original rear) adjusting for the variable move distance.
- If evading in the direction of the charge, the battle group must first turn 180 or 90 degrees (player's choice) unless its existing facing is closer to the direction of the charge. It must then wheel until it is facing a direction parallel to the chargers' indicated direction of charge. It then completes its evade move directly forwards, adjusting for the variable move distance.
- When making a 90 degree turn whilst evading, the normal rules for 90 degree turns are followed, except that the positioning of the turned battle group is different: The old side edge nearest the chargers becomes the new rear edge. The old front edge of the battle group becomes the new side edge.
- If an evading battle group encounters any obstructions, the following rules apply:
  - It interpenetrates friends if allowed to do so. (See ***Interpenetration*** in the ***General Movement*** section.)
  - It can shift sideways up to one base width to get past friendly troops it cannot interpenetrate, enemy troops, a camp or terrain, or to avoid leaving the table. All bases must end in edge to edge and corner to corner contact with another base of the battle group. The battle group cannot split.

## SEQUENCE SHOWING A SIMPLE EVADE MOVE OF LIGHT HORSE HERGULETIERS AWAY FROM FULLY ARMOURED GENDARMES WITH A SMALL SHIFT

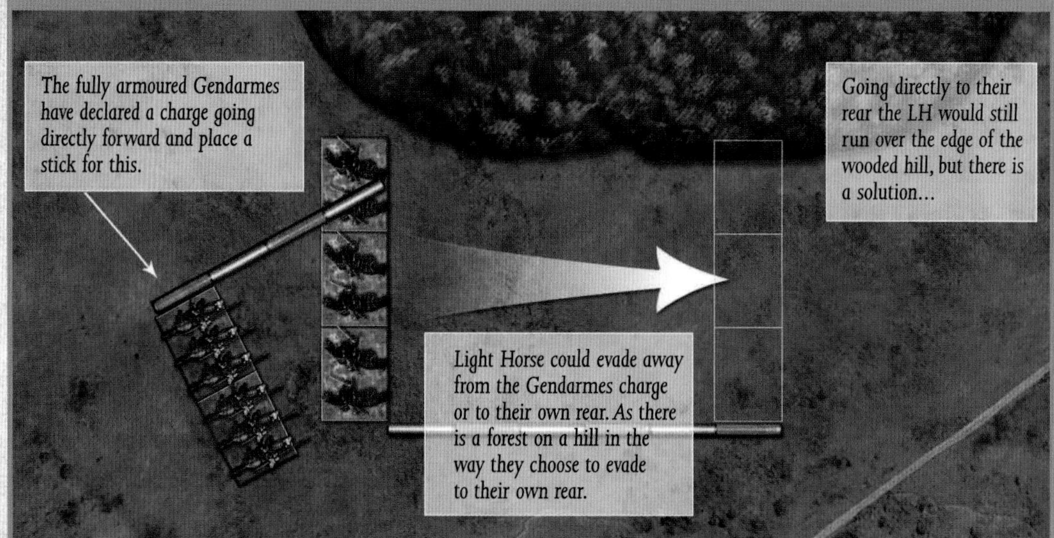

- Provided that they do not shift more than one base width sideways, bases that cannot get past an obstruction can be moved to the rear of those bases that have been able to complete their evade move. In this situation the battle group is more likely to get caught, as its rear will not move as far as its front.
- The evade move can include both of the above provided that no individual base shifts more than 1 base width sideways in total from the path it would have followed if there had been no obstruction.
- If the above would not allow all front rank bases to complete their evade move the battle group:
  - must instead burst through any friendly battle group in its normal evade path, with

DECLARATION OF CHARGES
LEGAL CHARGE CONTACT
CHARGING WITH YOUR BATTLE GROUPS
FORMATION CHANGES WHEN CHARGING OR BEING CHARGED
CHARGING TO CONTACT AND STEPPING FORWARDS
CHARGING A FLANK OR REAR
CHARGING THE FLANK OR REAR OF A TERCIO
CHARGING THE FLANK OF A KEIL
TROOPS WHO CANNOT CHARGE
ATTEMPTS TO CHARGE MOUNTED BATTLE TROOPS OR ELEPHANTS WITH FOOT BATTLE TROOPS
ATTEMPTS TO CHARGE OR RECEIVE A CHARGE WITH LIGHT TROOPS
ATTEMPTS TO CHARGE WHEN DISRUPTED OR FRAGMENTED
ATTEMPTS TO CHARGE WHEN COUNTING THREATENED FLANK
BEING CHARGED WHILE FRAGMENTED
BEING CHARGED WHILE ROUTING
POSSIBLE RESPONSES TO CHARGES
SEQUENCE OF CHARGES AND RESPONSES
RESOLVING IMPACT PHASE COMBAT

no shifting or contraction being allowed at all. The battle group is moved to the full extent of its evade move and any battle groups even partially burst through drop 1 level of cohesion immediately. (Note that battle groups passed through by evaders who can normally interpenetrate them do not count as burst through.)

- must instead halt 1 MU away from any enemy battle group in its path, with no shifting or contraction being allowed at all, and if it starts closer to them than 1 MU, does not move at all.

• If the evading battle group meets terrain it cannot enter, or has too little move to enter, or a camp, it turns 90 degrees and wheels to move parallel to the edge of the terrain or camp in whichever direction is closest to its original evade direction. (If equal, the evading player can choose.)

## BG TURNING 90 DEGREES TO EVADE

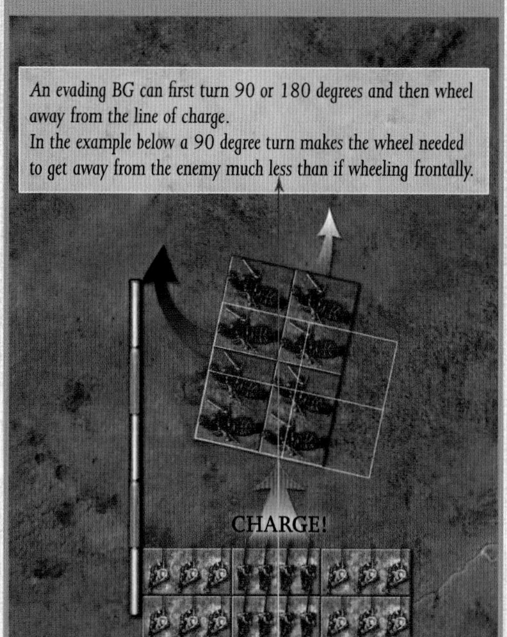


• Battle groups that cannot complete an evade move by any of the above means move as far as they can, and are likely to be caught.

• If the evading battle group meets a side table edge or the opponent's rear table edge, it can choose to turn 90 degrees and wheel to move parallel to the table edge in whichever direction is closest to directly away from the chargers (if equal, the evading player can choose); otherwise it leaves the table if any base even partly

## BG TURNING 90 DEGREES TO EVADE

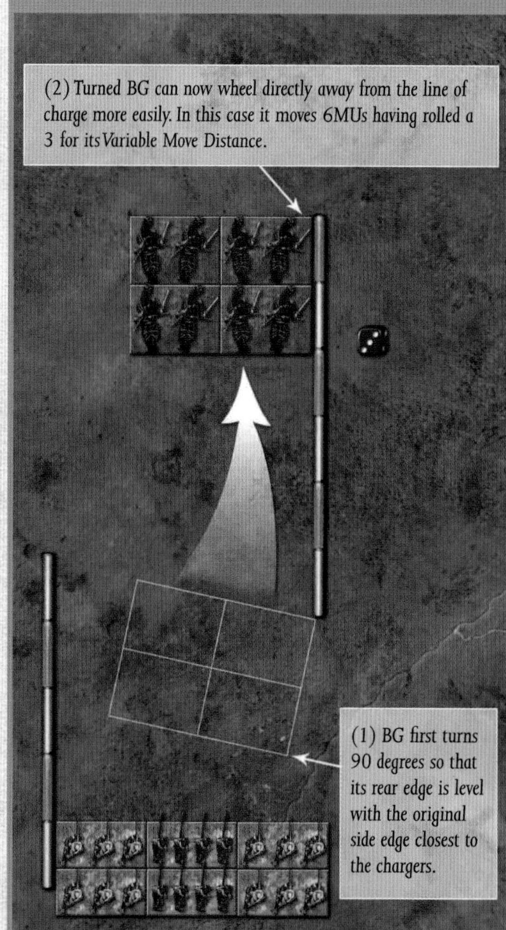

crosses the table edge. It cannot turn to avoid leaving its own rear table edge. Troops that evade off the table take no further part in the game and count as 1 attrition point towards army rout.

- The chargers now move their charge move, adjusting the move distance by a VMD roll if all their charge targets evaded. If all target battle groups evade out of the original path of the charge, the chargers can wheel in an attempt to catch them. A charging battle group whose move would take any part of it off the table edge instead halts its move at the table edge.
- Evaders who are contacted by chargers **always count as having been charged in flank/rear.**

## TIP!

Try to leave gaps for your troops to evade through. If you don't, they may burst through and disrupt your main battle line.

*The last stand of the Duke of Newcastle's Whitecoats, 1644, by Graham Turner © Osprey Publishing Ltd. Taken from Campaign 119:* Marston Moor.

# SEQUENCE OF CHARGES AND RESPONSES

*Charges and any responses* to them must be actioned in the order listed in the full turn sequence at the end of the book. The active player chooses the order of his charge moves. The non-active player chooses the order of his intercept moves. He also chooses the order (and direction) of his evade moves – before making any VMD rolls. Often, however, the results of charges declared in one area of the field cannot affect charges elsewhere, so it is usually convenient to fully resolve the sequence of pre-combat events in one area before proceeding to the next. Once all responses and all charge moves have been completed, impact combat is resolved.

# RESOLVING IMPACT PHASE COMBAT

*The combat for all bases* that have made contact this impact phase is now resolved. Note that where battle groups already had some bases in contact which fought in a previous turn, they do not fight now. Only new impact combats are resolved now. See the ***Combat Mechanism*** section.

# MANOEUVRE PHASE

*The battle of the Chikumagawa ford, 1561, by Wayne Reynolds © Osprey Publishing Ltd. Taken from Campaign 130:* Kawanakajima 1553–64.

*In the manoeuvre phase* the active player can move any available battle groups or commanders as permitted by the movement rules. Battle groups that are broken, already in close combat or still pursuing routers, or that charged, pursued or evaded (unlikely but possible) in the impact phase, cannot make a move in the manoeuvre phase. (Reforming, conforming to enemy or feeding more bases into an existing melee do not count as moves so are not prevented. Turning on the spot or placing/picking up portable defences do, so are.)

Commanders cannot be moved in the manoeuvre phase if they are fighting in the front rank of a battle group in close combat or pursuit or are with a battle group that charged, pursued, evaded or made an initial rout move in the impact phase.

Below are specific movement rules that apply in this phase.

# REFORMING

*If, as a consequence of* previous events, (other than forming square), a battle group is no longer in a "legal" formation (see ***Battle Group Formations*** section), it can reform in **either side's** manoeuvre phase.

- It reforms into a legal formation facing the direction previously faced by any of its bases (player's choice) and level with the furthest forward base in that direction. The final position and formation of the reformed battle group must be as close as possible to its position and formation prior to reforming. Bases in contact with the front edge of enemy bases must remain in contact with the same enemy bases.
- A battle group must reform if it is to make any voluntary move. (Feeding more bases into an existing melee does not count as a move.)
- Reforming occurs at the start of the manoeuvre phase and does not affect any of the other manoeuvre phase rules.
- A battle group currently fighting in two or more directions against enemy battle groups in close combat (or that would count as doing so if it wasn't a tercio or keil) cannot reform.

REFORMING

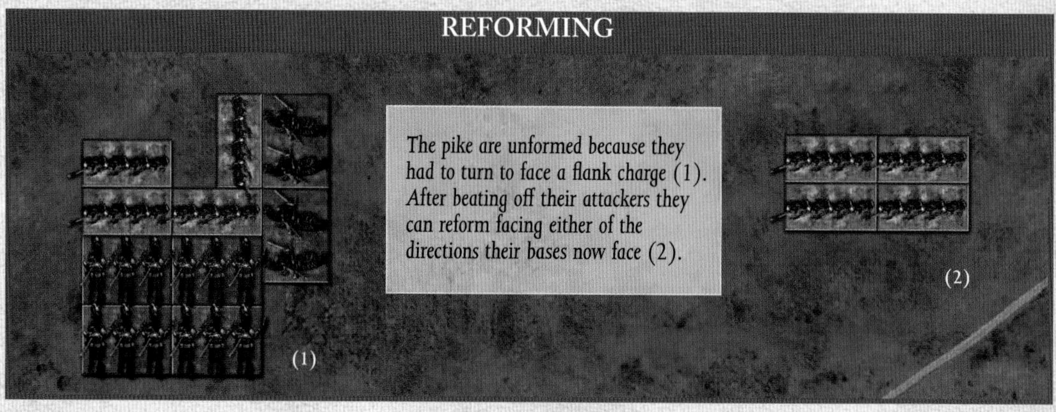


The pike are unformed because they had to turn to face a flank charge (1). After beating off their attackers they can reform facing either of the directions their bases now face (2).

- A battle group that has some of its bases facing enemy currently in contact with its flank or rear (and no enemy in contact to its front) is not forced to reform. If it does so, however, it must reform to face the enemy in contact.

# CONFORMING TO ENEMY IN CLOSE COMBAT

*At the start of the manoeuvre phase*, the active player's battle groups already in close combat with enemy **must** (unless otherwise stated below or physically impossible) pivot and/or slide bases by the minimum necessary to conform to the enemy bases in contact:

- Conforming usually means lining up each base in full front edge to front edge contact with an enemy base, or conforming to an *overlap position* (see below). If fighting against the flank of bases which were unable to turn to face, it means lining up in front edge contact with the enemy flank edge, with at least one base in front corner contact with an enemy front corner.
- The battle group must end its conform move in a normal formation (see ***The Basics*** section), except that each file steps forward to line up with the nearest file already in contact with enemy. This may result in additional enemy bases being contacted.
- If bases are in contact with the flank of enemy bases as a result of a charge that did not qualify as a flank or rear charge (unless the only reason it did not qualify is that the enemy bases are part of a tercio or keil), the battle group must pivot to conform with the front edge of the enemy battle group, sliding the minimum necessary to contact the front edge of at least one enemy base, or to an overlap position if this is not possible. This may sometimes look odd, but is a game mechanism to provide on-table clarification that the enemy battle group is not ***fighting enemy in 2 directions*** in the melee phase. This still applies even if conforming is not possible.
- Friendly battle groups not in contact with enemy must be shifted sideways sufficiently to make room for the above, provided that this is not blocked by enemy, impassable terrain or a camp and no bases would cross the table edge.
- Troops that cannot conform by any of the above methods do not move but continue to fight in an offset formation. They may however be able to conform at a later stage.
- A battle group is never required to conform if doing so will expose it to a flank or rear charge by an enemy battle group next turn (unless a flank or rear charge by that battle group is possible even if it does not conform).
- A battle group that has some bases facing at 90 or 180 degrees to the rest (due to enemy contacting its former flank or rear) does not conform to enemy.
- Battle wagons, artillery, troops in square and troops defending field fortifications, an obstacle or a riverbank, or in a river, do not conform to enemy.

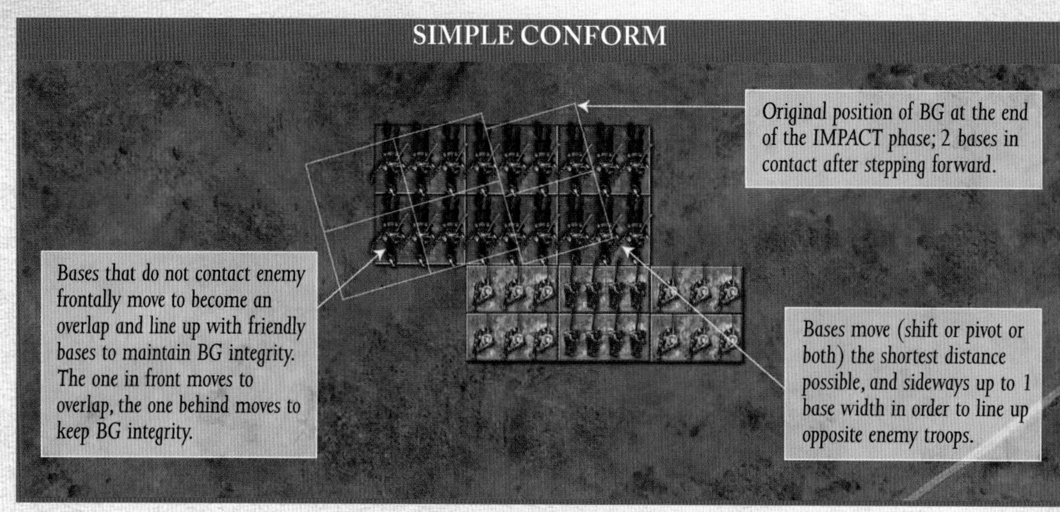


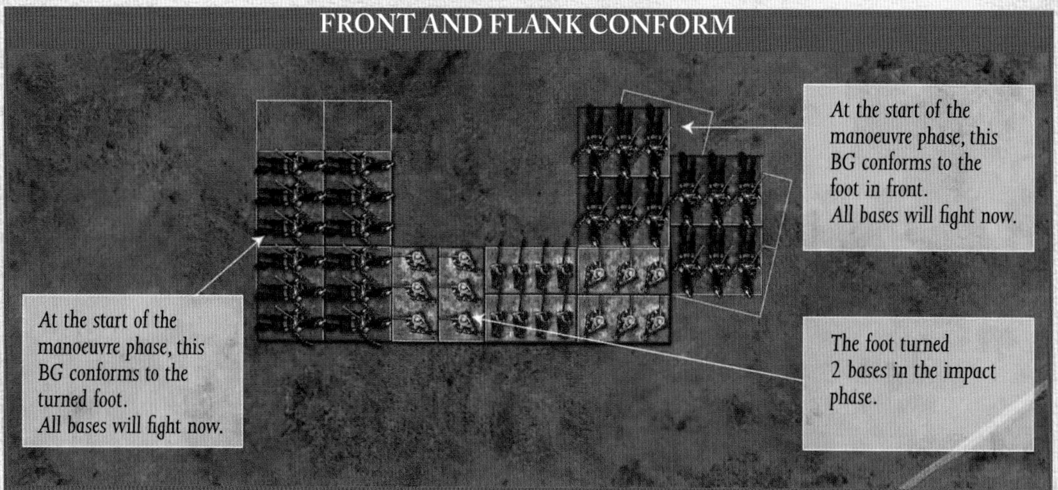


# FEEDING MORE BASES INTO AN EXISTING CLOSE COMBAT

A *battle group involved* in close combat can gradually feed in more and more of its troops until they are all fighting. The following mechanisms are used to represent this (the contraction and expansions mentioned are merely rule mechanisms to achieve this). They do not require a CMT and are not compulsory:

- If there is room to do so, a battle group that is already in contact with enemy can expand its frontage by one file (a base frontage) on one side only, unless that would result in an illegal formation. Special cases:
- Where a battle group is unable to expand its frontage without adopting an illegal

formation but has bases in its front rank which are unable to contribute even as an overlap to a melee, the whole battle group can be shifted sideways one base width instead. If it is fighting enemy on two or more sides, the shift cannot be made.

- Where a battle group is in a narrower than normal formation (e.g. a single base wide column), but cannot form a legal formation by expanding its frontage by one file, it can expand into a non-legal formation intermediate between its present formation and a wider legal formation.
- The active player makes his expansion or shift, if any, first. The non-active player can then expand or shift to match this expansion or shift, or to match a pre-existing overlap. He cannot expand or shift except to match the active player's new or pre-existing overlap.
- Alternatively, instead of expanding, either player can move bases currently unable to contribute to the combat into a non-front rank position provided that they could then contribute to the combat – (with dice or by creating a ***Point of Advantage*** **(POA)** (see ***glossary***) or denying the enemy a POA) – unless that would result in an illegal formation. This may result in contraction of the battle group frontage.
- Except when the whole battle group shifts as above, only bases that fulfil the following criteria can be moved:
  - They must not be in a position to contribute to combat prior to being moved (with dice or by creating a POA or denying the enemy a POA). Exception: Bases with heavy weapon or swordsmen capability in a file of Pike can be moved if sufficient Pike remain in the file to maintain the current POAs.
  - They must not have any enemy bases in front edge contact with them, nor able to fight them as an overlap.
  - Moving them must not result in contraction by more than one file on any side of the battle group.
  - If they are a 2nd rank base in a file that will fight as an overlap, troops of a type that normally fight in melee with 1 dice per base in the first 2 ranks cannot be moved into a front rank position.
- Subject to the restrictions above, troops can be moved out from non-front ranks, or from an unengaged end of a line to a non-front rank or the other end of the line. Tercios and mixed foot battle groups may be able to shift sideways instead. This represents a gradual spreading of the melee.
- A battle group can only expand into contact with a new enemy battle group if either of the following apply:
- The new enemy battle group was already fighting it as an overlap.
- The contact does not result in the previously unengaged enemy battle group entering close combat (with the expanding battle group) other than as an overlap.
- Bases cannot be "lapped round" the end of an enemy formation to get extra bases in front edge contact.
- Battle wagons never expand or contract in close combat.

**TIP!**

Make use of your numbers by feeding extra troops into combats to try to overwhelm the enemy.

## FEEDING MORE BASES INTO MELEE (1)

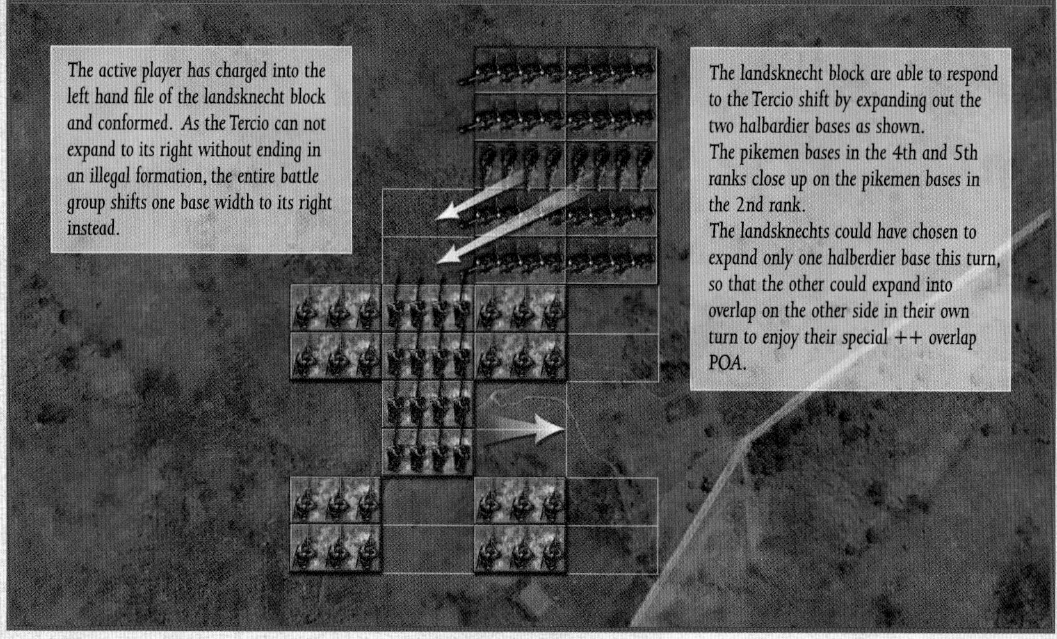


## EARLY TERCIOS

Early tercios are a special case. They can, if they are unable to shift as above, use the following methods to feed additional troops into combat. In each turn, they can move up to 2 bases (total) in any of the following ways:

- Turn a horn of shot to enter close combat.
- Move shot to a different horn.
- Move pike to a different pike file.
- Move pike to occupy a vacant file beside shot or pike already in close combat.

The resulting formation is deemed legal until the tercio is no longer in close combat or chooses to reform.

When moving bases as above, the following additional rules apply:

- No base can move outside the *footprint* of the tercio.
- Shot can only occupy the horn positions.
- Pike can only occupy the gaps between horn positions.
- The two front horn positions must always be connected by pike files at least 1 rank deep.
- The non-active player can match an overlap by the active player's troops, but not create a new overlap of his own.
- Bases cannot be moved if they are already in a position to contribute dice to close combat. (But can if they are only contributing to a POA).
- Bases cannot be moved if they have any enemy bases in front edge contact with them, or able to fight them as an overlap.
- Shot bases cannot be moved if this would leave any shot horn without at least 1 shot base.

FEEDING MORE BASES INTO MELEE (2)

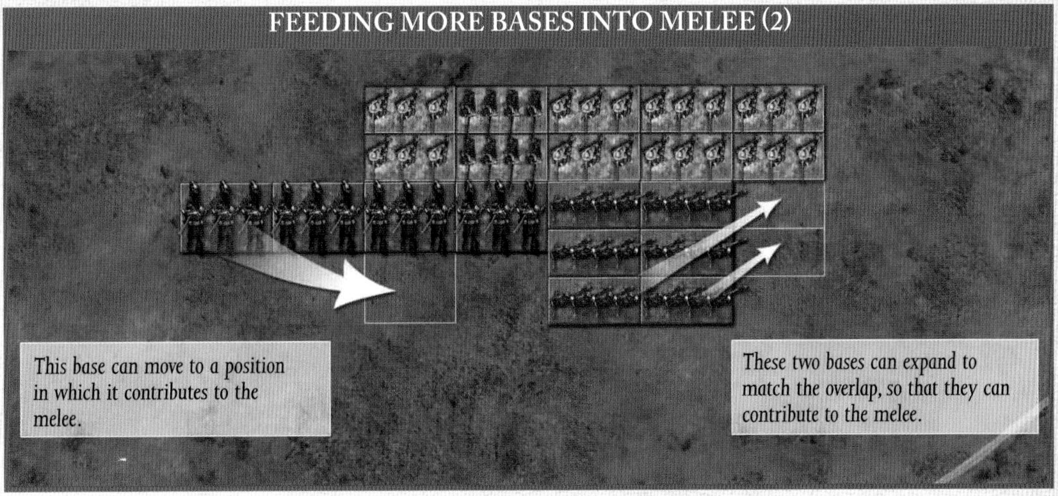




# RESTRICTED AREA

F*or normal movement* only, a battle group within 2 MU directly in front of an enemy battle group is considered to be pinned.

- It can only perform a limited number of actions:
  - Move straight ahead towards that enemy battle group.
  - Wheel towards that enemy battle group until its front is parallel to the enemy front (advancing thereafter if it wishes to do so), or wheel as far as it can towards such a position.
  - Remain in place. (It can expand, place portable defences, turn or use a formation change to change facing or form square, but it cannot contract – see below.)
  - Make a move that ends further away from that enemy battle group (i.e. the shortest distance between the battle groups is further at the end of the move than at the start).
  - Conform to an ***overlap position*** against another enemy battle group.
- In each of the above cases:
  - The battle group must end its move at least partly in front of the enemy battle group, or the move is not permitted.
  - No contraction is permitted. (Reduction in frontage that results from a 90 degree turn or forming square is not treated as a contraction.)
- If pinned by more than one enemy battle group it can choose which of these it responds

*Cavaliers enter restricted area of Parliamentarian foot*

to, and any restrictions apply relative to that battle group only.

- Battle troops ignore the restricted area of enemy light troops.
- Keils ignore the restricted area of all enemy troops.
- Battle wagons, artillery and troops in ***square*** exert no restricted area.
- The restricted area extends through friendly troops and passable terrain.
- The restricted area only applies in the manoeuvre phase. It does not affect moves (such as charges) that take place in other phases.

OPTIONS IN RESTRICTED AREA

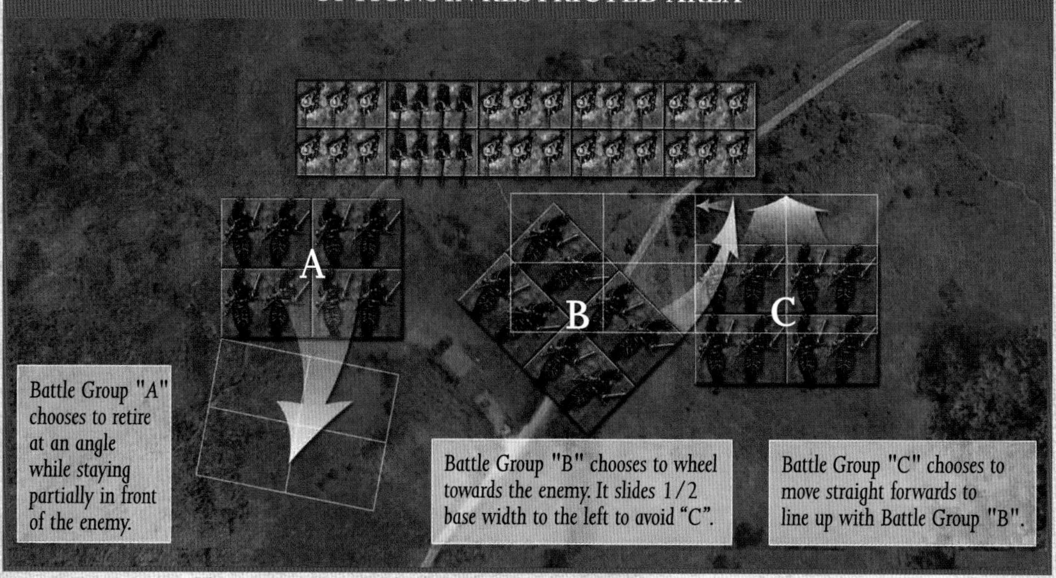


# SECOND MOVES

*Battle groups on their own* or forming part of a division, and commanders on their own, can move **twice** if they fulfil the following conditions:

- Neither the 1st nor the 2nd move can start, end or go within 6 MUs of any enemy (including the enemy camp but not enemy commanders' bases. Enemy in square can be ignored if the battle group or division is entirely of mounted troops and/or dragoons.).
- There must be a commander in line of command with the battle group or one battle group of the division at the start of the manoeuvre phase and he must remain with that battle group throughout the 1st and 2nd moves. He must be in command range of all of the battle groups comprising the division.
- The 1st and 2nd moves by a division and the 2nd move by a battle group must be an *advance*.
- The battle groups comprising a division must be specified to the opposing player

prior to the 1st move. Battle groups cannot be "dropped off" or "picked up" during the sequence of moves.

- If during a second move a battle group comes within visibility range of an enemy ***ambush marker*** (see ***Appendix 4***), the ambush is immediately revealed. Unless it was a ***dummy marker***, the move ends at that point if already within 6 MUs of the ambushers.

The second move must be carried out immediately after the first.

# THIRD MOVES

*Battle groups of mounted troops* or dragoons on their own or forming part of a division entirely of mounted troops and/or dragoons can move **three times** if they fulfil the following:

- Neither the 1st, 2nd nor 3rd move can start, end or go within 6 MUs of any enemy (including the enemy camp but not enemy commanders' bases or enemy in square).
- There must be a commander in line of command with the battle group or one battle group of the division at the start of the manoeuvre phase and he must remain with that battle group throughout the 1st, 2nd and 3rd moves. He must be in command range of all of the battle groups comprising the division.
- The 1st, 2nd and 3rd moves by a division and the 2nd and 3rd moves by a battle group must be an *advance*.
- The battle groups comprising a division must be specified to the opposing player prior to the 1st move. Battle groups cannot be "dropped off" or "picked up" during the sequence of moves.
- If during a third move a battle group comes within visibility range of an enemy ***ambush marker***, the ambush is immediately revealed. Unless it was a *dummy marker*, the move ends at that point if already within 6 MUs of the ambushers.

The 2nd move must be carried out immediately after the 1st, and the 3rd immediately after the 2nd.

*French Dragoons prepare to mount up*

# MOVING INTO CONTACT WITH ENEMY BATTLE GROUPS

*Battle groups cannot move* into contact with enemy battle groups in the manoeuvre phase, except to join an existing melee in an overlap position only. (Battle wagons and artillery can never move into contact with enemy, not even as an overlap.)

Such a move can include a sideways shift of up to half a base width. It is not a charge, so is not subject to the restrictions that apply to charges. It is not affected by the restricted area of other enemy battle groups.

Any other contact must wait until the next impact phase and is initiated by charging.

An **overlap position** is one with a base in any of the following situations:

- Full or partial side edge to side edge contact with an enemy base that is in front edge contact with friends.
- Front corner to front corner and side edge to side edge contact with a friendly base facing the same direction that has its full front edge in contact with an enemy base. (The base in overlap will therefore have a corner to corner contact with that enemy base.)
- Front corner to front corner and side edge to side edge contact with a friendly base facing the same direction that has all or part of its front edge in contact with the flank edge of an enemy base. (The base in overlap may therefore not be in contact with that enemy base.) This situation can occur when a flank contact is made on a base that is wider than it is deep.
- In cases where it was not possible to conform the troops already in melee: Front corner to front corner and side edge to side edge contact with a friendly base counting as fighting as if in front edge contact with enemy. (See the *Melee Phase* section.)

**TIP!**

Try to get as many overlaps as you can. Numbers have a quality all their own. Foot with swordsmen or heavy weapon capability and warriors are especially effective in overlap.

# BATTLE GROUPS ALREADY IN CONTACT BUT NOT YET COMMITTED TO CLOSE COMBAT

## FRONT CORNER TO FRONT CORNER ONLY

This can happen, for example, when a battle group breaks its frontal opponents and does not pursue. It may then be in front corner to front corner contact only with an enemy battle group that was fighting it only as an overlap. Battle groups in front corner to front corner contact only are not committed to close combat, and are free to move away. If they do not move away, no combat occurs unless they are eligible to fight as an overlap. If not, they can engage in melee as follows:

A battle group that is only in front corner to front corner contact with an enemy battle group, and not eligible to fight as an overlap, can shift 1 base width sideways to create a front edge to front edge contact, but only if both of the following apply:

- It is not in frontal contact with, nor eligible to fight as an overlap against, any other enemy battle group.
- It is not in the restricted area of another enemy battle group of a type it does not ignore.

No CMT is required. If the enemy are non-shock cavalry or camelry entirely *1 base deep* or light troops, and are not already in close combat other than only as an overlap, they can evade directly to their own rear. Otherwise the two battle groups fight normally in the melee phase. (There is no impact combat.)

## SIDE EDGE TO SIDE EDGE ONLY

This can happen, for example, when a battle group breaks its frontal opponents and pursues, leaving it in side edge to side edge contact with an adjacent enemy battle group. Battle groups in side edge to side edge contact are not committed to close combat, and are free to move away. If they do not move away, no combat occurs unless they are eligible to fight as an overlap. If not, they can engage in melee as follows:

A battle group that is in side edge to side edge contact with an enemy battle group can turn 90 degrees to face it, provided that it is not in the restricted area of another enemy battle group of a type it does not ignore. A CMT must be taken if this would normally be required for a stationary turn, and if it fails the CMT it cannot turn. If it does turn, it fights the enemy battle group as normal in the melee phase. (There is no impact combat.)

If the enemy are non-shock cavalry or camelry entirely *1 base deep* or light troops, and are not already in close combat other than only as an overlap, they can evade directly to their own rear or directly away from the turned battle group.

If it does not evade, the enemy battle group can choose whether or not to turn bases to face:

- If it does not turn bases to face, it will get no dice in the melee, but will not count as ***fighting enemy in 2 directions*** (see the ***Melee Phase*** section) if it is also fighting enemy to its front.

- If it does turn bases to face:
  - If it is already in close combat, it turns the contacted bases as if charged in the flank (see the ***Impact Phase*** section). It will then count as ***fighting enemy in 2 directions***.
  - If it is not already in close combat, it can either turn only the contacted bases as if charged in the flank, or the whole battle group can turn to face, using the normal rules for a 90 degree turn. In either case it will not count as ***fighting enemy in 2 directions***.

# MOVING INTO CONTACT WITH THE ENEMY CAMP

*Troops move into contact* with the enemy camp in the manoeuvre phase. This is not a charge.

*Camp guards defend against looters*

# SHOOTING PHASE

*The storming of Mirabello, 1525, by Graham Turner © Osprey Publishing Ltd. Taken from Campaign 44:* Pavia 1525.

In *the shooting phase* the effect of shooting with long-range missile weapons is resolved. Only bases that have a shooting capability listed in their troop description in our companion army list books can shoot.

Both players **must** shoot with all bases that are eligible to shoot in the shooting phase. Shooting is carried out in the order chosen by the active player. However, both sides shoot before any outcomes are resolved, so no advantage can be gained from choosing the order.

Shooting is only adjudicated if there is the potential to force a ***cohesion test*** or ***death roll*** on the target (see the ***Battle Group Deterioration*** section). If the number of dice to be rolled is less than the number of hits required to force either test, no dice are rolled. This speeds up play and reflects the historical reality that minor harassment would not materially affect the cohesion of large bodies of troops.

# RANGES

A *front rank base is* in range if a front corner or any part of its front edge is within range of the target. However, the pike base in point position of a battle group in Swedish brigade formation, regimental gun markers, commanders' bases and bases displaced by commanders' bases are disregarded when calculating ranges. Non-front rank bases shoot as if at the same range as the front rank, even if the front rank cannot shoot. The table below shows the range of different weapons in MUs.

| SHOOTING RANGES (MUs) | Short | Long |
|---|---|---|
| Musket, musket* and salvo | 3 | 6 |
| Foot bow, bow* and crossbow | 4 | 6 |
| Sling and mounted bow, bow* and crossbow | 4 | - |
| Arquebus and carbine | 3 | - |
| Bombs, pistols and javelins | 2 | - |
| Heavy artillery | 3 | 36 |
| Medium artillery | 3 | 24 |
| Light artillery | 3 | 8 |

# MOVEMENT AND SHOOTING

- Artillery whose battle group moved in any way during the preceding manoeuvre phase cannot shoot in the shooting phase. (This includes pivoting or turning.)
- The shooting of other troop types is not affected by having moved during the manoeuvre phase.
- No troops can shoot if they moved in the impact phase. (We judge that any shooting by chargers who failed to make contact and evaders would be too ineffective to have a significant effect.)
- No shooting takes place in the impact phase. Close range shooting is taken into account in the impact phase POA.

# TARGET PRIORITY

*An artillery base, when* more than 8 MUs from any eligible enemy target within *arc of fire* (see below), can shoot at any target within arc. Enemy light foot can be ignored unless within 3 MUs.

Otherwise, a front rank base that shoots can only shoot at its priority target. A base eligible to shoot from another rank has target priority as if in the front rank. A base which can shoot from more than one edge must shoot at whichever possible target has highest priority. A target must be legitimate in terms of line of sight, visibility and arc of fire (see below).

Targets are selected in the following order of priority:

- A targetable enemy base within short range and at least partly straight ahead. If there are two such targets, shoot at the nearest. If both are at exactly the same distance, shoot at the one most directly to the front.
- The nearest targetable enemy base in arc of fire. If two are at exactly the same distance, shoot at the one most directly to the front.
- If two targets are of equal priority, the shooting player chooses whether to target the one on the left or the one on the right. He cannot choose to target some of his bases to the left and some to the right in order to get extra bases shooting at the same battle group.

*Swiss Guard deliver a volley*

# ARC OF FIRE

Subject to target priority:

- A base can shoot at an enemy base that is not directly ahead, provided that some part of the enemy base is inside a straight line projecting forward parallel to, and at the following distance from, the shooting base's side edge:
  - 2 base widths if no base of the shooting battle group is within short range of that enemy battle group.
  - 1 base width otherwise.
- For the purpose of determining their arc of fire and target priority, regimental guns are treated as if in the central file of their battle group (or in one of the central files – owner's choice – if the battle group has an even number of files).
- A base can only shoot at an enemy base if at least part of the enemy base is forward of a straight line extending the shooting base's front edge.
- Light horse with bow capability can also shoot backwards (with a negative modifier), treating their rear edge as their front edge.

- Early tercio shot can shoot from their front, flank or rear edge, and later tercio shot from their front or flank edge, treating the shooting edge as their front edge.
- Battle wagons can shoot from either long edge of their base, as chosen by the shooting player. They shoot as if 2 bases side by side. The arc of fire and target priority is determined separately for each half. The long edge that is shooting is treated as their front edge. They cannot shoot from a short edge.

# LINE OF SIGHT AND VISIBILITY

*Line of sight is always* drawn from the front rank of the shooting battle group, even if the front rank is not shooting. A file can shoot at a target base if it is possible to draw straight lines from both front corners of its front rank base to a single point on the target base without passing through:

- Terrain that would block line of sight.
- Friendly troops, except as specified in the overhead shooting section below.

Troops permitted to shoot from an edge other than their front edge (see above) measure the above lines from the corner and mid-point of the shooting edge in the case of battle wagons, otherwise from the two corners of the shooting edge.

If any target is thus disqualified, the shooter moves on to its next target priority until a permitted target (if any) is found.

ARC OF FIRE AND LINE OF SIGHT

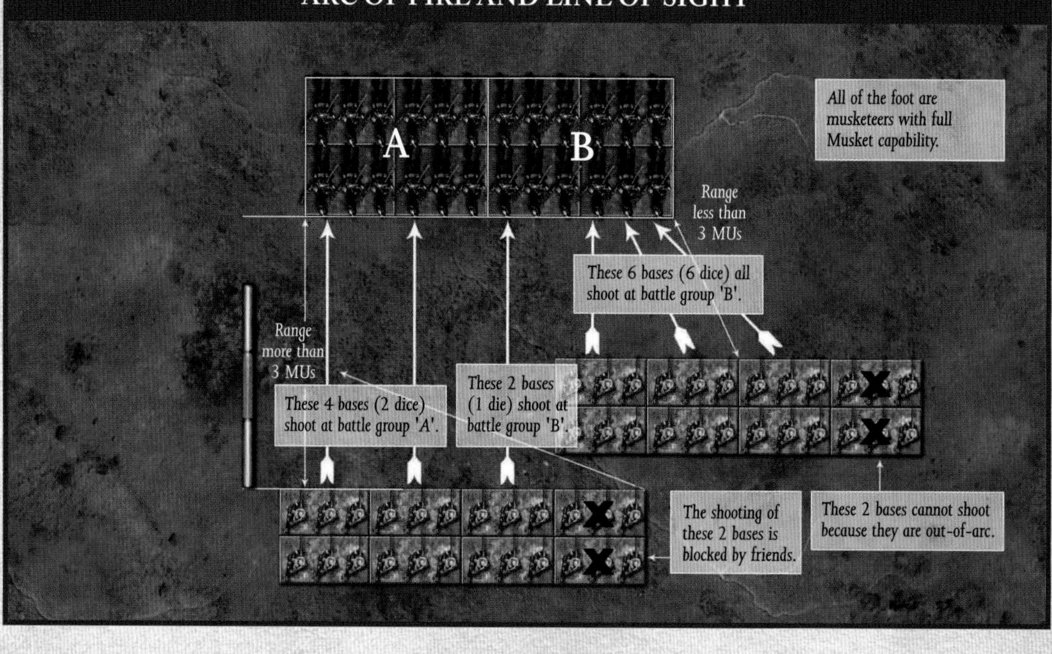

## ARC OF FIRE AND TARGET PRIORITY AT EFFECTIVE AND MAXIMUM RANGES

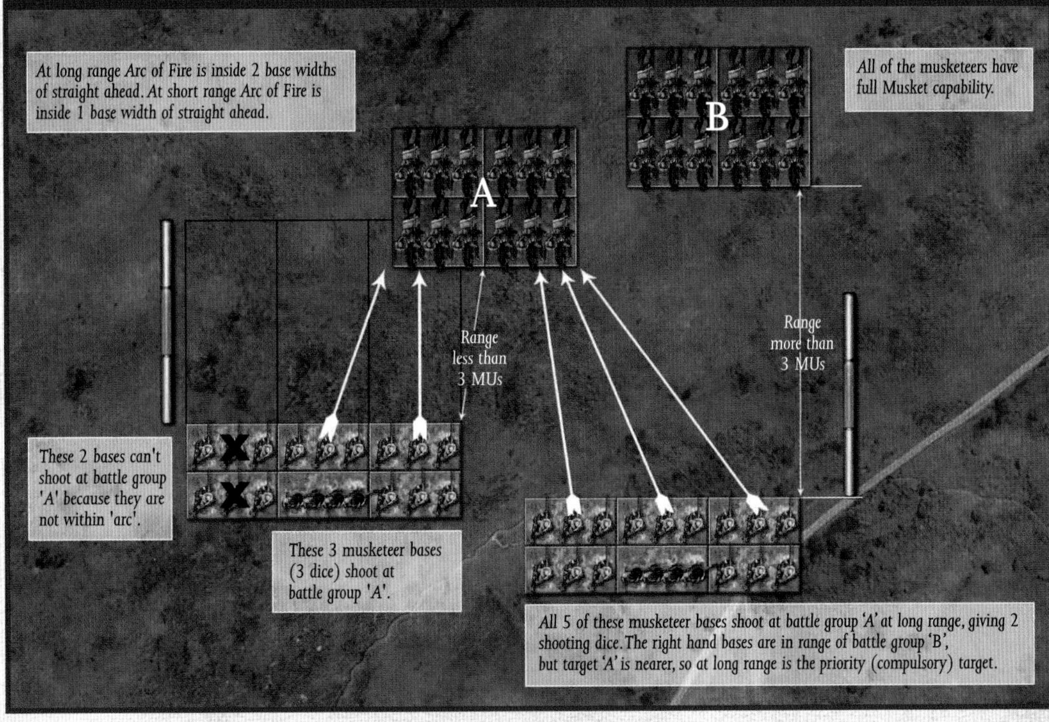


# OVERHEAD SHOOTING

- Artillery and dragoons only shoot with their front rank. Battle wagons only shoot with one file.
- Horse with pistol shoot only with bases in the 1st, 2nd and 3rd ranks.
- Other troops shoot only with bases in the 1st and 2nd ranks. However:
  - Light horse or tercio shot shooting to their rear treat their rearmost rank as their front rank.
  - Tercio shot shooting to their flank treat the shooting file as their front rank.
  - When a battle group in Swedish brigade formation shoots, the pike base in point position is disregarded. This means the battle group shoots as if that pike base is not there. Regimental gun markers are similarly ignored.
- Artillery on higher ground can shoot over friends if the intervening friends are over 1 MU from the shooters and over 3 MUs from the target base, measured along the line of the shortest distance between shooter and target.
- Artillery can shoot over friendly and enemy light foot if these are more than 3 MUs away from any part of the artillery battle group.
- Medium and heavy artillery can shoot over enemy artillery at eligible enemy targets beyond these.

# SHOOTING AND CLOSE COMBAT

*Bases that are engaged* in close combat cannot shoot or be shot at. As a result:

- A base cannot shoot if it is in the 1st or 2nd rank of a file which could contribute any dice (or part of a dice) to a melee this turn.
- A base cannot be shot at if it is the 1st or 2nd rank base of a file which could contribute any dice (or part of a dice) to a melee this turn.
- A battle group cannot be shot at if it is pursuing routers and still in contact with them.
- A battle group can be shot at if attacking a camp but not if looting it.

The first two bullets above apply:

- In the case of rear supported artillery, if the rear supporting file could contribute any dice (or part of a dice) to a melee this turn.
- In the case of battle wagons fighting as an overlap, to the whole battle wagon base.

See the ***Combat Mechanism*** section for **resolving shooting**

## SHOOTING AND CLOSE COMBAT

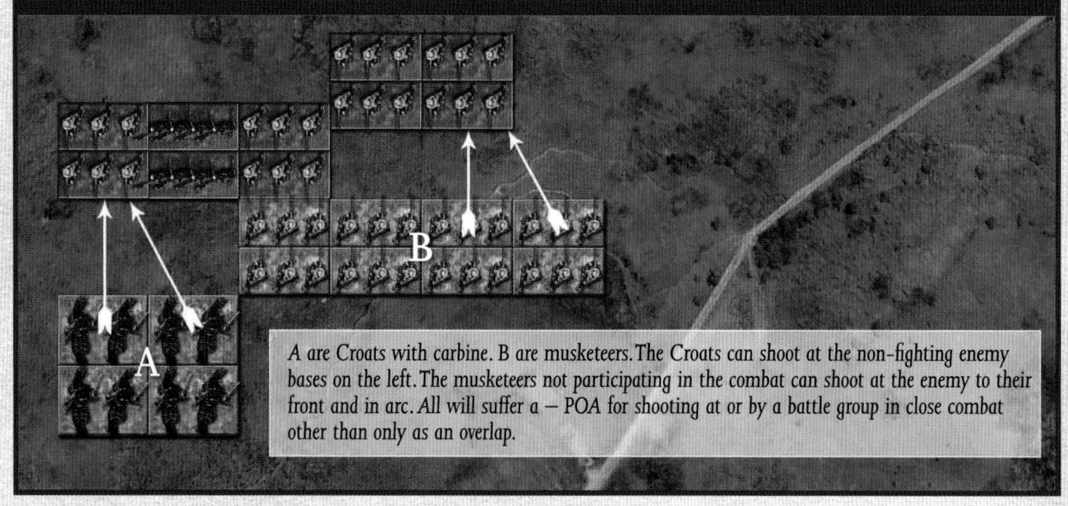


*A are Croats with carbine. B are musketeers. The Croats can shoot at the non-fighting enemy bases on the left. The musketeers not participating in the combat can shoot at the enemy to their front and in arc. All will suffer a – POA for shooting at or by a battle group in close combat other than only as an overlap.*

# MELEE PHASE

*The siege of Tenochtitlan, 1521, by Adam Hook © Osprey Publishing Ltd. Taken from Warrior 32:* Aztec Warrior.

*In the melee phase*, all bases in front edge contact with unbroken enemy, or in an overlap position, and who are not themselves broken, are eligible to fight in close combat. Other ranks can also be eligible to fight if so specified in the combat section. Battle groups which survived combat in the impact phase, and remain in contact with an unbroken enemy, will fight for a second time in the turn, often with more bases engaged as they are fed into the melee (see the ***Manoeuvre Phase*** section).

# OVERLAPS

*Overlap positions are defined* in the manoeuvre phase section. Each overlapping file fights with 1 dice, normally at the same net ***Points of Advantage*** (POA) (see the ***Combat Mechanism*** section) as if it was in front edge contact with the overlapped enemy base.

Foot with swordsmen or heavy weapon capability and warriors, however, always fight at a final overall ++ POA, when fighting as an overlap. No other POAs apply. (This means that they always need 3s to hit.)

## RESTRICTIONS:

- A battle group can only be overlapped by one file at each end of any of its four edges, even if it is stepped forward.
- A base that is in contact with the front edge of enemy bases on more than one of its edges cannot be overlapped on the corner between two contacted edges.
- A file overlapping two enemy battle groups can only contribute a melee dice against one of them (as chosen by the player whose battle group they belong to).
- A file that can contribute to close combat to its front, with dice or by creating a ***Point of Advantage*** (POA) or denying the enemy a POA, cannot fight as an overlap.

**BASES ELIGIBLE TO FIGHT IN MELEE**

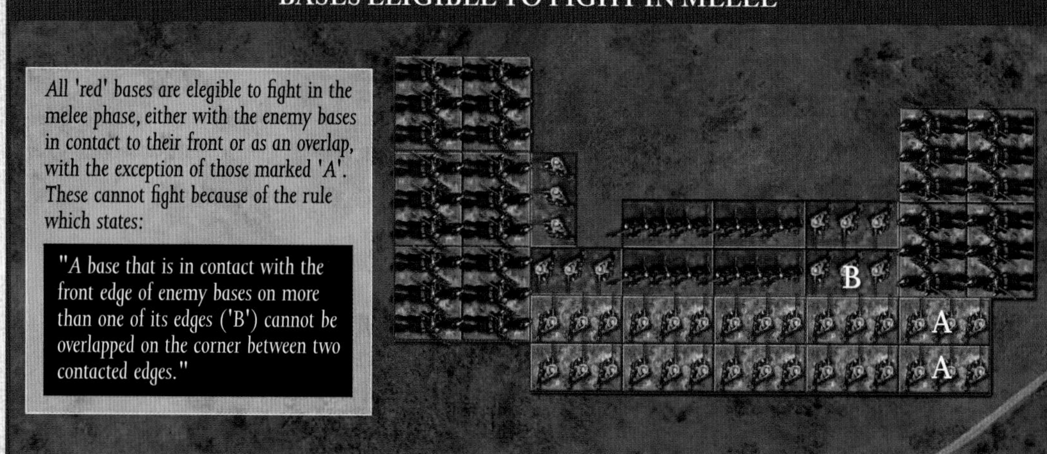

# MELEES THAT CANNOT LINE UP

*If it is not possible* for battle groups in contact to line up, they continue to fight in an offset position with the same number of bases counting as 'in front edge contact' or 'overlapping' as if they had conformed. If two bases would conform to the same enemy base then the one which has the shortest distance to conform fights against it. If the distance is equal their player chooses which fights.

Only the ends of a line of bases counting as 'in front edge contact' can be overlapped, even if it is stepped forward. One enemy file can fight as an overlap at each end.

## BASES THAT CANNOT LINE UP

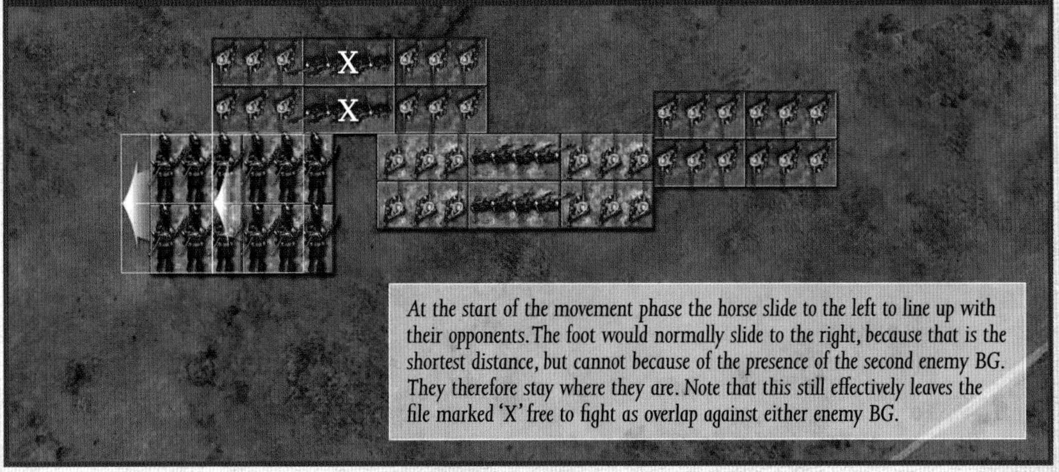


*At the start of the movement phase the horse slide to the left to line up with their opponents. The foot would normally slide to the right, because that is the shortest distance, but cannot because of the presence of the second enemy BG. They therefore stay where they are. Note that this still effectively leaves the file marked 'X' free to fight as overlap against either enemy BG.*

# FIGHTING ENEMY IN TWO DIRECTIONS

*A battle group only counts* as **fighting enemy in 2 directions** in melee if it has bases turned at 90 or 180 degrees to each other and it is in melee with different enemy battle groups on different facings. However, a battle group never counts as fighting enemy in 2 directions as a consequence of a charge unless it was a legal flank or rear charge.

Thus, early tercios never count as fighting enemy in 2 directions; keils and later tercios only do so if contacted on at least 2 sides, one of which was their rear when contacted.

# RESOLVING MELEES

See the *Combat Mechanism* section.

# SACKING CAMPS

*An unfortified camp contacted* by any part of the front edge of an enemy battle group counts as immediately sacked, and no combat takes place.

A fortified camp is assumed to be defended by camp guards, who must be defeated before the camp can be sacked. For simplicity, this is dealt with as follows. In the melee phase of each turn, each enemy battle group with any part of its front edge in contact with the camp rolls one dice, the defenders none. Mounted troops need to roll a 6 and foot troops or elephants a 5 or a 6 to sack a fortified camp successfully. Quality re-rolls apply.

Once a camp is sacked by any of the enemy battle groups in contact with it, all such battle groups must pass a CMT in the joint action phase to stop looting. If they succeed, they are free to move normally in their next turn. If all battle groups looting a camp stop looting, the camp is removed from the table.

Until the camp has been sacked, any enemy battle groups in contact with it can move away using the normal movement rules, but there is no free turn to do so.

*Fortified Camp under attack*

# THE COMBAT MECHANISM

*Akbar's Mughul cavalry, late 16th–early 17th centuries, by Angus McBride © Osprey Publishing Ltd. Taken from Men-at-Arms 263:* Mughul India 1504–1761.

*Combat between unbroken* battle groups, whether by impact, shooting or melee, uses the same combat mechanism. This always has the following sequence:

- Decide how many dice to roll.
- Roll dice to score hits and thereby decide (in close combat) which battle group(s), if any, have "lost" (i.e. inflicted fewer total hits on all their close combat opponents combined than the total hits they received from all their close combat opponents combined).
- Take cohesion tests.
- Take death rolls and remove any lost bases.
- Roll for commanders fighting in the front rank to see if they are lost. (In close combat only.)
- Take cohesion tests for nearby battle groups seeing a battle group break or a commander lost.
- Make compulsory moves as a result of combat.

"Close Combat" is a general term for impact and melee combat. Once such combat has been joined, battle groups are deemed to be in close combat until one side breaks off, breaks or is destroyed (or a battle group fighting only as an overlap moves away).

Note that **no shooting or close combat is calculated against routers.** Instead they lose bases automatically if pursuers remain in contact at the end of each pursuit move (see the ***Joint Action Phase*** section).

**TIP!**

When rolling cohesion tests and death rolls take them together by rolling 2 dice of one colour and one of another. It saves time.

# DECIDING HOW MANY DICE TO ROLL

## IN THE SHOOTING PHASE:

The shooting chapter specifies which bases are eligible to shoot. The number of dice to roll are as follows:

Battle wagons are treated as if 2 bases side by side when shooting.

| SHOOTING DICE | |
|---|---|
| Artillery (except when on battle wagons) | 1 dice per base at short or long range |
| Regimental gun | 1 dice per marker at short or long range |
| Dragoons | 1 dice per front rank base at short range |
| | 1 dice per 2 front rank bases at long range |
| Foot battle troops with musket* or mounted battle troops with carbine, bow or crossbow | 1 dice per base of 1st shooting rank at short range |
| | 1 dice per 2 bases of 2nd shooting rank or at long range |
| Horse with pistol | 1 dice per base of 1st shooting rank |
| | 1 dice per 2 bases of 2nd and 3rd shooting ranks |
| Foot with salvo capability | 1 dice per 2 bases at short or long range |
| Other foot battle troops with arquebus, musket, bow or crossbow | 1 dice per base at short range |
| | 1 dice per 2 bases at long range |
| Battle wagons | 1 dice per base width from long edge only at short or long range |
| Foot or mounted with other shooting capability (including any troops with bombs, bow*, javelins or slings and light foot or light horse with musket, arquebus, carbine, bow or crossbow) | 1 dice per 2 bases at short range |
| | 1 dice per 3 bases at long range |

| | | |
|---|---|---|
| DISRUPTED or DISORDERED | Lose 1 dice per 3* | Dice loss for Disruption, Fragmentation, Disorder or Severe Disorder is not cumulative, but whichever is worst applies.<br>*including dice for regimental guns |
| FRAGMENTED or SEVERELY DISORDERED | Lose 1 dice per 2* | |

DECIDING HOW MANY DICE TO ROLL
ALLOCATING COMBAT DICE
SCORING HITS - POINTS OF ADVANTAGE
PROTECTION
ARTILLERY IN CONTACT WITH ENEMY
ACCUMULATING HITS AND TAKING COHESION TESTS
SHOOTING IN THE IMPACT PHASE
COMMANDERS IN CLOSE COMBAT
FIGHTING BROKEN TROOPS
MOVEMENT OF BROKEN TROOPS AND PURSUERS
AN EXAMPLE OF COMBAT

## IN THE IMPACT PHASE:

This is the initial clash as the charge goes in. The front ranks are the key troops at impact, greater numbers being less important at this point. The question is, have the charging lancers broken into the front ranks of their foot opponents or have the foot stood firm?

Only bases coming into contact as a result of a charge in this impact phase fight. Combat between bases already fighting in the previous melee phase is not resolved until the next melee phase. If a new battle group charges into a battle group that was already in melee, there is an impact phase combat between the new charger and the bases it has just contacted. In the subsequent melee phase, all three battle groups will fight.

Turn any bases required to turn to face a flank or rear charge, move any tercio, keil, Swedish brigade or late 17th century pike bases required and proceed as follows: All bases that charge into front edge contact with enemy, or into front corner contact with an enemy edge, are eligible to fight. All enemy bases in contact with them are also eligible to fight. This includes bases contacted to their flank or rear which were unable to turn because they are already engaged to their front.

Both sides fight with the **same number of bases** determined as follows:

- If both sides have an **equal** number of bases eligible to fight, all of them fight. As far as possible, these are paired off to fight, so that each base fights one enemy base. If it is possible to do this in more than one way, the active player chooses which.
- If the number of eligible bases is **unequal**, both sides fight with the **lower** number of bases. The side with the higher number of bases chooses which of his bases will not fight. His choice must leave every eligible enemy base paired off against one of his.

Note that if multiple battle groups are involved in an impact combat, the above rules apply to the whole combat.

### TROOPS ELIGIBLE TO FIGHT AT IMPACT

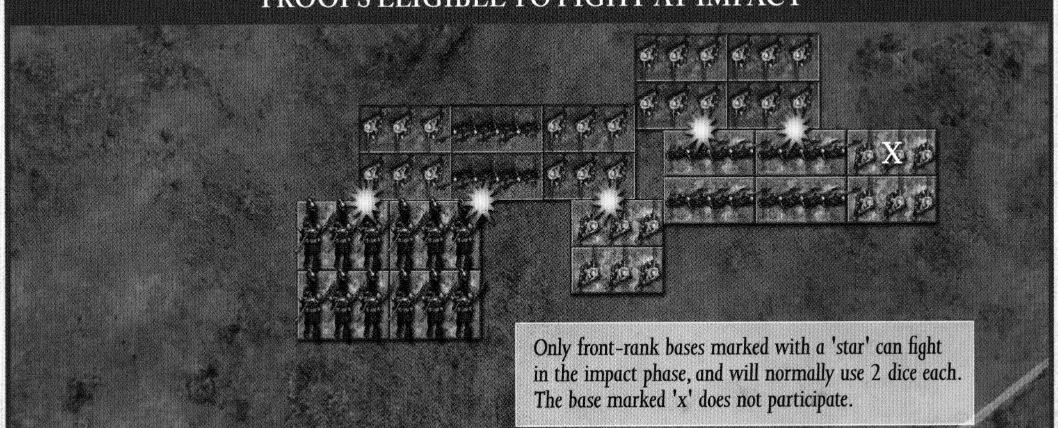


Only front-rank bases marked with a 'star' can fight in the impact phase, and will normally use 2 dice each. The base marked 'x' does not participate.

The number of dice to be rolled is as follows:

<table>
<tr><th colspan="3">IMPACT PHASE DICE</th></tr>
<tr><td>Battle wagons</td><td colspan="2">2 dice per front rank base width</td></tr>
<tr><td>Other troops</td><td colspan="2">2 dice per front rank base</td></tr>
<tr><td>Regimental guns</td><td colspan="2">1 dice</td></tr>
<tr><th colspan="3">REDUCTIONS</th></tr>
<tr><td>Light foot or light horse</td><td colspan="2">Lose 1 dice per 2 unless:<br>• Light Foot fighting against Light Foot.<br>• Light Horse fighting against Light Horse or Light Foot.<br>• Any fighting FRAGMENTED enemy.</td></tr>
<tr><th colspan="3">THEN</th></tr>
<tr><td>DISRUPTED or DISORDERED</td><td>Lose 1 dice per 3*</td><td rowspan="2">Dice loss for Disruption, Fragmentation, Disorder or Severe Disorder is not cumulative, but whichever is worst applies.<br>*including dice for regimental guns</td></tr>
<tr><td>FRAGMENTED or SEVERELY DISORDERED</td><td>Lose 1 dice per 2*</td></tr>
</table>

Battle wagons are treated as if 2 bases side by side when fighting on their long base edge, 1 base when fighting on their short base edge.

Regimental guns only get dice in the impact phase if at least some files are fighting to the battle group's front. They can never get dice against flank or rear chargers. Their dice is added to the effect of the fighting file nearest the battle group's centre. (Owner's choice if two fighting files are equally near the centre.)

## IN THE MELEE PHASE:

In drawn out melees a battle group's width and depth can be an advantage as it allows extra troops to be fed into the combat. Also troops in overlap positions and rear ranks that did not fight at impact can become involved in the combat.

- All bases whose front edge is in contact with enemy fight.
- An overlap fights against the same enemy base as the friendly base for which it provides an overlap. If able to provide an overlap on either side, its own player chooses which enemy base it fights.
- Rear ranks of an eligible troop type (see the combat dice table below) can fight if they belong to the same battle group as the front rank they are behind.
- The Melee Phase section above describes how to deal with melees if the battle groups have been unable to line up.
- A base contacted in front and flank and/or rear will now have more than one front rank enemy base fighting against it. It fights against its front edge opponent (even if it fought the impact round against a different base).

| MELEE PHASE DICE | | |
|---|---|---|
| Elephants, gendarmes, cavaliers or determined horse | 2 dice per front rank base. No dice for rear rank bases of any type. | |
| Battle wagons | 2 dice per front rank base width. No dice for rear rank bases of any type. | |
| Other troops | 1 dice per base in first 2 ranks. | |
| Troops in overlap | 1 dice per overlapping file (irrespective of the number of ranks). | |
| REDUCTIONS | | |
| Light foot or light horse | Lose 1 dice per 2 unless:<br>• Light Foot fighting against Light Foot.<br>• Light Horse fighting against Light Horse or Light Foot.<br>• Any fighting against FRAGMENTED enemy. | |
| THEN | | |
| DISRUPTED or DISORDERED | Lose 1 dice per 3 | Dice loss for Disruption, Fragmentation, Disorder or Severe Disorder is not cumulative, but whichever is worst applies. |
| FRAGMENTED or SEVERELY DISORDERED | Lose 1 dice per 2 | |

Battle wagons are treated as if 2 bases side by side when fighting on their long base edge, 1 base when fighting on their short base edge. When fighting on their long base edge, they count the file nearest the enemy as their front rank.

**TROOPS ELIGIBLE TO FIGHT IN MELEE**

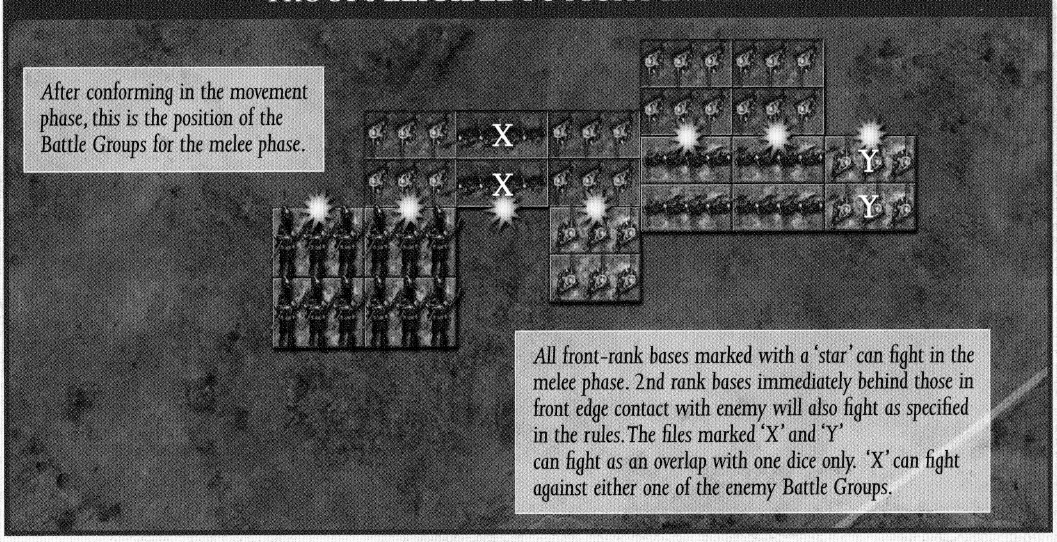


# ALLOCATING COMBAT DICE

*It is sometimes necessary* to split up a battle group's combat dice, e.g. if it is fighting more than one enemy battle group, or if some bases are fighting on different *Points of Advantage* (POA) – see below; or to combine shooting dice from several battle groups shooting at the same target:

- If a battle group is fighting against more than one enemy battle group, roll combat dice separately against each enemy battle group.
- If some bases have different POAs, roll separately for them.
- If more than one battle group is shooting at the same target, add the total number of bases to which a '1 dice per x bases' rule applies before calculating the number of dice to roll. A dice that is made up from bases from more than one battle group with different POAs rolls at the worst POA applicable. A dice that is made up from bases from more than one battle group of different qualities re-rolls as the worst quality applicable.
- If a battle group which is losing shooting or close combat dice (due to DISRUPTION, FRAGMENTATION, DISORDER, SEVERE DISORDER or being light foot or light horse in close combat) is fighting against more than one enemy battle group, first determine the total number of dice the battle group should lose. Then apportion the lost dice, if possible, in proportion to the number of bases fighting each enemy battle group, leaving at least 1 dice (if possible) against each enemy battle group.
- Similarly, if fighting at different POAs against parts of the same enemy battle group, apportion lost dice, if possible, in proportion to the number of bases fighting each part of the enemy battle group, leaving at least 1 dice (if possible) against each part of the enemy battle group.

The extra dice for regimental guns in impact combat is allocated to the fighting file closest to the centre of their battle group.

**TIP!**

Combine dice from multiple battle groups only if shooting the same target – close combat dice are always rolled battle group vs. battle group.

*Colonel Devereux's Regiment of Foot*

# SCORING HITS - POINTS OF ADVANTAGE

*If the numbers fighting in close* combat are equal, a combination of troop type, armour, combat capabilities and situation will make all the difference. This could result in a finely balanced match, or an advantage (or big advantage) to one side or the other. In *Field of Glory Renaissance*, rather than using numerical values we use **Points of Advantage** (POAs for short) to see who has the upper hand.

The roll required to score a hit depends on the "points of advantage" (POA).

- When shooting, a base will have its own overall POA.
- When in close combat, compare the overall POAs of opposing bases and take the difference as the net result e.g. a base with three pluses fighting against a base with a single plus will be on a net plus two (++). Its opponent will be on a net minus two (- -).
- If a base is fighting in close combat at a net +, the opposing enemy base fights at -. If a base is fighting in close combat at a net ++, the opposing enemy base fights at - -.
- ++ is the maximum net advantage. - - is the maximum net disadvantage. Additional net POAs are ignored.
- In close combat, each front rank base uses its own POAs. Rear rank bases use the same net POAs as the front rank.
- With the single exception of pike mixed with troops with heavy weapon or swordsmen capability (see below), close combat POAs that require a minimum number of ranks only apply if **all** those ranks have the required capability.

The scores needed to get a hit are different for shooting and close combat as follows:

## SHOOTING ROLLS TO HIT: (QUALITY RE-ROLLS APPLY.)

| Advantage | PoA | Minimum score to hit |
|---|---|---|
| Big advantage | ++ | 2 |
| Advantage | + | 3 |
| No advantage | No PoA | 4 |
| Disadvantage | - | 5 |
| Big disadvantage | - - | 6 |

## CLOSE COMBAT ROLLS TO HIT: (QUALITY RE-ROLLS APPLY.)

| Advantage | PoA | Minimum score to hit |
|---|---|---|
| Big advantage | ++ | 3 |
| Advantage | + | 4 |
| No advantage | No PoA | 4 |
| Disadvantage | - | 5 |
| Big disadvantage | - - | 5 |

The key to success is to make sure that you fight with + POAs. These can come from a base's troop type, armour, combat capabilities or the situation. Some of these may be advantages to the enemy, hence disadvantages to you. In the tables below, POAs are listed as '+' when in a base's favour and '-' when not. Each '+' cancels a '-'.

## SHOOTING POAS

If shooting at a battle group that has mixed armour classes, the shooters' POAs are determined not by the armour class of the targeted base, but as follows:

- Unless the shooting base is entirely behind a straight line extending the target battle group's rear edge, by the armour class of the front rank of the target battle group. If that has mixed armour classes, by the majority

| SHOOTING POAS | | | |
|---|---|---|---|
| **Nearest rank of target is:** | | | **If shooting with:** |
| Any one of | Unarmoured mounted battle troops unless entirely 1 base deep | + | Bow, bow*, sling or javelins |
| | Fully armoured gendarmes | - | Bow, bow*, sling or javelins |
| | Any mounted troops | - | Musket, musket*, salvo, arquebus, carbine, pistol |
| | Elephants | + | Any except bow, bow* or sling |
| | Battle wagons | - | Any except bombs or artillery |
| | Artillery | - - | Artillery |
| | Fully armoured foot | - - | Bow, bow*, sling, or javelins |
| | | - | Artillery, carbine, pistol or crossbow |
| | | | Any of the following at long range: musket, musket* or salvo |
| | Armoured or heavily armoured foot | - | Artillery, carbine, pistol, crossbow, bow, bow*, sling, or javelins |
| | | | Any of the following at long range: musket, musket* or salvo |
| | Unarmoured foot | - | Artillery, carbine, pistol or crossbow |
| | Any target | 0 | Regimental guns |
| Any one of | Any | - | Any, if shooting at a battle group in close combat other than as an overlap only |
| | Any | | Any, if shooting by a battle group which is in close combat other than as an overlap only |
| | Any | | Any, if shooting to rear (Light Horse with bow only) |
| | Any | | Captured or recaptured artillery |
| | Any foot | | Foot battle troops with ***threatened flank*** (see ***glossary***) |
| Battle troops which<br>• have any file of their battle group in 3 or more ranks (unless this is the 3 deep pike file of a Swedish brigade formation), or<br>• are a tercio, or<br>• are mob, or<br>• are in **square**, or<br>• are shot at from ***enfilade*** (see ***glossary***) | | + | Artillery |
| In cover or behind field fortifications or an obstacle | | - | Any except heavy or medium artillery |

type in the front rank e.g. when shooting at a pike and shot battle group with a single file of armoured pike flanked by files of unarmoured shot on each side, the target counts as unarmoured. If there are equal numbers of bases with different armour classes in the front rank, the target counts as having the lowest of these armour classes. Exception: When shooting at the front edge of a battle group in Swedish brigade formation, the shooters' POAs are determined by the armour class of the front rank pike base.

- When the shooting base is entirely behind a straight line extending the target battle group's rear edge, use the rearmost rank's armour class (determined as above) to determine POAs.

## TIP!

When shooting it is usually easiest to roll all dice shooting at a single target together. Be careful to use different coloured dice if some troops have different POAs or re-rolls.

## IMPACT POAS

Battle wagons, elephants and mounted cannot defend fortifications or an obstacle.

| IMPACT POAS | | | | |
|---|---|---|---|---|
| Any one of | Foot using salvo. Pike in the same battle group as foot using salvo | | ++ | against any foot |
| | Impact foot. Pike in the same battle group as impact foot. | | + | against any foot |
| | Pike or protected shot, if not charging and not FRAGMENTED or SEVERELY DISORDERED | | + | against any mounted |
| | Spearmen in 2 or more ranks, if not charging and not FRAGMENTED or SEVERELY DISORDERED | | + | against any mounted |
| | Spearmen in 2 or more ranks, if not FRAGMENTED or SEVERELY DISORDERED | | + | against any foot except pike in 3 or more ranks, protected pike, protected shot, foot with bayonet or impact foot |
| | Heavy weapon | | + | against any foot except pike in 3 or more ranks, protected pike, protected shot, foot with bayonet or impact foot |
| | Foot with light spear unless they are charging mounted shock troops | | + | against any except pike in 3 or more ranks, protected pike, protected shot, foot with bayonet or impact foot |
| | Regimental guns | | 0 | against any |
| | Elephants | | + | against any |
| | Battle wagons | | + | against any mounted |
| | Pistol | | + | against any except elephants, battle wagons, impact mounted or non-charging STEADY foot who are any of pike, protected shot or foot with bayonet |
| | Heavy lancers | Only in open terrain (see *glossary*) | + | against any except elephants, battle wagons, pistol or non-charging STEADY foot who are any of spearmen, pike, protected shot or foot with bayonet |
| | Light lancers | Only in open terrain (see *glossary*) | + | against any except elephants, battle wagons, heavy lancers, pistol or non-charging STEADY foot who are any of spearmen, pike, protected shot or foot with bayonet |
| | Impact mounted | Only in open terrain (see *glossary*) | + | against any except elephants, battle wagons, heavy lancers or non-charging STEADY foot who are any of spearmen, pike, protected shot or foot with bayonet |
| Pike in 4 or more ranks whether charging or not, unless FRAGMENTED or SEVERELY DISORDERED | | Only in open terrain (see *glossary*) | + | against any |
| Any mounted | | Only in open terrain (see *glossary*) | + | against any light foot, dragoons, warriors or unprotected medium foot without bayonet |
| Protected cavaliers, protected horse or protected determined horse | | | + | If they are at an overall disadvantage against any mounted after all other POAs of both sides have been totalled and netted out (raising - to 0, worse to -) |
| *Uphill* or foot defending field fortifications, an obstacle or a riverbank | | | + | |
| Charge counting as on flank or rear | | | ++ | **Final overall POA regardless of all other factors** |

## MELEE POAS

Battle wagons, elephants and mounted cannot defend fortifications or an obstacle.

| MELEE POAS | | | |
|---|---|---|---|
| Any one of.... | Pike or protected shot, unless FRAGMENTED or SEVERELY DISORDERED | + | against any mounted |
| | Pistol | + | against any except:<br>• elephants<br>• STEADY foot who are any of pike, protected shot or foot with bayonet<br>• mounted swordsmen if the pistoliers are not STEADY |
| | Swordsmen | + | against any except elephants, STEADY pistols, or STEADY foot who are any of spearmen, pike, protected shot or foot with bayonet |
| | Spearmen in 2 or more ranks, unless FRAGMENTED or SEVERELY DISORDERED | + | against any except pike in 3 or more ranks, protected pike, protected shot or foot with bayonet |
| | Heavy Weapon | + | against any except pike in 3 or more ranks, protected pike, protected shot or foot with bayonet.<br>Also cancels enemy 'better armour' POA if any. |
| | Elephants | + | against any |
| Pike in 4 or more ranks, unless FRAGMENTED or SEVERELY DISORDERED | | + | against any |
| Protected cavaliers, protected horse or protected determined horse | | + | If they are at an overall disadvantage against any mounted after all other POAs of both sides have been totalled and netted out (raising - to 0, worse to -) |
| Better Armour (front rank) | | + | against any except shot, heavy weapon, elephants or battle wagons |
| Fighting enemy in two directions | | - | unless early tercio, or later tercio/keil not in contact to its rear |
| *Uphill* or foot defending field fortifications, an obstacle or a riverbank | | + | |
| If fighting as an overlap - foot with swordsmen or heavy weapon capability or warriors | | ++ | **Final overall POA regardless of all other factors** |

## POAS REQUIRING RANKS

Some POAs require troops to be in a certain minimum number of ranks. With the single exception of pike files including bases with heavy weapon or swordsmen capability (see below), all of those ranks must have the specified capability. E.g. For a file to count as spearmen in 2 ranks, both the 1st and 2nd rank bases in the file must have spearmen capability. (Note that all POAs apply on a file-by-file basis.)

Exception: Pike count as being in 3 or 4 ranks for POA purposes even if some of the ranks in the file have heavy weapon or swordsmen capability, provided that there is a base with pike capability in the front rank, the file includes at least 2 bases with pike capability, and all of the 3 or 4 bases are facing in the same direction. E.g. A file which has its first 2 ranks with pike capability, a 3rd rank with heavy weapon capability and 4th rank with pike capability will fight in the impact and melee phases as "pike in 4 or more ranks…" if they are not fragmented or severely disordered.

POAs that do not specify a minimum number of ranks apply even if there is only one rank with the relevant capability. E.g. Steady spearmen negate the impact POA for heavy or light lancers or impact mounted in open terrain even if the spearmen are only 1 rank deep.

# PROTECTION

*Shot and pike in a mixed* battle group are able to provide mutual support. This is called "protection". It occurs when a file of shot has an adjacent file of the same battle group with a front rank of pike. The files must be facing in the same direction and in at least corner to corner contact (e.g. after one of the files has stepped forward when charging). The pike give "protection" to the shot and the shot give "protection" to the pike. The shot and pike are "protected". Typically, a mid C17th infantry battle group will be formed with a file of 2 pike bases in the centre in 2 ranks flanked on each side by a file of shot in 2 ranks.

Pike and shot battle groups are in fact a specific case of a general rule: In mixed battle groups of medium foot with a shooting capability and heavy or determined foot, when a file of medium foot has an adjacent file with a front rank of heavy or determined foot (of the same battle group) facing in the same direction and in at least corner to corner contact, both files count as "protected".

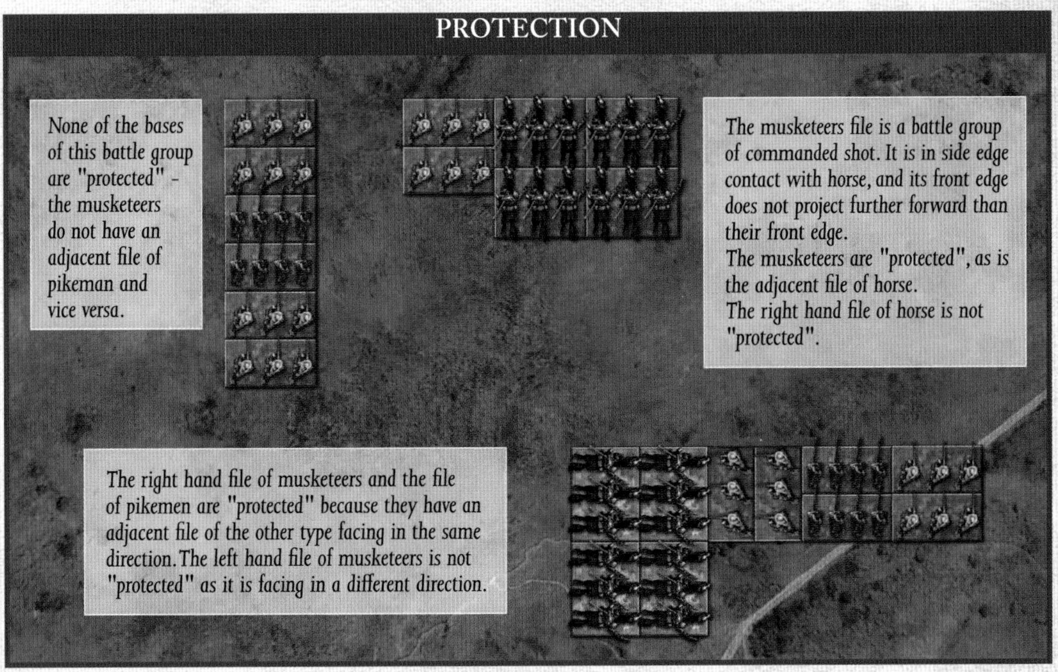

Only the adjacent files are "protected" – other files of the same battle group are not "protected".

In the French Wars of Religion, Henri IV introduced arquebusiers into his cavalry battle line to provide support against enemy cavalry. Gustavus did the same with musketeers from around 1627 and the practice was used in the English Civil War by both sides. In the C17th, these supporting infantry were called "commanded shot".

Accordingly, when troops are designated in our companion army list books as "commanded shot", they can give to, and receive "protection" from, cavaliers, horse or determined horse belonging to other friendly battle groups. To give or receive "protection", a file of commanded shot must be in at least partial side edge contact with a file of friendly cavaliers, horse or determined horse, and its front edge must not project further forward than their front edge. Only the adjacent files are "protected" – other files of the same battle group are not "protected".

In addition, foot bases entirely in enclosed fields or a village also count as "protected".

# ARTILLERY IN CONTACT WITH ENEMY

*Artillery bases* **never** take part in close combat.

Limbered artillery are automatically destroyed and removed from play if the artillery or their limber markers are contacted by any part of any non-broken enemy battle group.

When any base of an unlimbered artillery battle group is contacted by an enemy base in a way that would normally result in close combat, the whole artillery battle group is automatically captured unless all contacted bases have **rear support** (see below). If the artillery loses its rear support (e.g. if the supporting troops rout or break off) while the enemy are still in such contact, it is captured.

Rear support:

- When an unlimbered artillery base has the front edge of a base of unbroken friendly foot battle troops lined up in edge to edge and corner to corner contact with its rear edge, it has rear support.
- Artillery base depths vastly over-represent their actual historical depth. Hence a battle group in a position to give rear support to artillery is treated for all purposes as if its front edge was in the position of the front edge of the artillery, except that the files actually providing rear support cannot shoot.
- When an artillery base with rear support is in contact with enemy in the impact or melee phase, close combat takes place between the supporting troops and the enemy in contact with the artillery base. (The artillery crews are assumed to have withdrawn behind their friends but the artillery base is left in place and takes **no** part in close combat. If the enemy cease to be in contact with the artillery battle group and it has not been captured, the crews are assumed to return and the artillery then functions normally again.)

A captured artillery battle group counts as 2 attrition points towards its original side's break

## ARTILLERY IN COMBAT

It is the impact phase. Each of the artillery bases has rear support because it has a base of friendly foot battle troops in full front edge contact with its rear edge. The gunners are assumed to retire through the friendly foot but the artillery bases remain in position. Close combat occurs between the two pike and shot battle groups as if they were in contact with each other.

It is the impact phase. Although the two artillery bases on the left have rear support the right hand base is unsupported. Therefore the entire artillery battle group is automatically captured by the opposing player. Because it was captured by pikemen and/or shot, until recaptured, the artillery battle group is under the control of and can be used as part of the army of, the opposing player. In the meantime, combat proceeds between the opposing pike and shot battle groups as if the artillery was not there. If the battle group at the bottom succeeds in routing their opponents the artillery is recaptured.

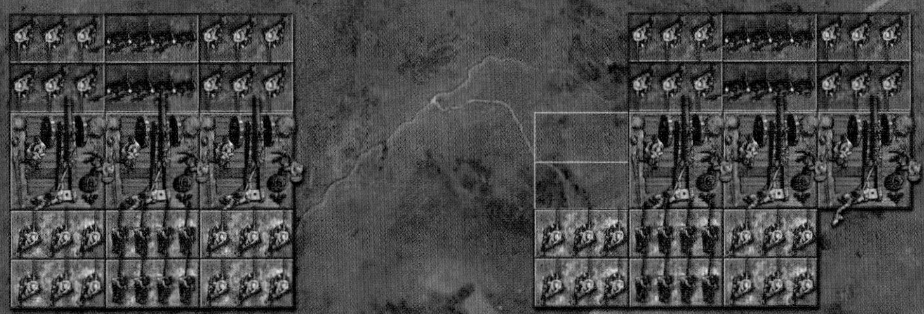

point. These attrition points are recovered if the artillery is recaptured (even if by troops other than pike and/or shot), lost again if the enemy captures it again, and so on.

Once captured, artillery cannot be recaptured until either:

- A battle group belonging to the previous owner, and already in contact, routs (all) the capturing enemy battle group(s).
- A battle group belonging to the previous owner **moves** into contact (in a way that would normally result in close combat) with an artillery base that does not have rear support from the current owner's troops.

If captured or recaptured by pike and/or shot, captured or recaptured artillery is subsequently controlled by the capturer or recapturer. If so, it is treated as a normal battle group of the army controlling it. (It is not necessary for the pike and/or shot battle group to remain in contact.) While under the control of the original enemy, it does not affect their break point, nor does its subsequent recapture or destruction cause them any attrition points.

If captured or recaptured by any troops other than pike and/or shot, artillery remains uncontrolled (out of action) until a battle group of pike and/or shot of the same side moves into contact with it, or it is recaptured by a battle group of pike and/or shot of the opposing side. (It is not necessary for the pike and/or shot battle group to remain in contact.) While it is uncontrolled it cannot move, shoot or suffer drops in cohesion. Uncontrolled artillery does not count as enemy to either side.

When control of a battle group of artillery switches, it becomes steady immediately, but it is treated as Poor and shoots at reduced effect. It can subsequently move as normal, with the additional option of turning 180 degrees if it passes a CMT.

# ACCUMULATING HITS AND TAKING COHESION TESTS

*Determine all of the hits* inflicted by both sides before taking cohesion tests and death rolls. Place a dice behind each battle group (or file, when necessary) to record the hits received. In close combat, use a separate dice for each battle group that inflicts hits, as you need to know who caused them in order to determine which battle groups (if any) lost the combat. By using this simple method you can keep track of multiple battle group combats. After all hits inflicted or received have been noted, take any outcome tests that are required. There is no need to record anything past this stage as there are no knock-on effects on unconnected combats.

A battle group has **lost** a close combat if the **total** number of hits it received from **all** of its opponents this phase is greater than the **total** number of hits it inflicted on **all** of its opponents this phase.

Next take any ***cohesion tests*** or ***death rolls*** caused by shooting or combat (see the ***Battle Group Deterioration*** section). If any battle group breaks, turn its bases around. It will rout at the end of the phase.

Cohesion tests are caused by shooting and combat in the following circumstances:

- Test a battle group after all shooting dice have been rolled if it suffered either of the following: (If both apply, this does **not** count as more than 1 reason to test.)
  - At least 1 shooting hit per 3 bases (1 HP3B). (See the ***Glossary*** for the full definition. Some troop types calculate HP3B differently and not all ranks count.)
  - At least 2 shooting hits from artillery and it is warriors.
- Test a battle group after all close combat dice have been rolled if it lost an impact or melee close combat.

There are some additional reasons to test cohesion and these are covered in the ***Cohesion Test*** section in the ***Battle Group Deterioration*** section.

# SHOOTING IN THE IMPACT PHASE

*Field of Glory Renaissance* differs from the original Field of Glory rules for Ancient and Medieval warfare in that shooting in the impact phase is subsumed into the Impact phase POAs rather than giving additional dice for Support Shooting.

# COMMANDERS IN CLOSE COMBAT

*Commanders can inspire* their troops by fighting in the front rank. As you might expect, this carries significant personal risk. The commander's base is representative only and gets no dice in combat.

- A commander can be declared to be fighting in the front rank of a single battle group in close combat. This improves its fighting ability by enhancing its quality re-rolls on close combat "to hit" rolls. The declaration is made before any close combat dice are rolled.
- A commander with the battle group who is not declared to be fighting in the front rank, does not affect quality re-rolls and is not at risk of being lost.
- A commander fighting in the front rank is placed anywhere in the front rank in contact with the enemy (player's choice) to show that he is fighting. The base(s) he displaces is (are) placed behind him, but still fight as if they had not been displaced. Once declared as fighting in the front rank, the commander cannot leave the front rank of that battle group until it is no longer in close combat and no longer pursuing enemy routers.
- If a commander is fighting in the front rank of a battle group that suffers a total of 2 or more hits in close combat, the opposing player rolls 2 dice (no re-rolls) after post-combat cohesion tests and death rolls. If the commander's battle group lost the combat, the commander is lost if these total 11 or 12. If it won or drew the combat, he is lost if they total 12. A lost commander is removed from play, and the bases he displaced are put back into their previous position before measuring to see if any friendly battle groups are in range to test cohesion for seeing him lost (see ***Cohesion Tests*** in the ***Battle Group Deterioration*** section).
- A commander who is fighting in the front rank can only influence the complex move tests or cohesion tests of the battle group he is with. He cannot affect those of other friendly battle groups.

*Ottoman General leads the attack from the front*

## TIP!

Risking your commander in the front rank is a serious step and commits him for an unknown period of time, during which he is preoccupied with hand to hand combat, losing his ability to control his other battle groups and putting him in real danger. However, commanders in this period typically led from the front and usually the risk will be worth it, especially if you need a quick break through or if things are getting desperate. The choice is yours!

# FIGHTING BROKEN TROOPS

*There is no explicit shooting* or close combat against, or by, broken troops. Damage inflicted on broken battle groups is assessed in the joint action phase.

**TIP!**

Light troops can be very useful to pursue broken enemy troops and prevent them from rallying..

# MOVEMENT OF BROKEN TROOPS AND PURSUERS

*When a battle group breaks* after shooting or close combat, or for any other reason, other nearby battle groups may have to take a cohesion test (see ***Cohesion Tests*** in the ***Battle Group Deterioration*** section). This is done after all combats and post-combat cohesion tests, death rolls and rolls to inflict commander losses have been resolved, but before the broken troops are moved. Each newly broken battle group makes an ***initial rout***, which, unless it is the result of being charged when fragmented, happens at the end of the phase. Winning battle groups may have to make an ***initial pursuit***.

## INITIAL ROUT

Roll to determine the variable move distance adjustment.

- If a battle group breaks as a result of being charged when fragmented, shooting or while in close combat, it routs directly away from the enemy charging, shooting at or in close combat with it. If there is more than one such enemy, bisect the angle between them.
- If a battle group breaks in other circumstances, it routs towards its side's rear table edge, making wheels and/or turns as appropriate to end its move as close to the rear table edge as possible.
- If any obstructions would prevent completion of a routing battle group's move, adjust as per evade moves (see the ***Impact Phase*** section) to get past these, but not to avoid leaving the table. It must go round a fortified or enemy camp, but can pass through its own unfortified camp. If its path is obstructed by unbroken enemy that cannot be bypassed, the battle group is destroyed at the end of the phase.
- A commander who is with a battle group at the moment it breaks must rout with it once. Until the joint action phase he cannot leave the battle group and cannot influence any complex move tests or cohesion tests.
- Battle wagons and artillery never make a rout move. Instead, they are destroyed (unless they are artillery who have been captured in close combat – see above) and removed from the table. Their opponents do not pursue.
- Regimental guns are lost if their battle group breaks. Their marker is permanently removed from play.

**COMPLEX PURSUIT MOVE**

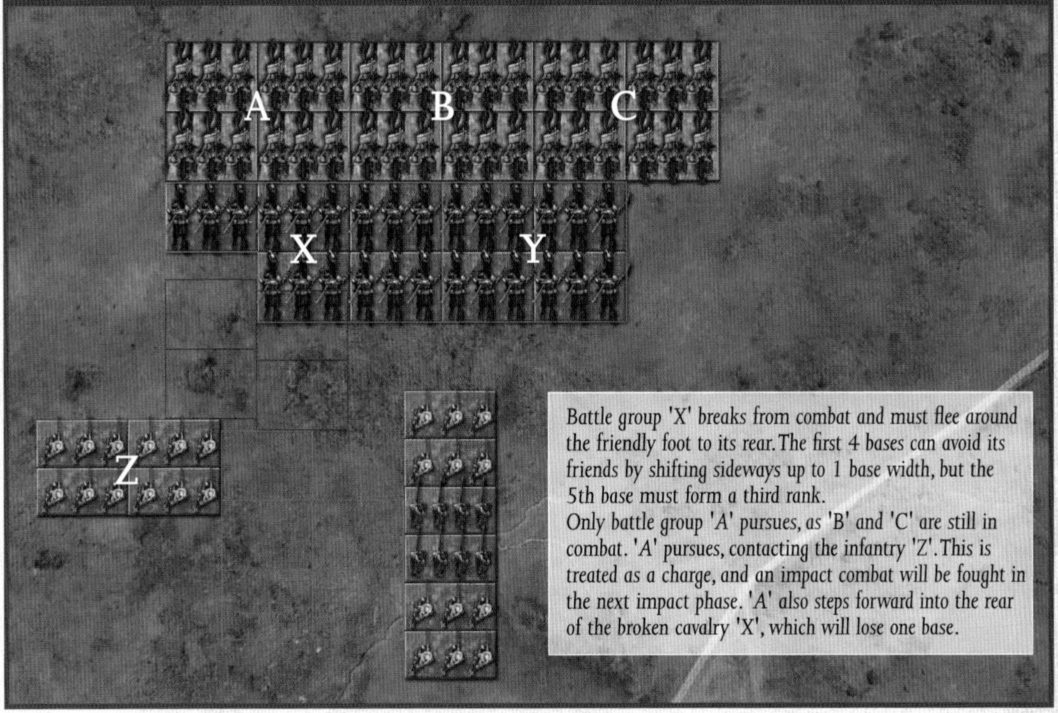


*Battle group 'X' breaks from combat and must flee around the friendly foot to its rear. The first 4 bases can avoid its friends by shifting sideways up to 1 base width, but the 5th base must form a third rank.*
*Only battle group 'A' pursues, as 'B' and 'C' are still in combat. 'A' pursues, contacting the infantry 'Z'. This is treated as a charge, and an impact combat will be fought in the next impact phase. 'A' also steps forward into the rear of the broken cavalry 'X', which will lose one base.*

## INITIAL PURSUIT

- An unbroken battle group, all of whose close combat opponents (except those only fighting it as an overlap) have broken and routed this phase, always pursues (even if it only fought as an overlap) unless:
  - It is foot who have broken mounted opponents, in which case the foot can choose to pursue by passing a CMT.
  - It has bases facing in more than one direction.
  - It is battle wagons or artillery.
- If some of a battle group's close combat opponents break, and some don't, it does not pursue unless it was fighting the unbroken enemy only as an overlap.
- A pursuit move made by a battle group which was providing rear support to artillery, or has captured or recaptured artillery to its front, measures its pursuit move from the original front edge of the enemy battle group it has broken.
- Pursuers make a variable movement distance roll and adjust their move accordingly.
- Pursuers who remain in contact with routers at the end of an initial pursuit move inflict losses (bases are removed from the routing battle group) and may inflict commander losses, as detailed in the *Joint Action Phase* section.
- Initial pursuits obey the same rules as pursuits in the joint action phase for moving multiple pursuing battle groups, following routers, avoiding friends or encountering the table edge, terrain or fresh enemy. See the *Joint Action Phase* section.

DECIDING HOW MANY DICE TO ROLL
ALLOCATING COMBAT DICE
SCORING HITS - POINTS OF ADVANTAGE
PROTECTION
ARTILLERY IN CONTACT WITH ENEMY
ACCUMULATING HITS AND TAKING COHESION TESTS
SHOOTING IN THE IMPACT PHASE
COMMANDERS IN CLOSE COMBAT
FIGHTING BROKEN TROOPS
MOVEMENT OF BROKEN TROOPS AND PURSUERS
AN EXAMPLE OF COMBAT

# AN EXAMPLE OF COMBAT

Let's *take a later tercio* battle group of 14 bases of Spanish foot charging into a battle group of 6 bases of Dutch foot from the late sixteenth century. There is another battle group of 6 bases of Dutch foot ready to charge into the flank of the tercio, but not within reach to intercept it. Both Dutch battle groups are deployed in two ranks with one file of pike flanked on each side by a file of arquebusiers. The tercio has 2 files of 4 pike bases flanked on each side by a single file of 3 arquebusier bases. Initially, it is a straightforward head to head clash against the Dutch battle group to the tercio's front. The charge of the Spanish takes place in the impact phase.

- The Spanish pike are classified as superior armoured heavy foot, pike and the arquebusiers as superior unarmoured medium foot, arquebus.
- The Dutch pike are classified as average armoured heavy foot, pike and the arquebusiers as average unarmoured medium foot, arquebus.

A few comments on these classifications: The tercio will have considerable resilience owing to its depth. The Dutch would usually prefer to shoot from a distance but they appear to be in the better tactical position. However, the tercio is of superior quality and will get to re-roll its 1s (see *Quality Re-rolls* in the *Battle Groups* section).

**SPANISH vs DUTCH**

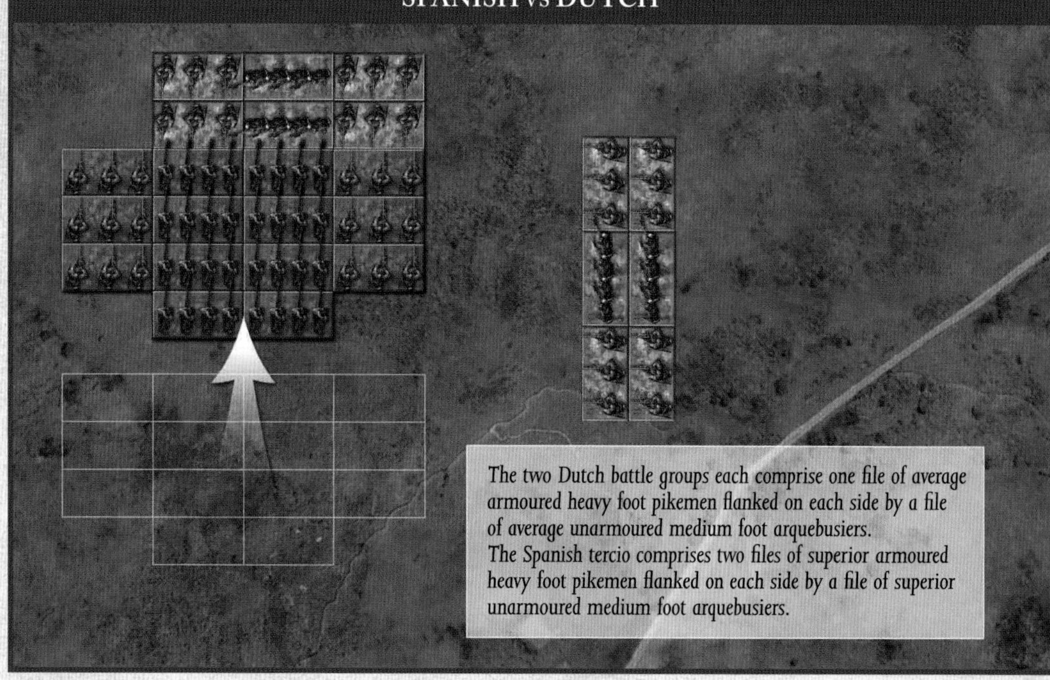

The two Dutch battle groups each comprise one file of average armoured heavy foot pikemen flanked on each side by a file of average unarmoured medium foot arquebusiers.
The Spanish tercio comprises two files of superior armoured heavy foot pikemen flanked on each side by a file of superior unarmoured medium foot arquebusiers.

The Spanish have charged in: it's the impact phase combat resolution stage. In the impact phase dice table under 'other troops', you find that both sides get **2 dice per front rank base** in contact. There are no overlaps in the impact phase, so even though the Spanish have more troops, this does not affect the situation yet. It is 6 dice for the Dutch versus 6 dice for the Spanish.

The pikemen and the shot have no basic POA against each other in the impact phase. However, the Spanish pikemen are 4 ranks deep and get a + POA for pikemen in 4 or more ranks. Each of the Dutch files facing 4 ranks deep pike therefore fight at a net – POA. Now refer to the 'Score to Hit' table. The Dutch have 4 dice at – POA, needing 5 or higher to hit, and 2 dice at 0 POA, needing 4 or higher to hit. The Spanish have 4 dice at + POA and 2 dice at 0 POA. All 6 need 4 or higher to hit. The Spanish are Superior and will re-roll any scores of 1.

## IMPACT AND SHOOTING DICE ROLLS

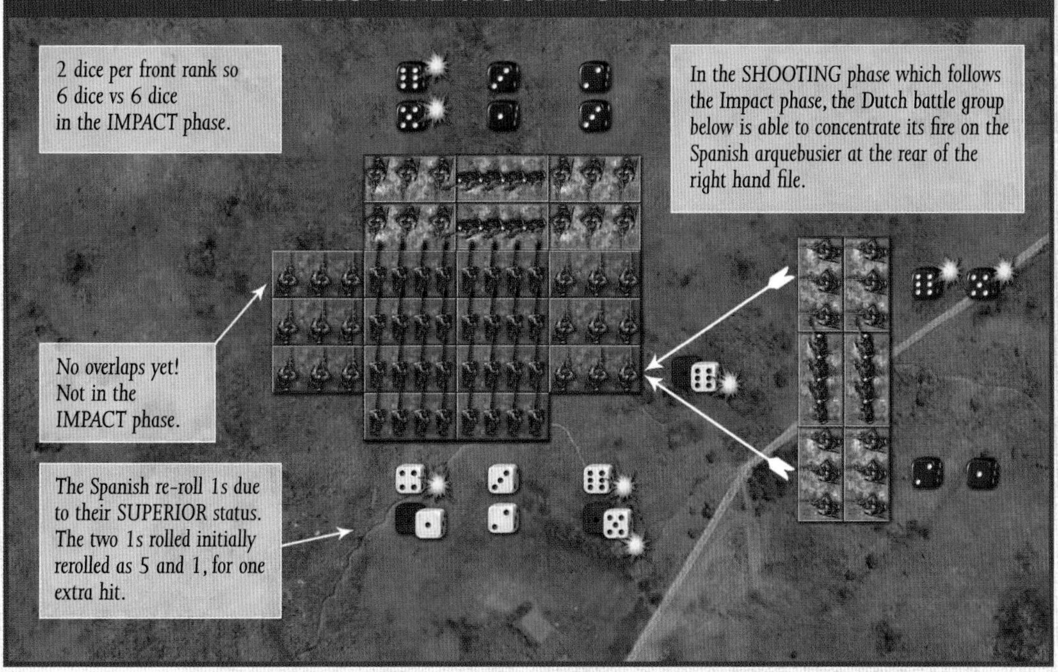


The Dutch roll 4 blue dice (needing 5 or higher) scoring 6, 5, 3, and 1, and 2 black dice (needing 4 or higher) scoring 3 and 2. This gives them just 2 hits on the tercio battle group. The Spanish roll 6 white dice (all needing 4 or higher) scoring 6, 4, 3, 2, 1 and 1. Only 2 hits so far, but they have two 1s. Being superior, they can re-roll these. They roll 5 and 1. Only one more hit, for a total of 3. The final result is 2 hits on the Spanish and 3 hits on the Dutch. **The Dutch have lost the impact phase combat.**

This is when it gets worrying for the Republic: the Dutch must now take a *cohesion test* (see the *Battle Group Deterioration* section). This is done by rolling 2 dice. The score to pass is 7. There are only a few modifiers in most circumstances. In this case, the only modifier is -1 for suffering >= 1 hit per 3 bases. The Dutch roll 5 and 1 for a total of 6, and deduct 1 for the modifier, giving a final score of 5. The modifiers are easy to remember. Usually it is either a -1 for a loss (-1 for 1 hit per 3 bases) or -2 for a bad loss (-1 for 1 hit per 3 bases and -1 for suffering at least 2 more hits than inflicted) and there are the few -1s that apply occasionally, such as for losing against shock mounted or foot using salvo in the impact phase. The negative modifiers can be mitigated by having supporting troops in the right place, or a commander with the battle group.

The Dutch scored 5, so **fail** their cohesion test. They drop one cohesion level from STEADY to DISRUPTED.

The Dutch now need to make a ***death roll*** (see the ***Battle Group Deterioration*** section) to decide if any bases are lost. This is straightforward. Roll more than the number of hits received to pass this test. As the Spanish battle group did not lose the combat (it inflicted as many or more hits than it received) it adds 2 to its dice roll so it cannot fail to score more than 1 and the Spanish player does not need to make a death roll. **Not losing combats is crucial:** Losers get both a cohesion test and a much bigger chance of losing bases on the death roll. The Dutch need 4 but roll 1 and lose a base. The Dutch choose to remove an arquebusier base. Note that there are no re-rolls on death rolls – if the Spanish had lost the combat, being superior would not have helped them here.

There will be a break in the action now while the manoeuvre phase is played.

In the shooting phase, the unengaged Dutch battle group will pour a volley into the right rear (3rd rank) base of tercio arquebusiers, who can return fire, as they can shoot from a side edge. (The 1st and 2nd rank cannot shoot, or be shot at, as they will be involved in the upcoming melee.) The Dutch get a - POA for shooting at a battle group involved in close combat, so they hit on a 5 or higher. The Dutch roll 6, 5, 2 and 1 (2 hits). This is not enough hits to trigger a cohesion test (1 hit per 3 bases) but it does trigger a death roll from shooting (with no automatic +2 on the dice as the shooting is mainly by firearms or artillery). The Spanish roll a 2 and lose an arquebusier base. However, this still gets to shoot this turn, as shooting is simultaneous, and cohesion tests and death rolls are not performed until after all shooting is complete. The Spanish are also on a - POA because their battle group is in close combat. They roll a 1, but re-roll it as a 6, which is a hit. This is not enough to trigger a cohesion test on the Dutch, but they roll a 1 on their death roll and lose a base.

We return to the fight in the melee phase. **Each base in the first 2 ranks gets 1 dice.** Overlaps now join the fight. The Spanish overlap the Dutch on one side and get 7 dice (an overlapping file only contributes 1 dice to the melee). The Dutch have lost a base, so have 5 bases. This would be 5 dice if they were STEADY. However, they are DISRUPTED and lose 1 dice per 3, ending up with 4 dice to roll. (Consider the 5 as 3+2. Each complete three reduces to a two, giving 2+2.)

POAs in the melee phase are not always the same as in the impact phase (e.g. foot using salvo get a ++ POA at impact against some troops for the effect of their close range volleys, but are no better than other shot types in the melee). In our example, the POAs are the same as before. Before losing a dice for Disruption, the Dutch have 2 arquebusier dice against shot (no POA); 2 pike dice against 4 deep pike (- POA), and 1 arquebusier dice against 4 deep pike (- POA). Note that the unarmoured arquebusiers get no additional - POA against the armoured pikemen because "better armour" does not give a POA against "shot". So the Dutch have 2 dice needing 4 or higher and 3 dice needing 5 or higher.

## MELEE DICE ROLLS

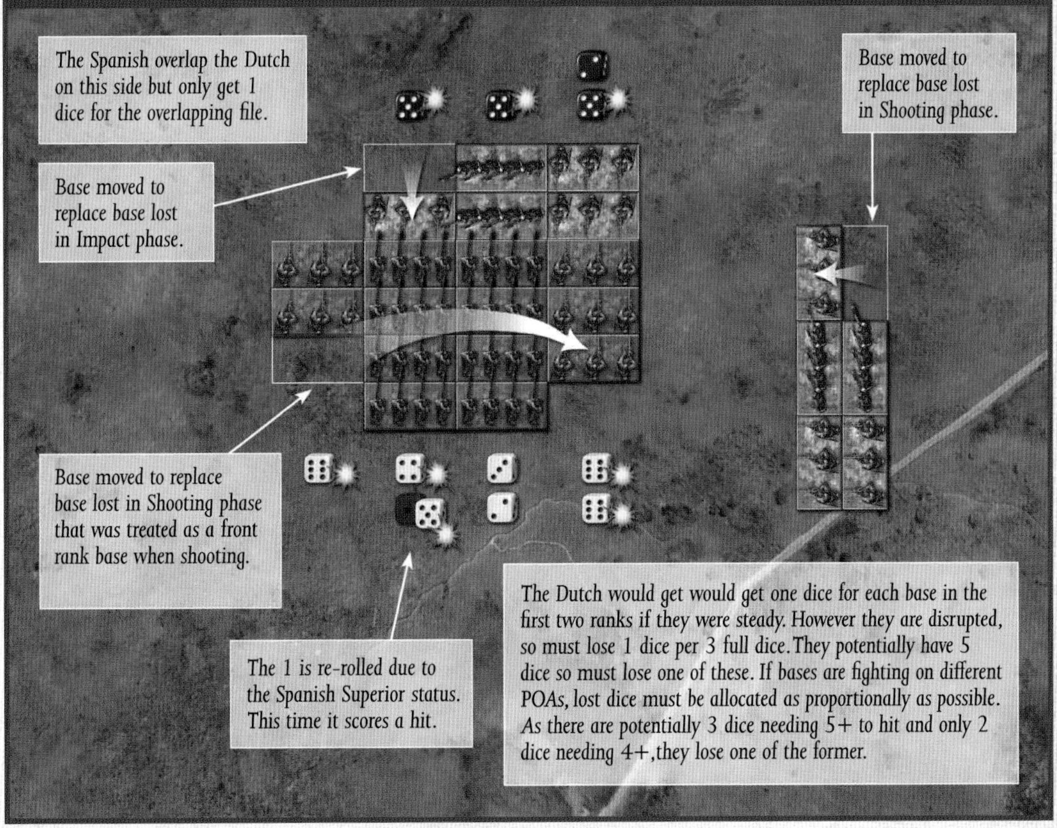


However, as calculated above, they must lose a dice owing to Disruption. As they have dice requiring different scores to hit, they must remove the lost dice as near in proportion as possible, so lose 1 of the 3 dice requiring 5 or higher. So the Dutch throw 2 blue dice requiring 5 or higher, and 2 black dice requiring 4 or higher.

The dice the Spanish get for their overlap is for arquebusiers vs arquebusiers, so is at 0 POA. Therefore the Spanish get 3 dice at 0 POA and 4 dice at + POA. All 7 dice need 4 or higher to hit.

The Dutch roll 2 blue dice (needing 5 or higher) scoring 5 and 5, and 2 black dice (needing 4 or higher) scoring 5 and 2, which gives 3 hits. The Spanish roll 7 dice (needing 4 or higher) and get 6, 6, 6, 4, 3, 2 and 1 which gives 4 hits. They re-roll the 1 and get a 5, to make a total of 5 hits. **The Dutch have lost the melee phase combat.** The smaller and shallower Dutch formation is being ground down by the Spanish veterans.

The Dutch must now take a cohesion test. They lost by 5 hits to 3. The Dutch have a -1 as 5 hits is more than 1 per 3 bases, a second -1 as they lost the melee by 2 or more hits (a bad loss) and a third -1 as they are already DISRUPTED. They roll 2 and 4 totalling 6. Subtracting a net -3 brings this down to 3, so they fail the test though not quite badly enough to lose 2 cohesion levels. They are now FRAGMENTED and will lose 1 dice in 2 for combat next time. With only half their original dice, they are in real trouble but help is at hand!

The death roll. The Dutch took five hits: they need a 6 to pass as losers of a melee, and get it! The Spanish suffered 3 hits, but get +2 on their roll as they did not lose the combat, so need to roll a 2 to pass. They roll a 1 and lose a base! They have already lost a shot base, so must remove a pike base next according to the ***proportional loss rule*** (see ***Base Removal*** in the ***Battle Group Deterioration*** section). They choose to remove the front rank pike base from the left hand file and shuffle up the other 3 bases to fill the space.

In the next impact phase, the unengaged Dutch battle group charges into the side of the tercio. This will not count as a flank charge because the target is a tercio. The two tercio pike bases in the 3rd and 4th rank will respond by moving into position behind the 1st two ranks of the right-hand file of arquebusiers, facing the chargers. The 3rd rank of arquebusiers is relocated to make room.

Note: If a 3rd Dutch brigade was available and charged in on the tercio's left side, the overlapping arquebusiers (which are not in contact with enemy to their front) would turn to face the attack, at least one Spanish pike base would be moved to take up position beside them (in the position normally occupied by the 3rd rank of arquebusiers on that side, but facing the flank) and any displaced arquebusiers would be relocated to make room. In summary, the Spanish player would have a total of 7 pike bases facing in three directions; because both flank attacks occur in the same impact phase, and he can choose whether to face each one with one or two pike bases, he is effectively free to choose which of the front rank pike bases the three pike bases eligible to be in the 2nd rank will be behind.

*English Civil War Pikemen*

# JOINT ACTION PHASE

*Highlanders at Auldearn, 1645, by Angus McBride © Osprey Publishing Ltd. Taken from Warrior 21:* Highland Clansman 1689–1746.

*The final phase is a common phase* in which various outcome moves are actioned. In addition, **both sides'** commanders get a chance to move to new positions and attempt to bolster or rally unsteady troops.

The order rarely matters, but the active player moves his troops first, or decides the sequence of events, should either side feel this is necessary.

*Count von Tilly Commander of the Catholic League*

# OUTCOME MOVES IN THE JOINT ACTION PHASE

## VOLUNTARY BREAK OFFS

In battles of this period, when close combat with steady enemy was not going well, mounted and foot troops would often fall back to regroup, either to charge again or to engage in a (sometimes indecisive) fire fight. *Field of Glory Renaissance* simulates this in the joint action phase as follows:

The following battle groups cannot break off:

- Elephants, artillery and battle wagons.
- Any battle group with bases facing in more than one direction.
- Any battle group which pursued into contact with fresh enemy but has not yet fought any combat with them.

Otherwise:

- Mounted troops can break off if they are DISRUPTED or FRAGMENTED and at least half their close combat opponents are STEADY non-shock mounted troops or elephants.
- Mounted troops can break off if at least half their close combat opponents are STEADY foot.
- Foot can break off if they are DISRUPTED non-shock troops or FRAGMENTED and all their close combat opponents are STEADY non-shock foot.

(In each case count only enemy front rank bases in contact other than only as an overlap.)

When breaking off, a battle group moves straight back. Move distance is not measured normally. Instead:

- Mounted end the break off move separated from their opponent by a full normal move, facing them, in the same formation as before. They will thus be in position to charge the same enemy again in their next turn.
- Foot end the break off move separated from their opponent by 4 MUs, facing them, in the same formation as before.
- If the breakers-off were stepped forward, they end their break-off move with a level front rank, measuring the break-off distance from the enemy contacted by their furthest forward base.

The distance from the enemy is reduced in the following circumstances:

- If the move is blocked by a friendly battle group (even if of a type the breakers-off could normally interpenetrate) or camp, the battle group halts when it touches this.
- If the move would otherwise leave the table, the battle group halts when it touches the table edge.
- If the move is blocked by an enemy battle group or camp, the battle group halts 1 MU from this.
- If the move passes through terrain, the distance is reduced to the normal move distance in that terrain.
- If the move reaches terrain when the distance has already exceeded the normal move distance in that terrain, the battle group halts when it touches the edge of the terrain.

If, as a result, the battle group is unable to move back at least 1 MU, the break off is cancelled and the melee continues next turn.

When battle groups can mutually break off, the active player decides whether to break off first. If he does, the non-active player cannot also break off.

**BREAKING OFF**

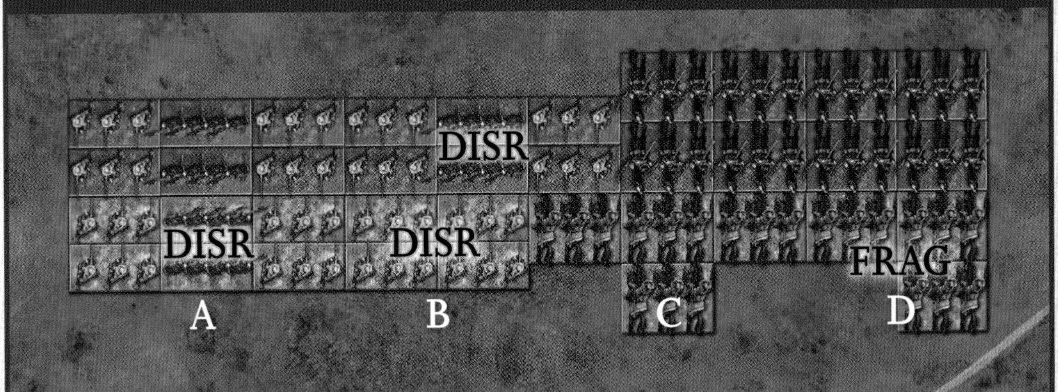


Battle group A is disrupted and all its close combat opponents are steady non-shock foot. So it can choose either to break off or remain in place. If it breaks off, it moves straight back, ending 4 MUs away from its melee opponents, facing them, in the same formation as before. If it had files stepped forward, it would end its break off move with a level front rank.

Battle group B cannot break off because its opponents are disrupted.

Battle group C and D are cavaliers. The opposing mounted troops are horse. Battle group C cannot break off because it is steady and less than half of (in fact none of) its opponents are steady foot. Battle group D can choose to break off or remain in place because it is fragmented and at least half of (in fact all of) its close combat opponents are steady non-shock mounted. If it breaks off, it moves straight back, ending 5 MUs away from its melee opponents, facing them, in the same formation as before.

## STOPPING LOOTING

Once a camp is sacked, battle groups in contact with it must pass a CMT in the joint action phase to stop looting. If they succeed, they are free to move normally in their next turn. If all battle groups looting a camp stop looting, the camp is removed from the table.

## ROUTERS AND PURSUERS

Broken troops (routers) and any pursuers move in every joint action phase as follows:

- Broken troops with enemy in contact at the start of this phase move directly away from the enemy in contact, bisecting the angle if the enemy are facing in more than one direction.
- Broken troops not in contact with enemy move towards their side's rear table edge, making wheels and/or turns as appropriate to end their move as close to the rear table edge as possible.
- Broken troops no longer being pursued move normal move distance. Broken troops still being pursued make a variable movement distance roll and adjust their move accordingly. Troops continuing their pursuit do the same.
- If any obstructions would prevent completion of a routing battle group's move, adjust as per evade moves (see the ***Impact Phase*** section) to get past these, but not to avoid leaving the table. It must go round a fortified or enemy camp, but can pass through its own unfortified camp. If its path is obstructed by unbroken enemy that cannot be bypassed, the battle group is destroyed at the end of the phase.
- Pursuers who remain in contact with routers must pursue if they are gendarmes, cavaliers or warrior impact foot. Other troops must pursue unless they pass a CMT to stop pursuing. (Normal quality re-rolls apply.)
- Gendarmes, cavaliers or warrior impact foot who have lost contact with routers must continue to pursue until they pass a CMT to stop pursuing (quality re-rolls **do not** apply) or the routers are removed from the table. (This does not apply to routers whom they were neither in contact with when they broke, nor have contacted since.) Other troops who have lost contact with routers stop pursuing automatically. Pursuers who have lost contact with routers can only charge them again in the impact phase if they have stopped pursuing.
- Pursuers follow routers, wheeling if necessary to do so. They can contract frontage by dropping back bases if necessary to avoid friends.
- If more than one battle group is pursuing the same routing battle group, move the fastest pursuers first after rolling all VMD rolls. If the move distances are equal, the pursuer chooses which to move first.
- A pursuing battle group whose move would take any part of it off the table edge instead halts its move at the table edge.
- Pursuers can choose to stop at the edge of any terrain that would severely disorder any of their bases.
- Pursuers normally contact any fresh enemy in their path. However troops can choose to halt their pursuit 1 MU away from fresh

### TIP!

Deciding whether to stop pursuing or to continue the pursuit is often a difficult decision. Staying with the routers will certainly prevent them from being rallied, but sometimes there is more to be gained from leaving the pursuit to fight elsewhere.

*La Valette's counter-attack, 1565, by Christa Hook © Osprey Publishing Ltd. Taken from Campaign 50:* Malta 1565.

enemy (or immediately if already closer) in the following circumstances. If they do so, all their front rank bases stop on that line:

- Light troops can always choose to halt their pursuit rather than contact fresh enemy battle troops.
- Foot can always choose to halt their pursuit rather than contact fresh enemy mounted troops or elephants.
- Any troops can choose to halt their pursuit rather than contact fresh enemy battle troops if they pass a CMT to do so. (Normal quality re-rolls apply.)

- If pursuers contact fresh enemy in any phase, this is treated as a charge on the contacted enemy. Combat is adjudicated in the next impact phase. (Except that if contact occurred in the impact phase it is adjudicated in the same impact phase.)
- FRAGMENTED troops who would be contacted by enemy pursuers (other than light foot) in any phase must take a Cohesion Test (and make a rout move if they break) before the pursuers are moved.
- Non-shock cavalry or camelry entirely 1 base deep or light troops who would be contacted by enemy pursuers in any phase can evade (unless they are already in close combat other than only as an overlap).
- Light troops who would be contacted by pursuing battle troops must pass a CMT not to evade unless either of the following apply:
  - They are already in close combat other than only as an overlap – in which situation evading is never possible.
  - They are light foot or dragoons entirely in uneven, rough or difficult terrain or

defending fortifications, an obstacle or a riverbank.
- Troops who stop pursuing halt on the spot and can move normally in their next turn.

### REMOVING BASES FROM ROUTING BATTLE GROUPS

Pursuers who are in contact with a routing enemy battle group at the end of any pursuit move:

- Inflict 1 base loss on the routing battle group for each pursuing battle group in contact with it. **No other shooting or close combat occurs against routers.**
- Can roll to kill the enemy commander if there is one with the routing battle group (whether or not he had been fighting in the front rank in any previous close combat). Roll 2 dice. If these total 10 or more, the commander is lost. Roll only once even if there is more than one pursuing battle group in contact with the routers.

### REMOVING DESTROYED BATTLE GROUPS

At the end of the joint action phase, battle groups are destroyed and removed from the table if either of the following applies:

- They are ***autobroken*** (see the ***Battle Group Deterioration*** section) and all pursuers have ceased pursuit.
- They are reduced to 1 base.

If the battle group was not already broken when this happens, this will trigger a cohesion test for nearby friendly battle groups as if it had broken. Leave it in place until this has been adjudicated.

## COMMANDERS IN THE JOINT ACTION PHASE

### TIP!

Your decisions regarding your commanders in the joint action phase are some of the most important ones you will make in the game. Consider them carefully. It can be critical for a commander to be in the correct position next turn to influence a complex move test, modify cohesion tests if your troops are coming under pressure, or to fight in the front rank of a battle group that is about to be charged by the enemy. Bolstering your unsteady troops is vital in halting the deterioration of your army's fighting capability. Rallying routed troops could also save the day, but often you are faced with choosing the least worst option. These decisions often make the difference between an average player and a great one.

## MOVEMENT

Commanders of both sides can move once in the joint action phase. They cannot move a battle group with them.

## BOLSTERING AND RALLYING TROOPS

Commanders of both sides can bolster or rally troops in the joint action phase. As battle groups deteriorate they drop down the cohesion ladder. However, with encouragement from their commanders they can climb back up it. We call this bolstering when encouraging troops that are not yet broken and rallying when attempting to bring back a broken battle group.

The bolstering and rallying procedure is as follows:

- Battle groups cannot be bolstered or rallied if their Cohesion Level dropped in the current turn.
- Broken troops cannot be rallied if they are within 6 MUs of any enemy (excluding the enemy camp and commanders' bases).
- Otherwise a commander can attempt to bolster or rally a battle group that **he is with**. (Note that joint action phase movement of commanders occurs before bolstering and rallying, so he can, if he is within his move distance and free to move, move to join the battle group for this purpose.) If the battle group passes a ***cohesion test*** (see the ***Battle Group Deterioration*** section) its cohesion level rises one level. If it fails, its cohesion level stays the same. (Cohesion level cannot drop when testing to bolster or rally.)
- Each commander can only attempt to bolster or rally one battle group in each joint action phase.
- When attempting to bolster or rally a battle group, only the commander with the battle group can apply his modifiers. (Thus the extra +1 for a GC only applies if he is the commander with the battle group.)

*Ataman Jablonowski Polish Commander*

## TIP!

Bolstering troops is one of the most important functions of commanders. If no attempt is made to bolster a distressed battle group, its cohesion may drop further as the situation worsens. Pretty soon it will be too late – it will BREAK. This is particularly important when opposing armies engage in a prolonged shooting fight or an extended melee. If you leave the troops until they are broken before you attempt to rally them you are on a -3 when testing – so you will need a high score. Far easier to bolster troops when they are merely DISRUPTED.

- Only a commander in ***line of command*** (see ***glossary***) can bolster or rally a battle group.
- Only one attempt can be made per joint action phase to bolster or rally each battle group, even if more than one commander is present with the battle group.
- A commander who attempts to rally a broken battle group does not have to rout with it if it fails the cohesion test.

*Mounted Crossbowmen*

# BATTLE GROUP DETERIORATION

*The last stand of Sir James Campbell of Lawers' brigade, 1650, by Graham Turner © Osprey Publishing Ltd. Taken from Campaign 142:* Dunbar 1650.

# COHESION TESTS

*Battle groups deteriorate* primarily by failing cohesion tests. There are several reasons for a battle group to take a cohesion test (CT):

### FRAGMENTED TROOPS BEING CHARGED

- Test a FRAGMENTED battle group immediately if it is charged by enemy other than light foot. Battle groups about to be contacted by enemy pursuers test as if being charged.

### POST-COMBAT

- Test a battle group after all shooting dice have been rolled if it suffered either of the following: (If both apply, this does **not** count as more than 1 reason to test.)
  - At least 1 shooting hit per 3 bases (1 HP3B) (see the *Glossary* for the full definition. Some troop types calculate HP3B differently and not all ranks count.)
  - At least 2 shooting hits from artillery and it is warriors.
- Test a battle group after all close combat dice have been rolled if it lost an impact or melee close combat.

### SEEING FRIENDLY BATTLE GROUPS BREAK OR COMMANDERS LOST

- Test a battle group if a friendly battle group within 3 MUs breaks or friendly artillery within 3 MUs is captured for the first time:
  - Immediately if a FRAGMENTED battle group breaks in response to being charged. Otherwise at the end of the current phase after resolving all combats, post-combat cohesion tests, death rolls and tests for inflicting commander losses.
  - Measure the distance before removing any lost troop bases. Test before the broken troops make their initial rout move.
  - Only light troops need test if the broken friends are light troops.
  - If an as yet unbroken friendly battle group is destroyed as a result of base loss(es) test as if it was broken, before it is removed from the table.
- Test a battle group if a commander in ***line of command*** (see ***glossary***) is lost within 3 MUs:
  - At the end of the current phase after resolving all combats, post-combat cohesion tests, death rolls and tests for inflicting commander losses.
  - Measure from the nearest part of the battle group he was with, after removing his base and putting any troop bases he displaced back in their previous position.

Note – no cohesion test is required when artillery that has been captured earlier in the game is recaptured, broken or destroyed.

### BOLSTERING AND RALLYING

- Test in the joint action phase to bolster or rally a battle group with a commander (see the ***Joint Action Phase*** section for details).

# THE TEST

*The cohesion test* is a very simple pass fail test. Roll two dice and apply the adjustment factors in the table below.

The following rules also apply:

## COMMANDERS AND COHESION TESTS

- Only one commander can affect a cohesion test – count whichever gives the best modifiers.
- A battle group in close combat can only count a commander who is with it.
- A commander with a battle group in close combat can influence other eligible battle groups unless he is fighting in the front rank.

## MIXED BATTLE GROUPS

Mixed foot battle groups test as if entirely of whichever of their component types is latest in the following list: light foot, medium foot, warriors, heavy foot, determined foot.

## MULTIPLE CAUSES

If a battle group must test for multiple breaks due to charges, or multiple breaks or lost commanders at the end of the phase, it only tests once but with a -1 adjustment to the dice for "more than one reason to test".

## TESTING MULTIPLE BATTLE GROUPS

If several battle groups have to test at the same time for seeing friends break or commanders lost, their side's player decides which order to test them in. If further battle groups break as a consequence, those that have already tested do not have to test again. If pursuits result in the loss of a commander, battle groups that have already tested at the end of this phase for breaks/lost commanders do not have to test again.

*English Civil War Dragoons Advance*

## COHESION TEST

**Throw 2 dice (Quality re-rolls apply). Score 7 to pass.**

### MODIFIERS

| | | | |
|---|---|---|---|
| Battle group suffered at least 1 HP2B from shooting* | -1 | Commander in *line of command* (see *glossary*) in *command range* if battle group is not in close combat, or with the battle group if it is in close combat | +1 |
| Battle group suffered at least 1 HP3B from close combat** | -1 | Extra if he is a great commander | +1 |
| At least 2 more hits received than inflicted in close combat** | -1 | Battle group counts as *supported* (see *glossary*) | +1 |
| Battle group has lost at least 25% of its original bases | -1 | **Current Cohesion State** | |
| Foot battle troops with *threatened flank* (see *glossary*) | -1 | Disrupted or Severely Disordered | -1 |
| | | Fragmented | -2 |
| More than 1 reason to test | -1 | Broken | -3 |
| Any one of…<br>Any troops shot at by artillery*<br>OR<br>Elephants, cavalry, camelry or light horse shot at by firearms*<br>OR<br>Any troops testing for having lost close combat even partly against elephants**<br>OR<br>Medium foot, warriors or dragoons testing for having lost close combat even partly against mounted troops or heavy or determined foot in *open terrain*** (see *glossary*)<br>OR<br>Any troops testing for having lost impact phase combat even partly against lancers, impact mounted or foot using salvo**<br>OR<br>Foot testing for having lost impact phase combat even partly against impact foot** | -1 | * Only applies when testing as a result of shooting hits. The modifier for being shot at by artillery or firearms applies whether or not they scored the hits.<br>** Only applies when testing as a result of losing a close combat. The modifier for fighting specific enemy troop types applies whether or not these inflicted more hits on the battle group than it inflicted on them.<br>Other tests do not use these modifiers even if they occur in the same phase. | |

## RESULT

| If the final score is: | |
|---|---|
| **7 or more** | • Rise one cohesion level if testing to bolster or rally the battle group.<br>• Otherwise no change in cohesion level. |
| **3, 4, 5 or 6** | • Drop one cohesion level (ignore if testing to bolster or rally the battle group). |
| **2 or less** | • Drop two cohesion levels if:<br>  • Testing for losing a close combat in which the battle group received at least 2 more hits than it inflicted.<br>  • Testing for seeing friends break or commander lost.<br>• Otherwise drop one cohesion level (ignore if testing to bolster or rally the battle group). |

# THE EFFECT OF COHESION LEVELS

| COHESION LEVEL AND EFFECTS | |
|---|---|
| LEVEL | EFFECT |
| STEADY | All troops start the battle STEADY |
| DISRUPTED (DISR) | • -1 on all CMTs<br>• -1 on all further cohesion tests<br>• Battle group loses 1 dice per 3 in close combat and shooting<br>• Non-shock battle groups must pass a CMT to charge or intercept |
| FRAGMENTED (FRAG) | • -2 on all CMTs<br>• -2 on all further cohesion tests<br>• Battle group can make a simple move to retire away from all enemy within 12 MUs but must CMT for any other move<br>• Battle group loses 1 dice per 2 in close combat and shooting<br>• Shock troops are no longer so<br>• Battle group cannot charge or intercept<br>• Battle group must take a cohesion test if charged by any troops except light foot |
| BROKEN | • Battle group makes a rout move in the phase in which it breaks, and in each subsequent joint action phase<br>• -3 on cohesion tests to rally<br>• 1 base removed for each pursuing enemy battle group in contact at the end of its pursuit move |

## TIP!

The best way to develop a winning strategy in *Field of Glory Renaissance* is to avoid taking cohesion tests! Minimise your risks by stacking combat modifiers in your favour and by preventing your opponent from concentrating shooting. Avoid the risk of panic spreading by keeping your supporting battle groups far enough back from the front line.

# DEATH ROLLS

*In addition to dropping cohesion levels*, a battle group can also deteriorate by losing bases as a result of the **death roll**. This is a simple pass/fail roll on a single dice as follows:

Thus, if losing a close combat or being shot at mainly by artillery or firearms, the roll needs to be more than the hits received. If being shot at mainly by bows or crossbows for example, or winning/drawing a close combat, then no roll is required unless 3 or more hits are taken.

| DEATH ROLL |
|---|
| Roll 1 dice for the battle group. (No re-rolls). |
| • Add +1 to the dice score if the battle group started the battle with only 2 bases |
| • Add +2 to the dice score if the battle group won/drew a close combat or the hits suffered were from shooting (unless the majority of the shooting dice - whether they scored hits or not - were attributable to any combination of artillery, regimental guns and firearms). |
| If the score does not exceed the number of hits, remove a base. |
| If a base was removed, and there were more than 6 hits, deduct 6 from the hits and roll again for the remainder. (Use the same modifiers.) |

## EXAMPLE:

A battle group of horse suffers 9 hits from shooting. Ouch! Seven of the shooting dice were attributable to arquebusiers and six to bowmen so the majority of the shooting dice were contributed by firearms. It doesn't matter which dice scored the hits. The horse cannot exceed the number of hits on the score of one dice, so it loses 1 base. It must deduct 6 from the total hits, leaving 3. It must now roll to score higher than this. As it has no modifier on its score (more than half the shooting dice were from firearms), it will lose another base only if it rolls less than 4 on the dice.

If a battle group must take a cohesion test as well as a death roll, the cohesion test is always resolved **before** the effect of the death roll. (This means that you can roll the dice together, but base losses that will result from the death roll do not affect the cohesion test modifiers.)

# BASE REMOVAL

*Bases removed as a result* of failed death rolls or pursuits obey the following priorities for removal:

- **Long range shooting by artillery only:** If the target has different troop types or weapons, and they are currently in their original proportions, remove a base of the most numerous type

*Master gunner prepares to fire*

without a shooting capability, unless the target has only one such base; if there are equal numbers of such bases with different close combat capabilities, remove the type with the heavier armour. (This rule is intended to ensure that the densest part of the target battle group takes the highest casualties from artillery). If there is only one base without a shooting capability, or if the different types are no longer in their original proportions, follow the proportional loss rule – see below.

- **Other shooting**: The nearest base to the shooters that obeys the proportional loss rule – see below. Exception – when a battle group in Swedish brigade formation loses a base, and the majority of the shooting dice are attributable to enemy bases any part of which are directly to the target's front, always remove the pike base in point position (until only 1 pike base is left).
- **Close combat**: Any front rank base facing the enemy battle group which inflicted most hits on the battle group.
- **Routing**: Furthest base from pursuers of the same type as any in contact with them. (This is to prevent base removal from causing pursuers to lose contact.)
- If bases are of equal priority, the battle group's owner chooses which to remove.
- If a battle group is in close combat with two or more enemy battle groups, do not remove a base that would leave any of the enemy battle groups (except those fighting only as an overlap) without a base to face (unless you run out of bases).
- If the base that should be removed has been displaced by a commander fighting in the front rank, remove the displaced base instead of the commander.
- If both players must remove bases, the active player does so second.

Where there is a choice of which base to remove, a base must be removed in accordance with the **proportional loss rule**: After the first base loss to a battle group, base losses from mixed battle groups must always (when there is a choice) be taken in proportion to the relative strengths of the different constituents of the battle group until the original proportions are restored. For example, a later tercio starting with 6 shot and 3 pike bases loses a pike base due to artillery fire; then it loses another base, a shot base must be removed. If another base is lost then another shot base is removed, leaving 4 shot and 2 pike bases i.e. the same proportion of pike to shot as the battle group started with. If another base is lost, and the priority rules allow a choice, the player has a free choice of which type to remove.

If possible, other bases of the battle group are immediately moved to fill vacated front rank positions and retain a legal formation. All vacated front rank positions must be filled unless this would result in an illegal formation or the file was only 1 rank deep. Non-front rank bases must be used to fill the vacated position if any are available, and can be from anywhere in the battle group. Other bases are shuffled up as necessary. If no non-front rank bases are available, front rank bases that are not in close combat or are only in close combat as an overlap must be used. If there are no such bases available, and there is a gap in the front rank, bases must be shifted as necessary to fill the gap. The player owning the battle group chooses which direction to shift, but if possible, it must leave at least one base in contact with each opposing enemy battle group in close combat (except those fighting only as an overlap). If this is impossible, the player whose battle group suffered the base loss chooses which enemy battle group it loses contact with.

# AUTOBREAK

*Battle groups automatically break* immediately when they have lost a certain proportion of their original bases, so accumulated losses can get you in the end:

| Quality | Autobreak on |
|---|---|
| Elite | > 60% lost |
| Superior | > 50% lost |
| Average | > 40% lost |
| Poor | > 30% lost |

All the rules that normally apply when a battle group breaks due to failing a cohesion test also apply when a battle group "autobreaks". However, battle groups below their autobreak point cannot be rallied. They are destroyed and removed from the table at the end of the joint action phase if all pursuers have ceased pursuit or they are reduced to one base.

Battle groups with only one base left are always destroyed and removed from the table at the end of the joint action phase, even if not autobroken. Where a battle group has not already broken when this occurs, it will trigger a cohesion test for nearby friendly battle groups as if it had just broken.

Note that regimental gun and limber markers do not count as bases, so do not affect the autobreak point of their battle group. Likewise, a commander with a battle group does not affect its autobreak point.

*French Thirty Years War infantry*

# VICTORY AND DEFEAT

*The capture of Francis I, 1525, by Graham Turner © Osprey Publishing Ltd. Taken from Campaign 44:* Pavia 1525.

An army suffers an **army rout** if at the end of the current phase it has accumulated attrition points which equal or exceed its *break point* (see the ***Playing the Game*** section). Unless both sides suffer a simultaneous army rout, which is a draw, the enemy has achieved a **Decisive Victory**.

In stand-alone games the game is now over. In campaign or scenario games, additional rules may be provided to cover a retreat from the battlefield.

- If playing to a time limit and neither army is broken at the pre-set time limit:
- A side that inflicted at least 4 more attrition points than the enemy and >= 3:1 gains a **Major Victory**.
- Failing that, a side that inflicted at least 3 more attrition points than the enemy and >= 2:1 gains a **Moderate Victory**.
- Failing that, a side that inflicted at least 2 more attrition points than the enemy gains a **Marginal Victory**.

If none of the above apply, the game is a draw.

*Victory parade of the Elizabethan English infantry*

# SPECIAL FEATURES

*The windmill battery at Lützen, 1632, by Graham Turner © Osprey Publishing Ltd. Taken from Campaign 68:* Lützen 1632.

# ELEPHANTS AND CAMELS

*Horses generally* don't like camels or elephants.

- Gendarmes, cavaliers, horse, determined horse, cavalry and light horse are DISORDERED if they are less than 1 base width from elephants or camelry.
- Camelry are only so affected by elephants.
- Camelry treat soft sand as rough going, not difficult.
- Camelry otherwise move as if cavalry.
- Elephants cause a -1 modifier on the cohesion test when enemy lose a close combat against them.
- None of the above applies to commanders depicted as camelry or on elephants.

# NAVAL UNITS

*Field of Glory Renaissance* seeks to recreate the land battles of the sixteenth and seventeenth centuries. However, a number of engagements were fought on or near coastal beaches and the outcomes were significantly influenced by naval action, particularly at battle sites bordering the English Channel and the North Sea. We simulate this as follows.

Our companion army list books designate which armies may have naval units at their disposal. Each naval unit deployed beyond a coastline entitles its owner to 3 non-enfilading artillery shots (i.e. dice) at any enemy battle group within 6 MUs of any part of the coastline edge during the shooting phase of each turn.

If both armies have naval units, only the player who has more can deploy the number of units by which his naval contingent is larger than his opponent's e.g. player A has two naval units and his opponent player B has one. A can deploy one naval unit and B cannot deploy any. Each deployed naval unit must be represented by two ship models placed on the water surface by the coastline at the end of deployment. They cannot be targeted for shooting nor contacted by any battle group. Their main function is to remind players they are there.

Naval units are not battle groups and do not contribute to the attrition point threshold of the army for the purpose of calculating victory and defeat.

# FIELD FORTIFICATIONS

- Except in scenario or campaign games, field fortifications (FF) are only allowed when permitted in our companion army list books and paid for.
- FF have a front and rear and these must be clearly identifiable.
- A base counts as defending field fortifications if it is completely behind the

fortifications, with its edge touching the rear edge of the fortification.

- The front edge of FF is treated as the front edge of a battle group defending them, including for measuring shooting ranges.
- Troops defending field fortifications are not disordered or severely disordered by terrain.
- Troops defending FF cannot be charged in flank/rear across the fortifications, and suffer no POA penalty for fighting in more than one direction across them. If not already facing the part of the fortification being attacked, the defending bases turn to face it and the rest of the battle group is shuffled up to maintain contact with the turned bases.
- Other than as above, troops defending FF never conform to enemy attacking across them.
- Troops providing rear support to artillery which are defending FF also count as defending FF.
- Troops approaching FF defended by enemy must halt 1 MU from the FF, and troops charging enemy defending FF can only move 1 MU in the impact phase. "Move" here includes any step forward.
- Undefended field fortifications do not impede movement of troops (i.e. not sufficiently to be represented in the rules).

*Attack on Field Fortifications*

# PORTABLE DEFENCES

- Portable defences (PD) include various portable obstacles carried by foot to use as a defence against horse, e.g. stakes, swinesfeathers and man-portable chevaux-de-frise.
- PD are only allowed when permitted in our companion army list books and paid for. They must be assigned to a specific battle group.
- A battle group carrying PD can place them (or pick them up) in the manoeuvre phase as a full complex move. Enough are carried to cover the front of the battle group when it is 2 bases deep. Stands depicting appropriate PD are placed on the table in the position of the front of the battle group. The battle group is shifted back to make room. The front edge of the PD is treated as the front edge of the battle group, including for measuring shooting ranges.
- Once placed, only that battle group can defend them. PD are treated as field fortifications when their defenders are in close combat against mounted, but give no advantage against foot, elephants or shooting. However, PD have no effect on movement.
- Troops defending PD never conform to enemy attacking across them.
- PD can only be picked up if there are no enemy within 6 MUs of the battle group. The battle group is shifted forward level with the former front edge of the PD.
- If the battle group moves away without picking up its PD, the PD markers are removed.
- A battle group that has placed and not picked up its PD cannot place more PD.

# SQUARE

- Square is a special all round defensive formation permitted only to foot battle groups including bases with pike or spearmen capability.
- A complex move test (CMT) must be passed to form or leave square. A battle group can only form square if it starts no more than 4 files wide.
- Square formation is depicted by moving the bases back to back facing in four directions (see diagram). The battle group must be shifted so that the centre of its front rank is in the same position as before.
- A battle group cannot form square unless there are unbroken enemy (excluding camp or commanders) within 6 MUs.
- A battle group cannot form or leave square while in close combat.
- A battle group leaving square can face any of its four edges in its normal formation.

- A battle group in square:
  - Cannot charge or intercept.
  - Can move 1 MU in a direction perpendicular to any of its four edges in its side's manoeuvre phase.
  - Exerts no restricted area.
  - Never counts as charged in flank or rear and never turns to face enemy contacting its flank or rear nor conforms to enemy in close combat.
  - Fights in any direction with one quarter of its bases, rounded up. Half of these, rounded up, count as front rank bases.
  - Cannot be overlapped.
  - Suffers no POA penalty for fighting in more than one direction.
  - Cannot fight as an overlap for another friendly battle group.
  - Cannot count any pike or spearmen POAs but, if steady, counts as steady pike or spearmen (respectively) for the purpose of determining enemy POAs, even if the base(s) in contact with enemy are not pike or spearmen.
  - The normal rules for "protection" are suspended. Pike and shot in a square including pike and shot always count as "protected".

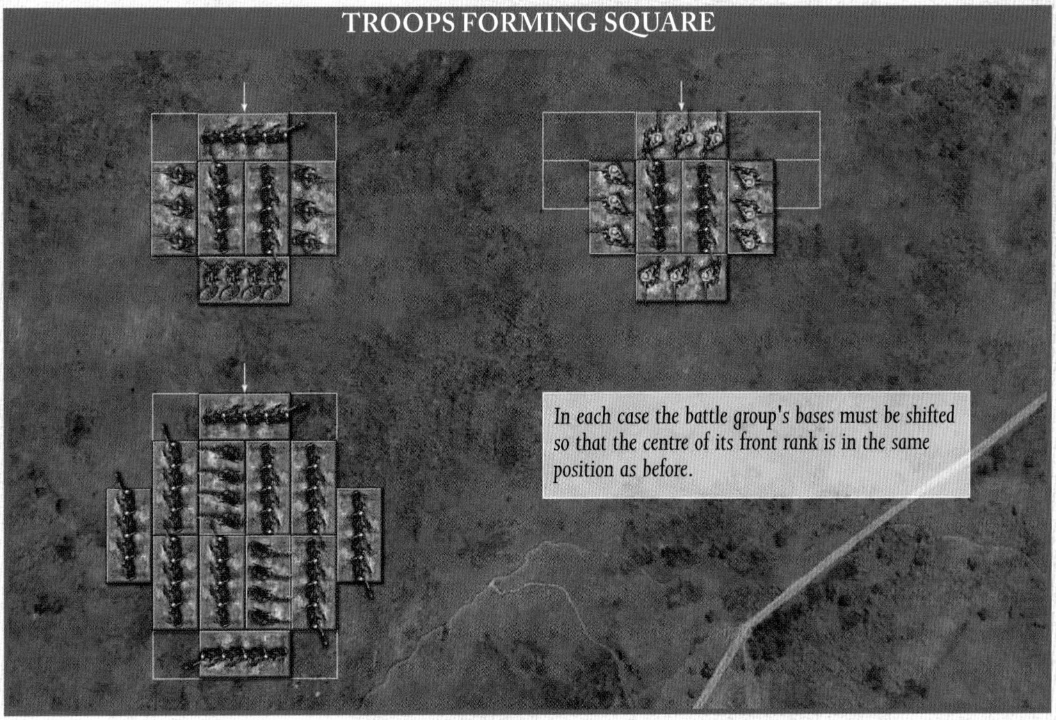

*Formed Square stands fast*

# REFERENCE SECTION

*English cavalry in Tangier, 1680, by Graham Turner © Osprey Publishing Ltd. Taken from Warrior 44:* Ironsides.

# SCALES

*Tabletop wargaming requires* a number of compromises to make our battle games enjoyable and to allow us to complete them in a reasonable period of time. This can of course work against us when attempting to recreate actual battles from history, but with a little care and preparation this is easily overcome. For normal club or competition games we are constrained by time, table space and our opponent's available armies. Love it or hate it, the modern phenomenon of wargaming anachronistic battles allows players to research and paint up armies from any location and time frame covered by the rules without worrying about the availability of historical opponents. As soon as we do this, we compromise literal figure scales, e.g. to make a "what if" battle between a Conquistador force and an Ottoman army work, we need to adjust the scale of the armies, as historically the Conquistadors could never field a force anywhere near the size of an Ottoman army. This is where our companion army list books and points values come into play and allow any combination of opposing armies to work. Obviously the approach differs for historical re-fights, and also for campaigns.

In *Field of Glory Renaissance*, the troop scale can be taken as roughly 100–250 men per base. In some important battles, however, only a few hundred combatants were engaged on each side, while others involved tens of thousands. In practice, therefore, we recommend ignoring theoretical troop scales and treating each army as a coherent whole, representing whatever full-sized army its prototype usually fielded. For example a tercio base represents more men in more ranks than a base forming part of a Williamite pike and shot battle group. Our companion army list books are specifically designed to create the correct SHAPE and feel of each army, allowing a good historical representation of how it fought. The rules generally assume that these lists are being used.

## FIGURE SCALE

The rules are compatible with all figure scales from 2mm to 28mm. All distances and ranges given in the rules are the same regardless of figure scale. Base sizes are listed below. The size for 15mm scale figures is shown first, followed by the size for 25/28mm scale figures in square brackets. For scales smaller than 15mm, it is recommended that the base sizes for the 15mm scale are used: simply add more figures to the base for visual effect. The base widths are standard for all bases. Base depths are always a compromise in tabletop armies and have been chosen to suit the size of the figures rather than the actual depth of the formation.

It is therefore apparent that the number of men represented by each base will depend on the size of battle being fought. Each base can be assumed to represent a body of troops in a battle formation of usually 3 to 5 ranks (or as few as 2 ranks towards the end of the period) with most battle groups being deployed 2 bases deep (4 to 10 ranks). Tercios and keils were even deeper in reality than these scales imply. Each base has a number of figures giving a visual representation of the formation that the battle group would most likely use.

The figures used should be an accurate representation of the troops they depict. This will assist your opponent to see at a glance what troops he is facing. In all games, but more especially tournament games, players must fully explain their troops at deployment or when asked.

Command bases are an exception to the figure scales. They are not fighting units, and are only used to indicate the location of the commanders on the battlefield. They do not add to the base count of any battle group they are with. Commanders are mounted on a single stand of a maximum 40mm [60mm] square or on a smaller stand of a suitable size for their troop type. They need not contain the same number of figures as their equivalent troop type, but must be easily identifiable as a commander, even when adjacent to a similarly armed combat battle group. Commanders' bases can therefore be as extravagant as you like.

## GROUND SCALE

The ground scale used is defined by effective (short) musket or bow range. The choice of scale is again a compromise and has been made with a view to making movement distances and missile ranges sufficient to ensure that players are faced with enough decision making to keep the game interesting while still maintaining a reasonable simulation of historical march rates and shooting distances.

All distances are specified in movement units (MUs). One movement unit, or MU for short, is usually either 25mm or 1 inch, as agreed by the players or decided by tournament organisers, regardless of figure scale. Alternatively, if using 25/28mm or larger figures on a table larger than 6 x 4 feet, a scale of 1MU = 1.5 inches or 40mm may be preferred.

## TIME SCALE

Each pair of game turns represents a varying amount of time on the battlefield, sufficient to encompass the majority of discrete battlefield actions. It also allows a reasonable period of time for battle groups to regroup during pauses in the action. The mass of minutiae that occur during battle are absorbed and incorporated into the cohesion, movement and combat mechanisms. Each turn represents a phase of battle rather than a fixed amount of time.

## BASE SIZES

Troop bases must be rectangles. For 15mm scale figures the width of all bases is 40mm. For 25/28mm scale figures the width is always 60mm. The depth varies according to troop type. The following tables show measurements for 15mm scale models. The 25/28mm scale equivalent is in brackets. Each base represents a body of men. The number of figures per base and the base depths are as follows:

Commanders will normally be depicted as one of their troop types. This is specified in the companion army list books. It is acceptable to use a slightly different number of figures to make the commander, his bodyguard and standard bearers easily distinguishable.

*Forlorn Hope defends Village*

| BASE SIZES | | |
|---|---|---|
| **Troop Type** | **Figures per base: 15mm [25/28mm]** | **Depth of base: 15mm [25/28mm]** |
| Heavy foot. Determined foot with pike | 4 | 20mm* [30mm] |
| Medium foot. Other determined foot. Warriors. | 3 or 4 [3] | 20mm [30mm] |
| Light foot | 2 [or 1] | 20mm [30mm] |
| Mob | 5-8 | 30mm [40mm] |
| Cavalry | 3 [or 2] | 30mm [40mm] |
| Light horse | 2 [or 1] | 30mm [40mm] |
| Camelry | 3 [or 2] | 30mm [40mm] |
| Gendarmes and cavaliers | 3 [or 2] | 30mm [40mm] |
| Horse and determined horse | 3 or 4 [3] | 30mm [40mm] |
| Dragoons | 4 or 5** | 40mm [60mm] |
| Elephants | 1*** | 40mm [80mm] |
| Artillery | 1 or 2*** | 40mm [80mm] |
| Limber markers | 2-4**** | 40mm [60mm] |
| Regimental gun marker | 1*** | 20-25mm [30-40mm] |
| Battle wagons | 1*** | 80mm [120mm] |
| Commander | As required | 40mm [60mm] or less |
| Fortifications or portable defences | Models of the defences | 15-20mm [20-30mm] |
| Supply camp | This will be a selection of tents, wagons etc. It is a rectangle 120mm [180mm] by 80mm [160mm]. It can be fortified if allowed in the army list. | |

* players may prefer to use 15mm [20mm] depth. This is acceptable but the game must be played so that no advantage or disadvantage accrues from using shallower bases and the rules are to be interpreted accordingly.

** this is the number of dismounted dragoon figures including horseholder recommended. The base should include one or two mounts as well.

*** the numbers given are for elephants, guns or wagons. Crew figures are additional.

**** the numbers given are for draught horses or similar.

## USING TROOPS BASED FOR OTHER SYSTEMS

As long as the correct base widths are adhered to, it is OK to use troops based for other rules systems. Modification to comply with *Field of Glory Renaissance* may require a little ingenuity. For example:

- Single-based figures can be "blue-tacked" on to temporary bases of the correct width.
- Lesser numbers of figures per base can be used if the figures or the stands they are attached to are too large to fit the normal number on our standard base widths.
- Base depths can be larger than standard if the figures or the stands they are attached to are too large to fit on our standard base depths.
- Some bases from some other systems may need to be placed side by side and treated as two bases one behind the other.

There are bound to be any number of other temporary fixes. If both players have troops based to the same system they can be used, as long as all bases are the same width. When using tercios and keils, the footprint of a battle group must be calculated as if the base depths specified by these rules are used. It may be convenient to mount such battle groups on movement trays using magnetic paper.

# TROOP TYPES IN DETAIL

*The troop types in these rules* are defined by their battlefield behaviour rather than their physical appearance or equipment alone. For example, the term 'heavy foot' is used to describe all infantry troop types that fight shoulder to shoulder in close formation. There are a number of individual troop types and these are described in the following table.

**TROOP TYPES**

| Troop Type | Ref | Description |
|---|---|---|
| Heavy Foot | HF | Foot troops who fight in close formation. These include most pikemen and billmen. |
| Determined Foot | DF | Heavy foot noted for their exceptional speed of advance, such as Swiss pikemen. |
| Medium Foot | MF | Foot troops fighting in looser formation than heavy foot and hence better suited than heavy foot to fighting in rough terrain. They are often principally reliant on missile weapons. They are capable of fighting alongside heavy foot in the open, particularly when they can be protected by pikemen, but are very vulnerable to a mounted charge if caught on their own in open ground. Medium foot cannot have pike capability. |
| Light Foot | LF | Foot troops who fight in a dispersed formation with missile weapons. They are best at harassing enemy from a distance and working in difficult terrain. |
| Warriors | War | Tribal or other close combat foot not part of the European or Chinese tactical systems, They are often fiercer but less disciplined than European or Chinese troops. They are very vulnerable to a mounted charge in open ground. |
| Mob | Mb | Untrained rabble, usually of low morale, fighting as a disorganised mass. They may be equipped with only peasant weapons or may have been hastily equipped with proper weaponry but not trained to use it effectively. They are treated as Medium Foot in all respects except that they are based differently. |
| Gendarmes | Gen | Usually drawn from a gentry skilled in horsemanship, these are armoured cavalry who rely on a fierce charge at the gallop with lance. They usually fight in less depth than other mounted troops, and can get carried away in the pursuit of defeated enemy. |
| Cavaliers | Cvls | Usually drawn from a gentry skilled in horsemanship, these are cavalry who rely on a fierce charge sometimes at the gallop. They usually fight in less depth than other mounted troops, and can get carried away in the pursuit of defeated enemy. Examples: Royalist horse of the English Civil Wars. |
| Determined Horse | DHo | Disciplined cavalry in shallow close order formations who mostly charge at the trot in a controlled manner. Examples: Swedish 30 Years War cavalry and Cromwell's Ironsides. |
| Horse | Ho | Cavalry who ride in close deep formations and charge at the trot. They include German men-at-arms and reiters trained to use the caracole. |
| Light Horse | LH | Lightly equipped horsemen specialising in skirmishing, usually with missile weapons. |
| Cavalry | Cv | Most other mounted troops fall into this category. They are capable of skirmishing or of forming a solid body to shoot or charge. They are not classified as light troops. |
| Camelry | Cm | Camel-mounted troops. They are treated as Cavalry, but they have less difficulty with movement over sand. Camelry disorder horses. |
| Dragoons | Dr | Infantry mounted on cheap horses who usually dismount to fight on foot in support of cavalry wings in battle. |
| Elephants | El | Indian elephants, whose strength is breaking into solid lines of enemy troops. Elephants disorder horses. |
| Light Artillery | LArt | Small cannon such as organ guns, falconets or galloper guns and drakes and also eastern rocket artillery. Treated as foot. |
| Medium Artillery | MArt | Moderately mobile pieces such as demi-culverins, quarter-cannon, sakers and falcons. Treated as foot. |
| Heavy Artillery | HArt | Heavy guns such as full cannon, demi-cannon and culverins or bombards. Intended more for sieges than for field battles and virtually immovable once deployed. Treated as foot. |
| Battle Wagons | BWg | Horse or ox drawn wagons, usually with missile-armed crew on board. Treated as foot. Not very manoeuvrable. |

## ARMOUR

The following is a guide to the characteristics of the armour classes in *Field of Glory Renaissance*. A number of considerations have been taken into account when determining the armour classes specified for historical troops in our companion army list books, e.g. where the various ranks in a battle group are armoured differently, or where individuals have a variety of armour levels, the troops are classified according to their average functional armour level. Reflecting significant differences between armour levels of different troop types within the same historical period has sometimes outweighed rigid adherence to standard descriptions.

| ARMOUR | |
|---|---|
| **Description** | **Distinctive features** |
| **Fully armoured** | Metal plate armour almost entirely covering the body. Horses mostly barded, at least for front ranks. |
| **Heavily armoured** | Horsemen in plate armour from head to knee riding unarmoured horses, or in more complete mail and plate on mounts with at least partial metal protection, or foot, either with plate armour for head and thorax, and thighs or a substantial shield or with additional metallic protection. |
| **Armoured** | Helmet and back and breast plate armour or more complete mail, leather or textile armour, if mounted, riding unarmoured horses. Also mixed battle groups of unarmoured and heavily armoured men resulting in an equivalent average level of protection. |
| **Unarmoured** | Equipped only with textile armour or buff coat; otherwise generally lacking armour of any kind. Contemporaries referred to unarmoured pikemen as naked. |

## COMBAT CAPABILITIES

*Field of Glory Renaissance* is function based. The mere possession of a weapon is not sufficient to qualify for a combat capability. For example, most western musketeers were equipped with a cheap sword but were not practised in its use (they mostly preferred to use their musket butt in close combat) and so do not have swordsmen capability.

Some weapons were used in different ways and at different times by different troops. Reiters preferred to wear down an opponent by shooting their pistols from a distance. Continental cuirassiers used their pistols to deliver a point blank range volley at impact.

The capabilities available to each historical troop type are specified in our companion army list books. Allocation of capabilities inevitably has a subjective element. In *Field of Glory Renaissance*, we have based our decisions on the most recent evidence available to us. The emphasis is always on establishing the historical role of each troop type, especially when fighting contemporary opponents. It should therefore be accepted that the descriptions below are not prescriptive and are for use only in *Field of Glory Renaissance*.

Capabilities are situational and may not result in a point of advantage in every combat.

## GLOSSARY OF COMBAT CAPABILITIES

| Capability | Phase | Description |
|---|---|---|
| Arquebus | Shooting | Foot whose missile weapons are mainly arquebus or caliver, though possibly including a proportion of musketeers. |
| Bayonet | Impact, Melee | Foot equipped with musket and either plug or socket bayonet. |
| Bombs | Shooting | Foot equipped with naptha bombs or grenades. |
| Bow | Shooting | Specialist foot bowmen or longbowmen, or horse archers (excluding crossbowmen). |
| Bow* | Shooting | Foot or cavalry making effective use of bows but only as a subsidiary weapon, or not all equipped with bow. Examples: C16th Highlanders. |
| Carbine | Shooting | Mounted equipped with carbine: the cavalry equivalent of the arquebus. |
| Crossbow | Shooting | Foot or mounted troops armed with crossbows. |
| Heavy Artillery | Shooting | Heavy artillery such as demi-cannon, culverins or bombards. |
| Heavy Weapon | Impact, Melee | Troops armed with pole arms or 2-handed swords, axes, and other weapons. Examples: English billmen, Irish Galloglaich and some Landsknecht and Swiss foot. |
| Impact Foot | Impact | Foot relying on a fierce charge to disrupt the enemy at impact. Examples: C17th French foot. Aztec and Indonesian foot warriors. |
| Impact Mounted | Impact | Cavalry, usually in shallow formations, who rely on the impetus of their charge, sword in hand or with light lance, to shatter the enemy formation, allowing the effective use of swords and similar in the ensuing melee. Examples: Polish winged hussars and 17th century French cavalry trained by Turenne. |
| Javelins | Shooting | Light foot or light horse with javelins. Examples: early Irish kerns, stradiots. Warriors with atlatl. Example: Aztec or other Mesoamerican warriors. |
| Lancers | Impact | Mounted troops specialising in charging with lance. Example: French and other gendarmes. French gendarmes used a heavy lance which proved significantly more effective than the light lance used by Spanish contemporaries. Therefore some troops have heavy lancers capability and others light lancers capability, which includes cavalry using a spear as a primary weapon such as early reiters. |
| Light Artillery | Shooting | Light artillery such as drakes or organ guns. |
| Light Spear | Impact | Foot battle troops armed with light spear, whether thrust or thrown. Example: Inca warriors. |
| Medium Artillery | Shooting | Field guns such as falcons, sakers and demi-culverins. |
| Musket | Shooting | Foot armed mainly with musket though possibly including a proportion armed with arquebus or caliver. |
| Musket* | Shooting | Foot in mixed battle groups with a low ratio of musketeers to pikemen e.g. early English Civil War Royalist foot. |
| Pike | Impact, Melee | Foot armed with long 2-handed pikes and forming a concentrated pike block. Most such troops are also armed with swords – the Pike melee POA already takes this into account. They never use 'Swordsmen' POA. |
| Pistol | Shooting, Impact, Melee | Mounted armed with pistols. Depending on their style of fighting, such troops may be given Pistol capability in Shooting or Impact and/or Melee phases. For example, 16th century German reiters preferred to use their pistols at a distance, so are given Pistol capability in the Shooting phase, but not in the Impact phase. Later in the century, cavalry started to withhold their pistol fire until the moment of impact, so are given Pistol capability in the Impact phase. Both could use spare pistols in the melee, so are also given Pistol capability in the Melee phase.<br>Troops with pistol capability can only use pistol in the phase(s) specified in their list in our companion army list books. |

| | | |
|---|---|---|
| Salvo | Shooting, Impact | 30 Years War Swedes were trained to withhold fire until very close range when usually at least 3 ranks would fire simultaneously. Such troops have an advantage in the impact phase to simulate the powerful effect of close range volley fire but shoot with reduced capability at short range in the shooting phase. |
| Sling | Shooting | Still used by some native Americans. |
| Spearmen | Impact, Melee | Foot usually fighting in close formation with thrusting spear. |
| Swordsmen | Melee | Foot using swords as their primary weapon. Example: Spanish sword and buckler men. Foot equipped with swords or equivalent weapons as secondary weapons, but ready and willing to fight hard hand-to-hand when required. Example: Early Ottoman janissaries. Mounted troops equipped with swords, maces or horseman's axes and ready and willing to fight hand to hand. Examples: French gendarmes and some horse archers. |

# FORTIFICATIONS

| FORTIFICATIONS | | |
|---|---|---|
| **Type** | **Ref** | **Description** |
| Field Fortifications | FF | Temporary earthworks or other obstacles used to enhance defensive positions. |
| Portable Defences | PD | Stakes, swinesfeathers or man-portable chevaux-de-frise used by infantry as a defence against cavalry. |

# APPENDIX 2 : BATTLEFIELD TERRAIN, VISIBILITY AND DISORDER EFFECTS

TERRAIN PIECE SIZES

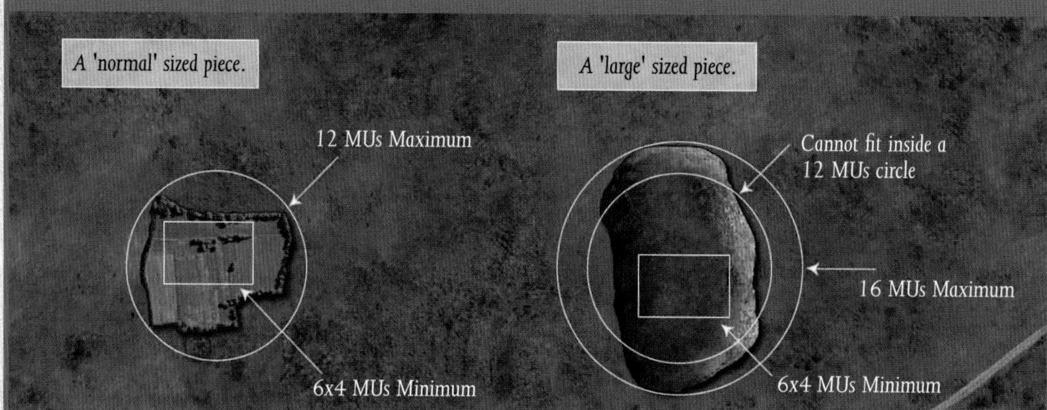

| TERRAIN DESCRIPTION, VISIBILITY AND COMBAT EFFECTS | |
|---|---|
| **OPEN** | |
| Open (O) | An open area of ground offering no impediment to movement. Full visibility. |
| **UNEVEN** | |
| Broken Ground (BG) | A mostly open area, with some rocks and/or scrub. An area of open fields broken up by shallow irrigation or drainage ditches, or muddy. |
| **ROUGH** | |
| Brush (B) | An area mostly covered by substantial brush or rocks or by small gullies or boggy ground. Light foot wholly inside are only visible within 4 MUs. |
| Enclosed Fields (EF) | An area of cultivated land divided by walls, hedges or deep irrigation or drainage ditches. Counts as *cover* for bases wholly inside. Light foot or dragoons wholly inside are only visible within 4 MUs. Foot bases entirely in enclosed fields count as *"protected"* (see the *Combat Mechanism section*). |
| Plantation (P) | An area lightly covered with fruit or olive trees, or other managed woodland with little undergrowth. Counts as *cover* for bases wholly inside. Troops wholly inside are only visible within 4 MUs. Troops inside can only shoot with their first shooting rank. Troops beyond a plantation cannot be seen. |
| Gully (G) | A gully is a depression in the ground. It is too uneven to provide any uphill advantage but can conceal troops. Troops in a gully are only visible from outside within 1 MU. Troops in a gully can see outside. |
| **DIFFICULT** | |
| Forest (F) | Dense woodland or jungle. Counts as *cover* for bases wholly inside. Troops wholly inside are only visible within 2 MUs. Troops inside can only shoot with their first shooting rank. Troops beyond a forest cannot be seen. |
| Vineyards (V) | A cultivated area of vines, usually planted in straight lines. Counts as *cover* for bases wholly inside. Light foot wholly inside are only visible within 4 MUs. |
| Marsh (M) | A very boggy area, which may include small ponds with occasional trees and shrubs. Light foot wholly inside are only visible within 4 MUs. |
| Soft Sand (SS) | An area of soft sand and some low sand dunes. Light foot wholly inside are only visible within 6 MUs. Camelry count it as Rough. |
| Village (Vg) | An area of buildings and sheds with a road passing through it. Counts as *cover* for bases wholly inside. Troops wholly inside are only visible within 2 MUs. Troops inside can only shoot with their first shooting rank. Foot bases entirely in a village count as *"protected"* (see the *Combat Mechanism* section). |
| Steep Hill (SH) | A steeply sloping hill which gives a close combat advantage to those higher up the slope. Troops on such a hill can shoot over troops below them. Troops beyond a crest line are only visible within 1 MU. Steep hills are always difficult, whether clear or covered by broken ground, brush, plantation, vineyards, forest or a village. |
| **IMPASSABLE** | |
| Impassable (I) | An area of extremely steep hills or a quarry, or a lake etc. No troops can enter. Any troops forced into it are destroyed. |
| **SLOPES** | |
| Gentle Hill (GH) | A gently sloping hill which gives a close combat advantage to those higher up the slope. Troops on such a hill can shoot over troops below them. Troops beyond a crest line are only visible within 1 MU. Slopes can be clear, uneven (if covered by broken ground), rough (if covered by brush or plantation) or difficult (if covered by vineyards, forest or a village). |
| **LINEAR** | |

| | |
|---|---|
| **Obstacle (Ob)** | Roadside ditches, hedges or walls or other linear hindrances to movement such as a high-banked stream or stretch of boggy ground. Its length must be at least 6 MUs and can be up to 18. If more than 12 MUs, it counts as 2 features. It can be from 1 to 2 fortification depths in width. It cannot be curved or angled. Light foot or dragoons whose front rank is defending an obstacle are only visible to troops within 4 MUs or behind a line extending the obstacle's rear edge. An obstacle is otherwise treated as if it was a *field fortification*. |
| **Road (Rd)** | A single base wide road or track that must pass through or touch a village if there is one, and must connect 2 different table edges, no more than one of them a short edge. The maximum length of the road is 60 MUs. |
| **Coastline (C)** | Extends up to 8 MUs in from the short table edge – May be the bank of a major river or the sea. Impassable to troops. |
| **River (Rv)** | Up to 4 MUs wide, entirely within 6 MUs of the side edge. The placing side dices for its difficulty when putting it down. 1 = uneven, 2,3 = rough, 4,5 = difficult, 6 = impassable. Troops can only move within 45 degrees of straight across. The river cannot have more than 2 bends. |

## VISIBILITY EFFECTS

Terrain blocks line of sight beyond the visibility distances specified above.

The visibility distances specified for plantations, forests and villages apply equally to:

- troops outside looking in at troops wholly inside.
- troops wholly inside looking out.
- troops wholly inside looking at other troops wholly inside.

When shooting, the total distance from the nearest front corner or part of the front edge of each shooting file to the target must be within the specified distance. (It makes no difference how much of the distance is in the terrain.)

Light foot in brush, enclosed fields, vineyards, marsh and soft sand or behind obstacles (and dragoons in enclosed fields or behind obstacles) cannot be seen from further away than the specified distance, but can see out normally. When they shoot they become (and subsequently remain) visible to all bases of the battle group they are shooting at – these can immediately shoot back.

## DISORDER EFFECTS

If a battle group's formation could not function well due to its situation (such as in terrain, or near camelry or elephants) it is DISORDERED or SEVERELY DISORDERED and therefore vulnerable. The terrain causing disorder or severe disorder for various troop types is shown in a table in the General Movement Rules section. The effects are listed in the table below.

| Terrain grade | Effect |
|---|---|
| NO EFFECT | |
| DISORDER | Does not count as STEADY |
| | -1 on complex move tests. |
| | Lose 1 dice per 3 for shooting and close combat. |
| | No cohesion test penalty. |
| SEVERE DISORDER | Does not count as STEADY |
| | -2 on complex move tests. |
| | Lose 1 dice per 2 for shooting and close combat. |
| | -1 on cohesion tests. |

- Only bases that are currently at least partly in the situation are affected.
- Bases not in the situation do not suffer penalty, so a long line of heavy foot may be disordered at one end and unaffected at the other.
- If any part of a battle group is DISORDERED or SEVERELY DISORDERED, it takes complex move tests (CMT) and cohesion tests (CT) as if entirely so. If it finds itself in combat, only those bases affected suffer any penalties.
- Lost combat dice for DISORDER or SEVERE DISORDER are **not** cumulative with dice loss for DISRUPTION or FRAGMENTATION. Only one state applies – whichever is worst.
- Troops defending field fortifications are not disordered or severely disordered by terrain.

Disorder effects are temporary and recover immediately that the cause is no longer present:

- Terrain effects cause DISORDER or SEVERE DISORDER to some troops. Bases at least partially in the terrain are affected. The effect ceases when they leave it.
- The elephants and camelry effect ceases when they are no longer within the disordering distance.

# APPENDIX 3 : GLOSSARY OF TERMS

| GLOSSARY OF TERMS | |
|---|---|
| < | Less than. |
| <= | Less than or equal to. |
| > | Greater than. |
| >= | Greater than or equal to. |
| **Active Player** | The player whose turn it currently is. |
| **Advance** | A move listed in the *Advance* section of the Simple and Complex Moves table in the *General Movement Rules* section. It must result in at least part of the battle group ending further forward than its original front edge. |
| **Army Rout** | An army suffers an army rout if at the end of the current phase it has suffered Attrition Points equal to or greater than its initial number of battle groups, counting each *grand battle group* as two battle groups for this purpose. |
| **Attrition Points** | Attrition points are received for various adverse events. If sufficient attrition points are accumulated, the army routs. See the *Playing the Game* section. |
| **Autobreak** | See the *Battle Group Deterioration* section. |
| **1 Base Deep** | Cavalry or camelry are considered to be "entirely 1 base deep" for the purpose of evading or being shot at if their battle group is entirely in a single rank of bases. This represents a formation in which smaller numbers of troops separated by gaps dash around harassing the enemy. |
| **Battle troops** | Any troops other than light foot, light horse and dragoons. |
| **Better Armour** | Fully armoured is best, then heavily armoured, followed by armoured and lastly unarmoured.<br>Elephants and battle wagons have no armour class. No enemy counts "better armour" against them, and they don't count "better armour" against any enemy. |
| **Charge Range** | A battle group is in charge range if it can make a 'legal' charge contact (See the *Impact Phase* section) within its normal move distance. |
| **Close Combat** | 'Close Combat' is a general term for impact and melee combat. Once such a combat has been joined, battle groups are deemed to be in close combat until one side breaks off, breaks or is destroyed (or a battle group fighting only as an overlap moves away).<br>Impact and melee phase combat use the close combat mechanisms. |

| | |
|---|---|
| **Cohesion Test (CT)** | A test taken to see if adverse events cause a battle group to drop down the Cohesion ladder. See the ***Battle Group Deterioration*** section. |
| **Column** | A battle group is a column if its formation is entirely 1 base wide. This is the only formation that can be 'kinked' – kinking at the point at which its front base wheeled to change direction. |
| **Command Range** | The distance at which commanders can influence troops – i.e. control divisions and affect complex move tests and cohesion tests.<br>This is:<br>• Great commander (GC): 12 MUs.<br>• Field commander (FC): 8 MUs.<br>• Troop commander (TC): 4 MUs.<br>• Command range is measured from the nearest point on the commander's base.<br>• A C-in-C or sub-commander can influence any troops except allied troops.<br>• An ally commander can only influence troops that are part of his own allied contingent. |
| **Commanded Shot** | Battle groups of shot designated as commanded shot by our companion army list books and capable of giving and receiving protection to and from friendly battle groups of cavaliers, horse or determined horse – see the ***Protection*** rule section in the ***Combat Mechanism*** section. Note that shot detached from pike and shot battle groups at deployment time, and shot-only battle groups not specifically designated in our companion army list books as "commanded shot", **cannot** be used as commanded shot. |
| **Complex Move Test (CMT)** | A test taken to see if a battle group can make a complex move as defined in the Simple & Complex Moves Table. See the ***General Movement Rules*** section. |
| **Cover** | Plantation, forest, village, vineyards, enclosed fields. These give cover to bases wholly within them. |
| **Death Roll** | A test taken to see if hits cause base losses. See the ***Battle Group Deterioration*** section. |
| **Defending a riverbank** | For a base to count as defending a river bank in close combat, the following must all apply:<br>• The entire fighting edge of the base must be facing the river and not in it.<br>• At least part of the fighting edge of the base must be within 1 MU of the river.<br>• The enemy front rank base must be at least partly in the river. |
| **Detached shot** | Shot who have been detached from their parent battle groups for the purposes of a game – see ***Detached Shot*** in ***Appendix 4***. |
| **1 Dice per x Bases** | '1 dice per x bases' = 1 dice per full x bases, i.e. round dice down. See also ***Appendix 8***. |
| **1 Dice per x** | 'Lose 1 dice per x' = Lose 1 dice per full x dice, i.e. round dice up. See also ***Appendix 8***. |
| **Early Tercio** | See ***Battle Group Formations*** in the ***Basics*** section. |
| **Enfilade** | Artillery shooting at a target from a position where, if the artillery were battle troops in charge range, it could deliver a legal flank charge. |
| **Field Fortifications** | Temporary earthworks or other obstacles used to enhance defensive positions. See the ***Special Features*** section. |
| **Fighting enemy in 2 directions** | A battle group only counts as fighting enemy in 2 directions in melee if it has bases turned at 90 or 180 degrees to each other and it is in melee with different enemy battle groups on different facings. However, a battle group never counts as fighting enemy in 2 directions as a consequence of a charge unless it was a legal flank or rear charge. Thus, early tercios never count as fighting enemy in 2 directions; keils and later tercios only do so if contacted on at least 2 sides, one of which was their rear when contacted. |
| **File** | A single front rank base and all the bases of the same battle group lined up behind it. |
| **Firearms** | Any of arquebus, bombs, carbine, musket, musket*, salvo or pistol capabilities. |
| **Footprint** | The footprint of a tercio is the rectangle enclosing the outmost edges of its original normal formation at deployment rounding up to an even number of ranks deep. The footprint remains the same despite any modification of the formation on account of lost bases.<br>Examples:<br>The footprint of an early tercio with 8 bases of shot and 8 bases of pike is a rectangle (square) of which the corners are the outer front corners of the front shot horns and the outer rear corners of the rear shot horns. The footprint of an early tercio which starts with 8 bases of shot and 6 bases of pike is the same as if it started with 8 bases of shot and 8 bases of pike.<br>The footprint of a later tercio is a rectangle of which the corners are the 2 front corners of the front rank and the other corners are where the rear corners would be if all files of battle group were the depth of the deepest rank, rounded up to an even number. |

| | |
|---|---|
| **Forlorn Hope** | Historically, the term "forlorn hope" could refer to a body of troops used for a variety of semi-suicidal tasks. For the purpose of these rules, it refers to a small battle group of medium foot shot deployed in terrain ahead of the main army to delay the enemy advance. See *Appendix 4*. |
| **Grand Battle Group** | Any battle group that starts the game with more than 12 bases. |
| **HP2B (Hits per 2 bases) & HP3B (Hits per 3 bases)** | 1 HPxB = 1 hit per x bases in the battle group, except that:<br>• Elephants and artillery count front rank bases only, but each counts as 2 bases.<br>• Battle wagons count the bases from one rank or file, whichever is the greater number. Each base counts as 2 bases.<br>• Other troops count the first 3 bases in each file (whether contiguous or not).<br>• Commanders' bases and regimental gun markers do not count.<br>• Limber markers do not count<br>Example: a 16 base early tercio will count as having twelve bases.<br>See also *Appendix 8*. |
| **Horns** | The positions at the corners of an early tercio pike block occupied by shot bases. See *Battle Group Formations* in the *Basics* section. |
| **Keil** | See *Battle Group Formations* in the *Basics* section. |
| **Later Tercio** | See *Battle Group Formations* in the *Basics* section. |
| **Light troops** | Light foot, light horse and dragoons. |
| **Line of Command** | The C-in-C and sub-commanders are considered in line of command for all troops in the main army, but not for any allied troops. Ally commanders are not in line of command for troops other than their own contingent. |
| **Mixed battle group** | A battle group which includes troops having different weapon capabilities. |
| **Movement Units (MU)** | All distances are specified in Movement Units (MUs). Each MU is usually either 25mm or 1 inch, as agreed by the players or decided by tournament organisers, regardless of figure scale. Alternatively, if using 25/28mm or larger figures on a table larger than 6 x 4 feet, a scale of 1MU = 1.5 inches or 40mm may be preferred. |
| **Naval Units** | See the *Special Features* section. |
| **Open Terrain** | The whole battlefield apart from areas of uneven, rough, difficult or impassable terrain counts as "open terrain".<br>POAs and Cohesion Test modifiers only applying 'in open terrain' do not count:<br>• If the base claiming the POA or causing the Cohesion Test modifier even partly enters uneven, rough or difficult terrain.<br>• If attacking or defending fortifications, an obstacle or a riverbank. |
| **Order of March** | The order in which an army's battle groups will be deployed. See *Appendix 4*. |
| **Overlap** | See the *Manoeuvre Phase* and *Melee Phase* sections. |
| **Partial edge contact** | When bases must be "in at least partial edge contact", this means that it isn't necessary for the bases to be in full edge to edge and corner to corner contact. However, it does not suffice for them to be in corner to corner contact only. |
| **POA - Points of Advantage** | POAs are combat advantages arising from troop type, armour, combat capabilities and situational factors. Troops often have different POAs in the different phases: Impact Phase, Shooting Phase and Melee Phase. See the *Combat Mechanism* section. |
| **Portable Defences** | See the *Special Features* section. |
| **Protection** | Certain troop types can provide each other with mutual "protection". See the *Combat Mechanism* section:<br>• In mixed battle groups of medium foot with a shooting capability and heavy or determined foot, when a file of medium foot has an adjacent file with a front rank of heavy or determined foot (of the same battle group) facing in the same direction and in at least corner to corner contact, both files count as "protected". Only the adjacent files are "protected" - other files of the same battle group are not "protected".<br>• Troops designated (in our companion army list books) as "commanded shot" can give to, and receive "protection" from, cavaliers, horse or determined horse belonging to other friendly battle groups. To give or receive "protection", a file of commanded shot must be in at least partial side edge contact with a file of friendly cavaliers, horse or determined horse, and its front edge must |

| | |
|---|---|
| | not project further forward than their front edge. Only the adjacent files are "protected" - other files of the same battle group are not "protected".<br>In addition, foot bases entirely in enclosed fields or a village also count as "protected". |
| **Quality Re-rolls** | A mechanism by which the effect of troop quality is represented. See the *Battle Groups* section. |
| **Rear support** | When an unlimbered artillery base has the front edge of a base of unbroken friendly foot battle troops lined up in edge to edge and corner to corner contact with its rear edge, it has rear support. |
| **Regimental Guns** | These are represented by markers. Regimental gun markers do not count as bases. In particular they are not counted for purposes of HPxB (see *glossary*) or Autobreak (see the *Battle Group Deterioration* section). Any rules applying to "artillery" do not apply to regimental guns. |
| **Restricted Area** | The area ahead of a battle group in which enemy movement is restricted in the manoeuvre phase. A battle group's Restricted Area is the rectangle directly in front of the battle group to a distance of 2 MUs. See the *Manoeuvre Phase* section. |
| **Shock Troops** | These include:<br>• any battle group including mounted with *heavy lancers*, *light lancers* or *impact mounted* capability, except light horse<br>• gendarmes<br>• cavaliers<br>• determined horse<br>• any battle group including foot with *impact foot* or *salvo* capability<br>• keils<br>They do not count as shock troops while fragmented. |
| **Shot** | Foot with arquebus, musket, musket* or salvo capability. |
| **Square** | A special all round defensive formation permitted only to foot battle groups including bases with pike or spearmen capability. See the *Special Features* section. |
| **Steady** | Bases count as STEADY if they are not DISRUPTED, FRAGMENTED, BROKEN, DISORDERED or SEVERELY DISORDERED. |
| **Supply Camp, Sacking** | See the *Melee Phase* section. |
| **Support** | A battle group counts as "**supported**" if the total number of bases currently in supporting battle groups equals at least half the original total number of bases in the supported battle group at deployment (after detaching any shot).<br>To qualify as supporting, a battle group must be battle troops and all of the following must apply to it:<br>• It is entirely behind a straight line extending the rear edge of the supported battle group.<br>• The supported battle group is at least partly in front of a straight line extending the front edge of the supporting battle group.<br>• If it is foot, its nearest base is within 6 MUs of the supported battle group, if mounted or elephants, 9 MUs.<br>• Its quality is not more than one level below that of the supported battle group (e.g. average troops can support superior troops, but not elites).<br>• It is entirely STEADY.<br>• It is not Artillery or Mob.<br>• It is not in close combat, unless only as an overlap.<br>Intervening friends and enemies do not block support.<br>Special cases:<br>• Battle wagons never count as supported.<br>• Early tercios always count as supported.<br>• If they do not qualify as supported as above, later tercios and keils count as supported unless they have any enemy (other than a commander, camp or any light troops) within 12 MUs and even partly behind a line extending their rear edge.<br>*See diagram below* |
| **Swedish Brigade** | See *Battle Group Formations* in the *Basics* section. |
| **Tercio** | See *Battle Group Formations* in the *Basics* section. |

| | |
|---|---|
| **Terrain Sizes** | Normal pieces: Each must be so sized and shaped that:<br>• A 4 x 6 MU rectangle can be fitted entirely within its footprint.<br>• Its entire footprint can be fitted within a 12 MU diameter.<br><br>Large pieces: Each must be so sized and shaped that all of the following apply:<br>• A 4 x 6 MU rectangle can be fitted entirely within its footprint.<br>• Its footprint cannot be entirely fitted within a 12 MU diameter circle.<br>• Its entire footprint can be fitted within a 16 MU diameter circle. |
| **Threatened Flank** | A battle group of foot battle troops counts as having a threatened flank if any of the following apply:<br>• Any part of the battle group is less than 12 MUs from a side table edge. It makes no difference which way the battle group is facing. Commanded shot are immune to this cause of threatened flank.<br>• Any part of the battle group is less than 6 MUs from either side's base table edge. It makes no difference which way the battle group is facing. Commanded shot are immune to this cause of threatened flank.<br>• The battle group has unbroken enemy mounted battle troops (who are not in close combat) within 12 MUs of a flank and at least partly on that side of a line extending its flank edge, unless it has unbroken friendly mounted battle troops within 12 MUs, or unbroken friendly foot battle troops (other than artillery) or elephants within 6 MUs, of that flank and at least partly on that side of a line extending its flank edge. See diagram below. The following are immune to this cause of threatened flank:<br>• Tercios.<br>• Keils.<br>• Battle groups with their flank edge or corner (on the potentially threatened flank) touching an obstacle, the rear edge of field fortifications, difficult terrain or impassable terrain other than a coastline, provided that lines extending the front and rear edges of the battle group both pass through the obstacle, fortification or terrain.<br>• Battle groups entirely in rough or difficult terrain.<br>• There are enemy battle troops capable of making a legal flank or rear charge on them in their next turn. Note: Later tercios and keils never count as charged in flank, so are immune to this cause of threatened flank unless the enemy are capable of charging them in the rear. Battle wagons, early tercios and troops in **square** never count as charged in flank or rear, so are immune to this cause of threatened flank. |
| **Uphill** | Unless a hill has clearly defined peaks or ridge crests, it is considered to have a single peak at the most central point of the terrain piece. A base is uphill if it is standing entirely on a hill, and the nearest peak or point on a ridge crest is behind a straight line extending its front edge. If both bases have their front edge touching a peak or ridge crest, or if both would count uphill using the above definition, then neither counts as uphill. |
| **Variable Movement Distance (VMD)** | See the *General Movement Rules* section. |
| **Within** | At or closer than. |
| **Zone of Interception (ZOI)** | The zone ahead of a battle group where it can intercept an enemy charge. A battle group's Zone of Interception (ZOI) is the rectangle directly in front of the battle group to a distance of 2 MUs if foot, 4 MUs if mounted troops or elephants. In the ZOI battle groups of some troop types have the option of making interception charges. See the *Impact Phase* section. |

## TROOPS PROVIDING SUPPORT

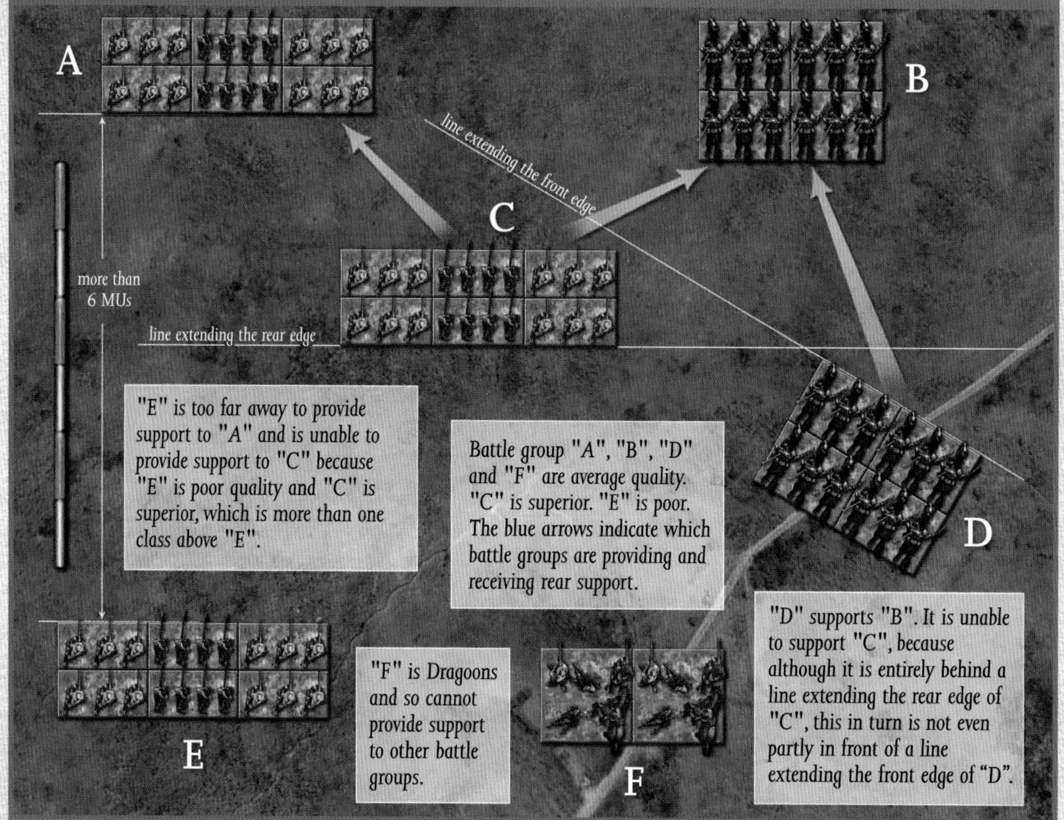


## THREATENED FLANK

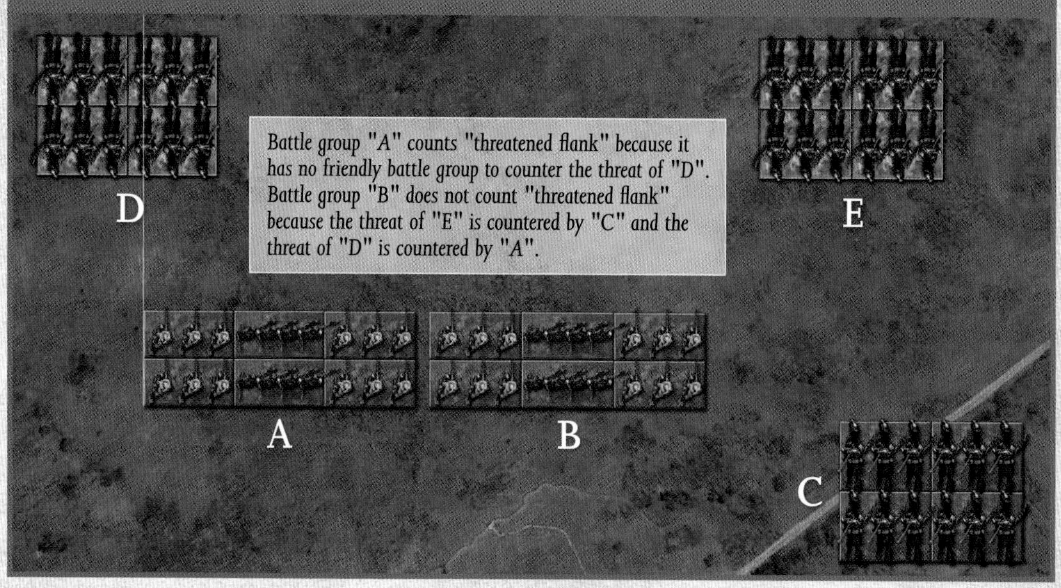

# APPENDIX 4: SET UP RULES

*The wargame may be* an historical re-creation, a scenario or part of a campaign. Various factors will determine the setup for such battles and it is likely that the opposing armies will be unequal. Parts of the following set-up rules covering items already decided can therefore be ignored.

In contrast, for tournaments, typical club or pick-up games, players will most likely be on a level footing. This type of game does not take into account events preceding the battle and only requires each player to supply an army (possibly anachronistic) to a fixed total points value. A later appendix describes how to use the information contained in our companion army list books to work out the composition of your army.

In multi-player games each side has one player designated to carry out the set-up procedure for his side.

## ORDER OF MARCH

Prior to set up, players design their armies to a fixed total points value in accordance with the constraints specified in our companion army list books. Each player writes down an "order of march" listing the army's battle groups in the order in which they will be deployed on table. The army's total initiative modifier, and the number of battle groups in each deployment batch, as described below, must also be noted.

## SETTING UP THE GAME

The following sequence of events precedes play:

- Dice for pre-battle initiative.
- Terrain choice and placement.
- Place camps and field fortification markers.
- Detach any shot.
- Place ambush markers.

*Dragoons march down sunken Lane*

- Record outflanking marches.
- Deploy battle groups.
- Deploy field fortifications and naval units.
- Commit to dismounting.
- Deploy commanders.
- The player who **lost** the initiative roll begins the game as the active player in the first turn.

## PRE-BATTLE INITIATIVE

Successful generals have always endeavoured to bring the enemy to battle in a place of their choosing, such as Prosper Colonna who took up a strong defensive position at Bicocca and tempted the unruly Swiss into a suicidal frontal assault, or Wallenstein who blunted the reputation of the Swedes behind the fortified lines of Alte Veste. Sometimes they achieved this through better battlefield intelligence, by employing fast moving mounted troops to scout out their opponents, but on other occasions armies blundered into each other and who had the initiative in the forthcoming battle was a matter of chance. In *Field of Glory Renaissance*, we reflect this by incorporating an element of luck in deciding which general has gained the initiative and can select the overall terrain type, reflecting the likelihood that he will have a greater influence on choosing the battlefield. His opponent also starts deploying first, revealing his initial dispositions, and makes the first move, which to some degree shows his hand. However, just as in reality, a good opponent will devise his own tactics to counter these disadvantages.

An army's total initiative modifier is pre-calculated and included in its order of march. At set up each player rolls a d6 and adds its total initiative modifier. If the total scores are equal, roll again, using the same modifiers. The high scorer has prebattle initiative.

| PRE-BATTLE INITIATIVE MODIFIERS | |
|---|---|
| +2 | C-in-C is a great commander |
| +1 | C-in-C is a field commander |
| +1 | The army has 10-24 bases of horse, determined horse, cavaliers, cavalry, light horse, camelry or dragoons, excluding commanders |
| +2 | The army has more than 24 bases of horse, determined horse, cavaliers, cavalry, light horse, camelry or dragoons, excluding commanders |

## TERRAIN CHOICE

Each army list in our companion army list books specifies a set of territory types characteristic of those typically found in the army's homeland.

The player gaining the initiative chooses a territory type from those available to either army. Terrain is then chosen and placed according to this territory type.

### TIP!

Choosing and positioning terrain is a very important aspect of your pre-battle planning. You want the terrain to favour your army and inconvenience the opposing army: e.g. mounted armies might prefer to fight on the open steppes, whilst armies with an advantage in light or medium foot or warriors will look for rough or uneven ground where they will have the advantage. Know what kinds of battlefield suit your forces.

The table below shows the terrain pieces available in each territory type. The maximum number of allowed pieces of each type is shown, followed by the priority pieces in brackets.

Both players make their terrain selections from the row relating to the territory type chosen by the player with pre-battle initiative.

| TERRAIN SELECTION | Maximum (priority) | | | | | | | | | | | | | | | | |
|---|---|---|---|---|---|---|---|---|---|---|---|---|---|---|---|---|---|
| **TERRITORY TYPE** | Open | BG | B | EF | P | G | F | V | M | SS | SH | Vg | I | GH | Ob | Rd | Rv/C |
| AGRICULTURAL | 2 | 3(2) | | 4(2) | 2 | | | 2 | | | 1 | 1 | | 2 | 2 | 2 | 1 |
| HILLY | | 3 | 3(1) | | 1 | 1 | 2 | | 1 | | 3(2) | 1 | 1 | 3 | 1 | 1 | 1 |
| WOODLANDS | | | 2 | | 2 | 1 | 4(2) | | 2 | | 1 | 1 | | 2 | 1 | 1 | 1 |
| STEPPES | 4(2) | 4 | 2 | | | 1 | | | | | | | | 1 | | | |
| MOUNTAINS | | | 2 | | 1 | 1 | 1 | | 1 | | 4(2) | 1 | 2 | | | 1 | 1 |
| TROPICAL | | | 2 | | | | 4(2) | | 2 | | 1 | 1 | 1 | 1 | | 1 | 1 |
| DESERT | 2 | 2 | 2 | | | 1 | | | | 4(2) | 1 | | 1 | 1 | | 1 | |
| **COLOUR KEY** | Open | Uneven | Rough | | | | | Difficult | | | | | Impassable | Special | | | |

A **river** or a **coastline** counts as 1 piece but 2 selections. A **road** counts as 1 piece and 1 selection.

Other terrain pieces come in 2 sizes: see the ***Glossary***. A large piece counts as 2 selections and as 2 towards the maximum of that type, unless it is one of the two compulsory pieces. Compulsory pieces can be chosen as either size.

A **hill** can be clear or can be wholly or partly covered with one of either **broken ground**, **brush**, **plantation**, **vineyards**, **forest** or a **village**. It counts as the number of selections for its size. The covering does not count as extra selections. However, both the hill and the covering each count towards the maxima (and minima) of their respective types.

Only the player with pre-battle initiative can choose a **river**, a **coastline**, or a **village**. He cannot choose both a **river** and a **coastline**.

The player with initiative selects a compulsory piece from the available priority pieces. The other player then selects a compulsory piece from the remaining priority pieces. A covered hill can be chosen as a compulsory piece only if either of the following apply:

- Hills are priority pieces.
- Hills are permitted and the covering is a priority piece and of at least normal size.

The player with initiative then makes from 2 to 4 other selections from the list of available terrain. Roads cannot count towards the 2 minimum pieces. The total pieces of any type, together with any compulsory piece of that type, cannot exceed the maximum of that type.

The other player then makes from 2 to 4 other selections from the list of available terrain. Roads cannot count towards the 2 minimum pieces. He cannot select any pieces that, together with those already chosen by both players, would exceed the maximum of that type.

All terrain selection is made before **any** are placed on the table.

## TERRAIN PLACING SEQUENCE

The order in which terrain is placed is as follows:

1. The player with initiative places any **river** or **coastline**.
2. The player with initiative places any **village** (including any integral hill).

3 The player with initiative places his **compulsory piece.**
4 The other player places his **compulsory piece.**
5 The player with initiative places any **open area**(s).
6 The other player places any **open area**(s).
7 The player with initiative places his remaining pieces except roads.
8 The other player places his remaining pieces except roads.
9 The player with initiative places any **roads.**
10 The other player places any **roads.**
11 **Open area** pieces are removed from the table.

No piece can be placed (prior to adjustment) closer than 4 MUs to any other piece except:

- Any piece can be placed closer than 4 MUs to a coastline, river or road.
- A road can be placed closer than 4 MUs to any piece and can pass through a village, but (for aesthetic reasons) not through other terrain pieces.
- A road must pass through or touch a village if there is one.

The use of open areas is to restrict the placing of other terrain.

The whole of the battlefield counts as open, except where terrain pieces are placed.

## TERRAIN PLACING DICE ROLLS

The placing player picks up the terrain piece he intends to place and rolls to determine where on the table it is to be placed. (If it cannot be placed in the indicated location, it is lost.) When a piece has been successfully placed, the other player makes an adjustment roll, which may allow the placement to be amended or negated. This process is repeated for each terrain piece in turn.

The placement roll:

1 = Touching the long edge – opponent's half.
2 = Touching the long edge – own half.
3 = Touching a side edge or coastline – opponent's half.
4 = Touching a side edge or coastline – own half.
5 = Anywhere over 8 MUs from edges – opponent's half.
6 = Anywhere over 8 MUs from edges – own half.

The initial placement roll is not required for **rivers, coastlines** or **roads.**

The adjustment roll is made after each terrain feature is placed:

0–2 = No change permitted.
3,4 = Can slide the piece up to 6 MUs in any direction.
5 = Can either slide the piece up to 12 MUs in any direction or pivot the piece on one point through any angle.
6+ = Can remove the piece entirely.

Modify the dice roll by:

**-1** if the piece is a **compulsory** piece
**+1** if it is **impassable** or a **river** or **coastline.**

**Rivers** and **coastlines** can be removed, but not slid or pivoted. **Roads** can be slid sideways but not lengthways, and cannot be pivoted.

When a piece 'slides' it must maintain its angle of placement relative to the table edges. To pivot, fix any point on the edge of the terrain piece and rotate the piece around this point. A piece cannot be slid or pivoted off table, nor to overlap another terrain piece.

TERRAIN PLACEMENT AND SHIFTS

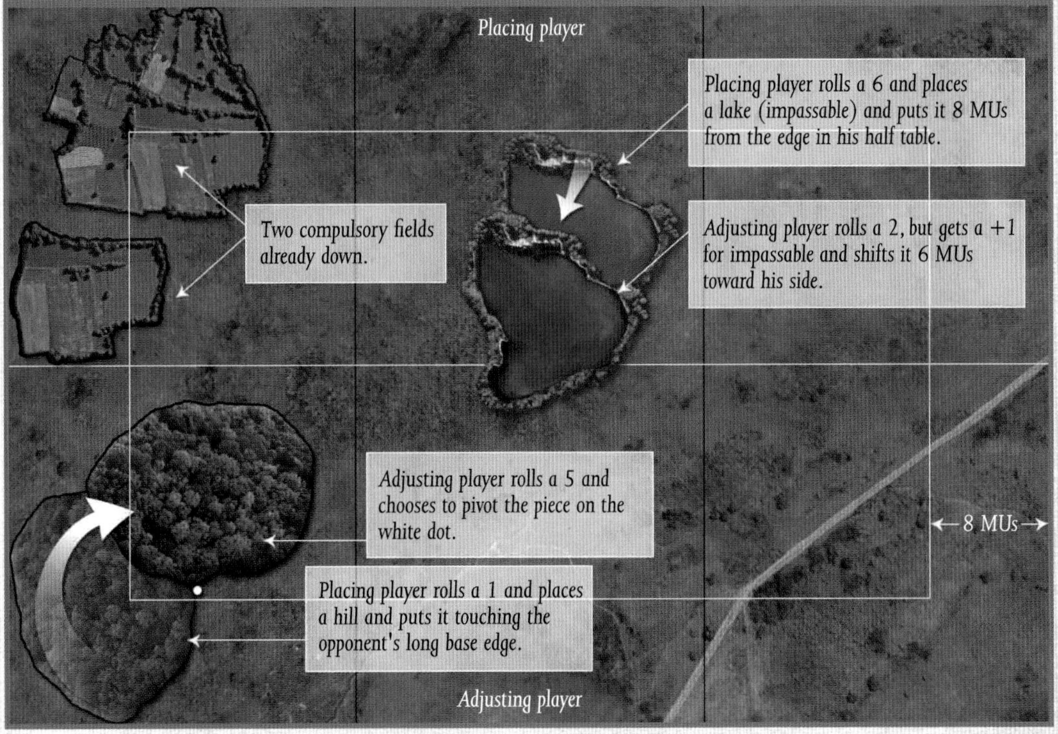




## SUPPLY CAMPS, DETACHMENTS AND MARKERS

The player without the initiative places his supply camp anywhere up to 10 MUs from his side's rear table edge. The supply camp cannot be placed in impassable terrain nor a river, nor in a position surrounded on more than two sides by impassable terrain. He also places any field fortification markers. The player with the initiative then does the same. In equal points games, fortified camps (and field fortifications) must be paid for with army points – see *Appendix 5*.

The player without the initiative then detaches any shot. The player with the initiative then does the same.

The player without the initiative then places any ambush markers. The player with the initiative then does the same.

## FIELD FORTIFICATIONS

Field fortifications (FF) can only be used when permitted by the army list in our companion army list books. A player can never have fewer than 4 FF bases unless he has none at all. They can be deployed anywhere (other than in impassable terrain) within 15 MUs of the owner's rear table edge and more than 12 MUs from the side table edges.

A player who has paid for FF bases can put down up to 3 FF base sized markers to indicate their approximate location on the battlefield (leaving sufficient room to deploy the FF within the above bounds). Each marker must represent at least 4 FF bases – dummy markers are not permitted. The number of FF bases represented by each one must be written on the bottom.

After deployment of all visible on-table troops, the player without the initiative deploys his FF

**FIELD FORTIFICATIONS**

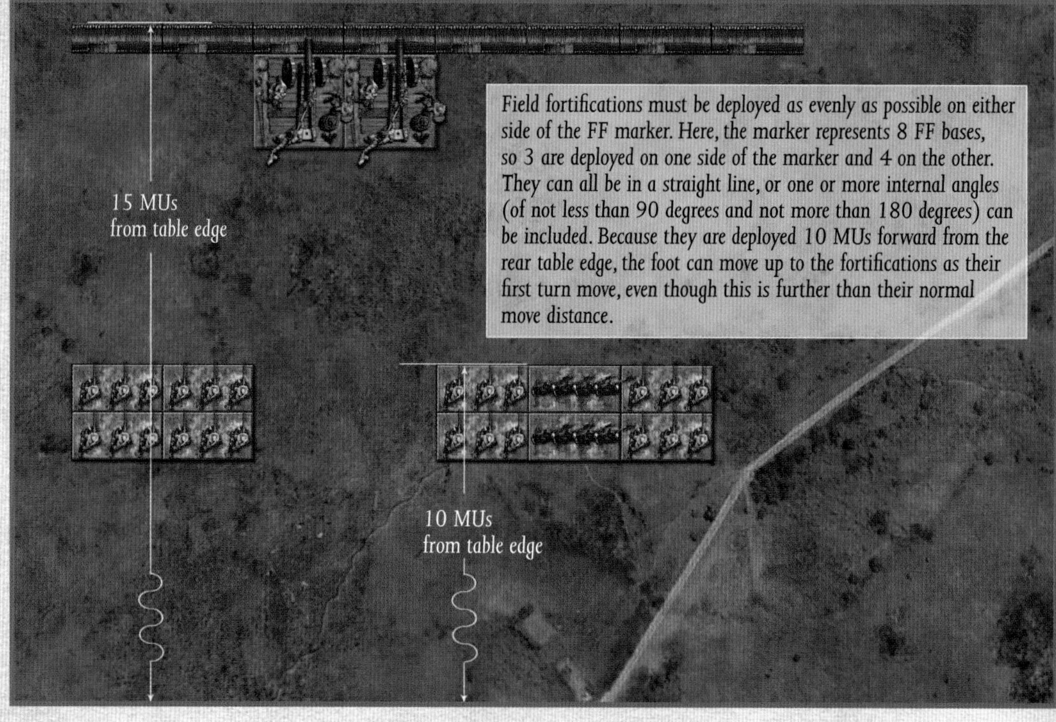


Field fortifications must be deployed as evenly as possible on either side of the FF marker. Here, the marker represents 8 FF bases, so 3 are deployed on one side of the marker and 4 on the other. They can all be in a straight line, or one or more internal angles (of not less than 90 degrees and not more than 180 degrees) can be included. Because they are deployed 10 MUs forward from the rear table edge, the foot can move up to the fortifications as their first turn move, even though this is further than their normal move distance.

bases on the designated marker(s). One base must be deployed in the exact position of the marker. The others must be distributed as evenly as possible on each side of the marker. They must each be positioned in side edge and corner to corner contact with another of the bases represented by that marker, or in corner to corner contact at an internal angle of not less than 90 degrees (and not more than 180 degrees). All must be in passable terrain within 15 MUs of the owner's rear table edge and more than 12 MUs from the side table edges.

The other player then deploys his FF bases in the same way.

Foot battle groups (other than battle wagons or artillery) whose entire front edge was deployed 10 MUs forward from their rear table edge can move up to defend fortifications placed parallel to the rear table edge as their entire first turn move, even if this exceeds their normal move. Apart from a shift of up to half a base width to match the fortifications, the move must be straight forward, and all front rank bases must end the move defending fortifications.

## DETACHED SHOT

It was common practice in this period for shot to be detached from the parent unit when circumstances required. Accordingly, after camps and field fortification markers have been placed, a player whose army includes mixed battle groups of pike and shot can detach shot bases from up to half such battle groups to create new "temporary" battle groups of between 2–8 medium foot shot bases. They have the quality and armament of the worst constituent, if different. The parent battle groups must be combined into composite battle groups so that the army has the same break point as before. All temporary and composite battle groups must conform to the general rules for battle group composition but need not conform to the composition of battle groups in their army list. Composite battle groups cannot adopt a formation with pike deeper than they would have been in the original battle groups unless all shot have been detached.

## EXAMPLE:

Essex's army finds itself on a battlefield choked with hedgerows and enclosures. The army includes 8 average pike and shot battle groups, each comprising 2 bases of heavy foot pike and 4 bases of medium foot shot. Essex detaches 2 shot bases from each of 4 battle groups to create two "temporary" battle groups of 4 shot each. As he now has two battle groups too many, he combines the 4 parent battle groups into two new composite BGs each with 4 shot bases and 4 pike bases.

The same rules apply to tercios, except that no more than half of the shot bases can be detached from a tercio. If the residue of two tercios (or the residue of a tercio and a normal pike and shot battle group) are combined, the resulting battle group must have at least 4 shot bases and is deployed as and treated as a later tercio for the rest of the game.

A grand battle group counts as 2 battle groups for break point purposes before making any detachment. If shot are detached, it must divide into, and subsequently be treated as, 2 normal battle groups for attrition purposes. The break point of the army remains unchanged.

The army's order of march must be adjusted by the minimum necessary to accommodate the reorganised battle groups. In tournaments, players wishing to use the detached shot option must have a second army list (differing only in this regard) pre-prepared and can only use their main list or that alternative list.

Detached shot are in fact a specific case of a general rule: In mixed battle groups of foot with a shooting capability and foot without, bases with shooting capability can be detached prior to deployment in the same way as described above for detached shot.

### FORLORN HOPE

Each army can deploy one battle group of up to 4 bases of medium foot shot (if it has one) between 10 and 15 MUs from its rear table edge as a forlorn hope. It must be entirely in non-open terrain or defending an obstacle.

### AMBUSHING

The player with pre-battle initiative can place ambushes up to half way across the table from his side's rear table edge, in the two outer thirds of the table's width. The other player can place ambushes up to 18 MUs forward from his side's rear table edge, in the two outer thirds of the table's width. Only mounted troops, commanded shot or light troops can be placed in ambush within 12 MUs of a side table edge. Battle wagons and artillery cannot ambush.

Ambushes must not be visible from any part of the enemy deployment area for light troops (even if the enemy have no light troops).

Ambushes are made by placing 'ambush markers' as follows:

- Each side can place up to 3 ambush markers on the table. An ambush marker is a 40mm

### AMBUSH DISCOVERED

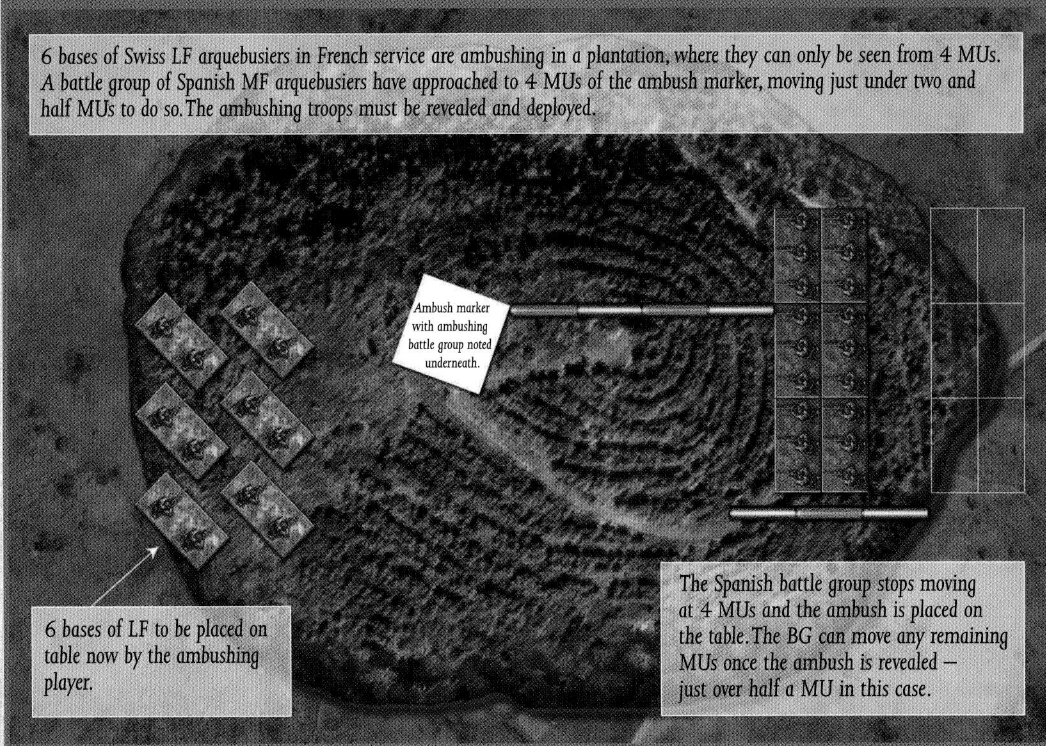


square in 15mm scale, 60mm in 25/28 mm scale. The player must clearly identify (by noting on the bottom of the marker) the single battle group from his order of march that this represents, and any commander who is to accompany it. Alternatively the marker can be left blank as a 'dummy marker' to confuse the enemy.

- If any enemy come within visibility range of the marker, the ambush (or its non-existence) is immediately revealed.
- When an ambush is revealed, place a base entirely on top of the ambush marker and then deploy the battle group around this base. It can face any of the edges of the ambush marker, and can be in any legal formation. A commander who was ambushing with it must be placed in legal contact with it. No base can be placed closer than the first base to any enemy battle group to which it would be visible. Only mounted troops, commanded shot and light troops can be placed within 12 MUs of a side table edge. A base that cannot be properly placed for any reason is lost. The enemy can then complete their move, unless it was a second or third move and they are within 6 MUs of the ambushers.
- Either player can reveal an ambush at any time in his own turn. He need not move the battle group to do so, but must place it on table in the correct position.
- When a friendly battle group will pass through an ambush marker, the ambush is revealed before the friends are moved.

AMBUSH DEPLOYED

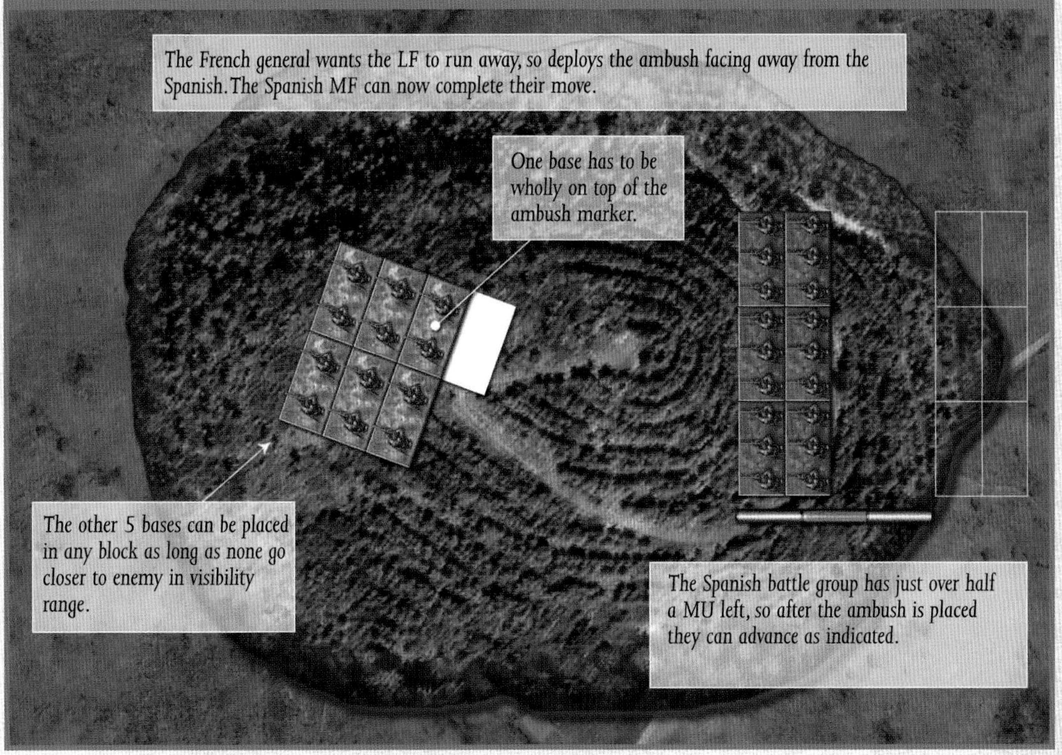


## OUTFLANKING MARCHES

Attempts to surprise the enemy by sending a force on a wide outflanking manoeuvre in this period were rare but did occasionally occur. If successful, this could turn a battle as at Wittstock (1636). This tactic is possible in *Field of Glory Renaissance* and therefore:

- Each player can choose to send up to 2 off-table outflanking marches, one on each flank. These are noted down before deployment, specifying on which side table edge they will arrive.
- Each outflanking march must include a single commander and between 1 and 3 battle groups. A grand battle group counts as two battle groups for this purpose. The C-in-C cannot flank march.
- An allied commander can only make an outflanking march with troops from his own allied contingent and must take his whole contingent.
- An outflanking march normally arrives anywhere on the specified side table edge (but see below).

The player testing for the arrival of his outflanking marches rolls two dice for each one at the beginning of each of his turns and consults the table below:

When an outflanking march successfully dices to arrive:

- The controlling player must immediately declare which flank the outflanking march is on and the number of battle groups it includes.

| OUTFLANKING MARCH ARRIVAL TEST | |
|---|---|
| **roll two dice for each outflanking march (no re-rolls)** | |
| **modifier** | |
| +1 | If the flank march is led by a field commander |
| -1 | If the flank march includes foot other than light troops |
| **score** | **Result** |
| 9 or less | Roll again next turn |
| 10 or more | Success – see below |

| STRAGGLING TEST | |
|---|---|
| On the turn when the outflanking march should arrive, roll two dice for each battle group to see if it is straggling. Straggling battle groups will not arrive in time for the battle. | |
| **modifier** | |
| +1 | Gendarmes, cavaliers, horse, determined horse, cavalry, camelry and light troops |
| -1 | Elephants, battle wagons and artillery |
| **A battle group is straggling (and will not arrive) if it scores less than 5. Quality re-rolls apply** | |

- Unless both armies have an outflanking march on that flank (see below), and unless they are straggling (see below), the outflanking battle groups and commander arrive in any legal formation in the manoeuvre phase of the controlling player's **next turn**, anywhere on that flank's side table edge. All battle groups must be in command range of their commander at the end of their first move on to the table.
- The player rolls for each battle group immediately before it would arrive to see if it is straggling.
- Straggling battle groups are assumed to be delayed sufficiently that they will not arrive in time for the battle. Each straggling battle group counts as 1 attrition point for the purposes of army defeat (2 if a grand battle group). If all the battle groups of an outflanking march are straggling, the commander is also assumed to be straggling.
- If both armies have an outflanking march on that flank:
  - The side with more battle groups, excluding battle groups entirely of light troops, drives the other back. A grand battle group counts as two battle groups for this purpose.
  - If equal, the side with more battle troops of all types drives the other back.
  - If still equal, both sides are driven back.
  - A driven back flank march arrives in the manoeuvre phase of its side's **next turn** following either side's successful dicing for arrival on that flank. It arrives on the side table edge up to 12 MUs from its army's rear table edge. Each battle group arrives in any legal formation and makes a full double move on to the table perpendicular to the table's side edge, ending its move facing away from that table edge. This counts as its full normal move for that turn. It does not have to be in command range of its commander.
  - If not themselves driven back, the enemy arrive in the manoeuvre phase of the following turn, using the normal rules for arrival (see above), except that they too must arrive in the same 12 MUs of the side table edge.

  - Both sides are subject to the normal rules for straggling, but this is not tested for until after determining which side is driven back.
- Battle groups within 6 MUs of the point of arrival of enemy flank marchers obey the following rules:
  - Unless already in close combat, battle wagons are destroyed and artillery is captured, their crews having fled and dispersed. (This does not cause friends to take a cohesion test.)
  - Supply camps are assumed to have been sacked, even if fortified.
  - Unless already in close combat, other types make an evade move perpendicularly away from the side table edge, even if of a type not normally able to evade. They do so as if evading in the direction of a charge from that direction (see the ***Impact Phase*** section).
- Arriving flank marchers (whether arriving normally or driven back) measure their move from the side table edge. Their first move must be perpendicular to the table edge. Normal restrictions on second or third moves apply to those arriving normally. Any battle groups that cannot fit onto the table this turn must arrive in their side's next turn or the first turn thereafter when space is available. They have no effect on enemy within 6 MUs.

## DEPLOYING BATTLE GROUPS

The total number of battle groups in the army is divided into 4 deployment batches **as evenly as possible**, with larger numbers allocated to the earlier batches (e.g. 8 becomes 2-2-2-2, 9 becomes 3-2-2-2 and 15 becomes 4-4-4-3). The size of these batches is noted in the order of march. Count each grand battle group as two battle groups for this purpose.

All battle groups except those in ambush or on an outflanking march are deployed in the order listed in the order of march. But note that:

- Battle groups in ambush or on an outflanking march are omitted, and the next battle groups in the order of march must be deployed instead. Thus the correct number of battle groups must be deployed in each batch, until all visible on-table battle groups have been deployed. As a result, there may be no battle groups left to deploy in the last batch.
- If a grand battle group's position in the order of march means that it "straddles" two batches, it is deployed in the earlier batch (unless it has been split into two normal battle groups by detaching shot). The remainder of the following batch is deployed as normal.

Other than when in ambush, light troops, artillery and forlorn hope can be deployed up to 15 MUs forward from their side's rear table edge and other battle groups up to 10 MUs from the side's rear table edge. Only mounted troops, commanded shot and light troops can be deployed within 12 MUs of a side table edge. No troops can be deployed in impassable terrain or a river. Battle wagons, heavy artillery and limbered medium artillery cannot be deployed in difficult terrain. Medium artillery can only be deployed in difficult terrain if it will be defending field fortifications.

It is not obligatory to deploy troops of an ally contingent close to each other and to their commander, but it is generally more historical and more effective under the rules to do so.

The deployment sequence is as follows:

- The player **without** pre-battle initiative deploys his first batch of battle groups.
- The player with initiative then deploys his first batch of battle groups.
- The players continue alternately deploying their second, third and fourth batches.

All battle groups must be fully defined to your opponent as they are placed on the table.

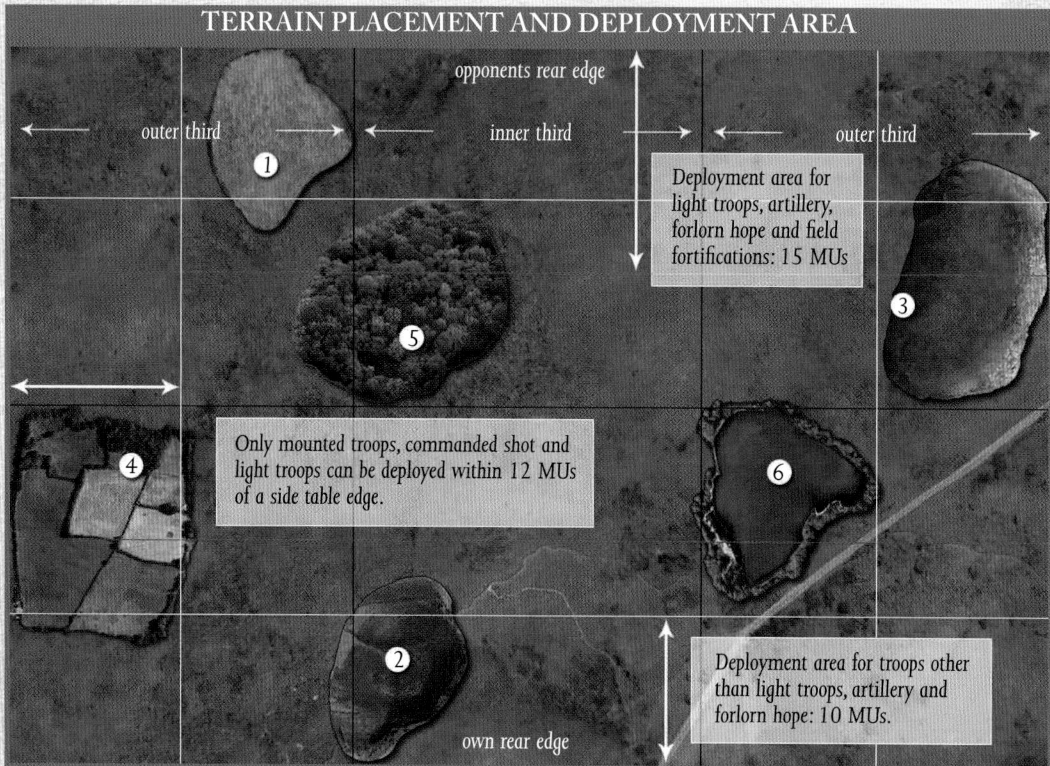


## DEPLOYING MOUNTED TROOPS DISMOUNTED

Mounted battle groups are only allowed to dismount if their list in our companion army list books indicates that they are permitted to do so. Each base dismounts as specified in the list.

They can only dismount at the following times:

- When first deployed on the table.
- Immediately after all non-ambushing on-table battle groups have been deployed by both sides. The player without initiative decides first.
- When their ambush is revealed. (But only if it was noted as dismounted on the ambush marker.)

Flank marchers cannot dismount.

## DEPLOYING COMMANDERS

Commanders, except those in ambush or on an outflanking march, are positioned after both armies have deployed all visible on table battle groups. The player without initiative deploys his commanders first. Commanders can be deployed anywhere up to 15 MUs forward from their side's rear table edge.

# APPENDIX 5: ARMY COMPOSITION AND THE POINTS SYSTEM

*In historical re-fights* or campaign battles, the armies are determined by actual battle accounts or by the campaign scenario. However, for one-off battles that provide a reasonable opportunity for either player to win, a points system can be very useful. To achieve balance, the more effective the troops, the more each base costs in points. The recommended total points value for a singles game of about 2 to 4 hours is between 600 and 800 points. We suggest 800 points for 15mm singles tournament games and 650 points for 25/28mm.

| POINTS VALUES | Basic cost | | | |
|---|---|---|---|---|
| **Commanders (-10 points if ally)** | **80(GC)** | **50 (FC)** | **35 (TC)** | |
| Quality: | Elite | Superior | Average | Poor |
| Foot battle groups | | | | |
| Fully-armoured | 12 | 10 | 7 | - |
| Heavily-armoured | 11 | 9 | 6 | 4 |
| Armoured | 10 | 8 | 5 | 3 |
| Unarmoured | 9 | 7 | 4 | 2 |
| Dragoons | 10 | 8 | 5 | 3 |
| Heavy artillery | - | 32 | 25 | 17 |
| Medium artillery | - | 26 | 20 | 14 |
| Limbers | - | 0 | 0 | 0 |
| Light artillery | - | 16 | 12 | 9 |
| Battle wagons | | | 14 | 8 |
| Battle wagons with light artillery | | | 20 | 14 |
| Regimental guns | 14 | 12 | 9 | 7 |
| Mounted battle groups | | | | |
| Armoured determined horse | 22 | 18 | 12 | 8 |
| Unarmoured determined horse | 18 | 15 | 9 | 6 |
| Fully-armoured or heavily armoured gendarmes | 22 | 18 | 12 | 8 |
| Armoured cavaliers | 19 | 16 | 11 | 7 |
| Unarmoured cavaliers | 16 | 13 | 8 | 5 |
| Heavily armoured cavalry or camelry | 18 | 15 | 10 | 6 |
| Armoured cavalry or camelry | 15 | 12 | 8 | 5 |
| Unarmoured cavalry or camelry | 11 | 9 | 6 | 4 |
| Heavily armoured horse | 16 | 13 | 9 | 5 |
| Armoured horse or light horse | 12 | 10 | 7 | 4 |
| Unarmoured horse or light horse | 10 | 8 | 5 | 3 |
| Others | | | | |
| Elephants | - | - | 25 | - |
| Naval units | - | - | 30 | - |
| Fortified camp | - | - | - | 24 |

| **Combat capabilities and other attributes** | |
|---|---|
| Foot (multiply cost by 3 for battle wagons) | |
| Bow, bow*, bombs | 1 |
| Arquebus, musket* | 2 |
| Musket, salvo | 3 |
| Impact foot, pike, heavy weapon | 1 |
| Swordsmen | 1 |
| Each base with bayonet in BG with no pikemen | 2 |
| Determined foot | 1 |
| Each shot base in BG with pikemen, or if commanded shot | 1 |
| Extra for BG using Swedish brigade | 4 |
| All other weapon capabilities | 0 |
| Mounted | |
| Heavy or light lancers | 1 |
| Impact mounted | 3 |
| Melee swordsmen | 2 |
| Pistol/carbine (shooting) | 2 |
| Impact pistol | 1 |
| Melee pistol | 2 |
| Bow | 2 |
| Bow* | 1 |
| Camelry | 1 |
| All other weapon capabilities | 0 |
| Defences per base frontage | |
| Portable defences | 3 |
| Field fortifications | 3 |

Each base has a basic cost determined by its type, armour and quality. The right hand side details the extra costs to be added for combat capabilities and certain battle groups.

To calculate the cost of your battle groups, take the basic cost from the table, add the additional cost for combat capabilities, then multiply the total by the number of bases in the battle group. Exception: the overall cost of bases comprising a Swedish brigade is increased by 4. An easier way is simply to look up the cost of each base in our companion army list books.

Points costs for portable defences and field fortifications are per base frontage. See the Special Features section for the restrictions on bases using portable defences.

The cost of a commander is reduced by ten points if he is the commander of an allied contingent.

Supply camps are compulsory but cost no points unless fortified. They are not battle groups.

When choosing an army it is recommended that players reference one or more of the companion army list books published to accompany these rules. A few opening lines from an example army list are shown below.

<table>
<tr><th colspan="11">NEW MODEL ARMY</th></tr>
<tr><td colspan="11">Territory Types: Agricultural, Hilly, Woodlands</td></tr>
<tr><td>C-in-C</td><td colspan="6">Great Commander/Field Commander/Troop Commander</td><td>80/50/35</td><td colspan="3">1</td></tr>
<tr><td rowspan="2">Sub-commanders</td><td colspan="6">Field Commander</td><td>50</td><td colspan="3">0-2</td></tr>
<tr><td colspan="6">Troop Commander</td><td>35</td><td colspan="3">0-3</td></tr>
<tr><th rowspan="2">Troop name</th><th colspan="3">Troop Type</th><th colspan="3">Capabilities</th><th rowspan="2">Points per base</th><th rowspan="2" colspan="2">Bases per BG</th><th rowspan="2">Total bases</th></tr>
<tr><td>Type</td><td>Armour</td><td>Quality</td><td>Shooting</td><td>Impact</td><td>Melee</td></tr>
<tr><th colspan="11">Core Troops</th></tr>
<tr><td rowspan="2">Horse</td><td rowspan="2">Determined horse</td><td rowspan="2">Armoured</td><td>Superior</td><td rowspan="2">-</td><td rowspan="2">Pistol</td><td rowspan="2">Pistol</td><td>21</td><td rowspan="2" colspan="2">4</td><td rowspan="2">8-32</td></tr>
<tr><td>Average</td><td>15</td></tr>
<tr><td rowspan="2">Foot</td><td>Medium Foot</td><td>Unarmoured</td><td>Average</td><td>Musket</td><td>-</td><td>-</td><td>8</td><td>4</td><td rowspan="2">6</td><td rowspan="2">12-64</td></tr>
<tr><td>Heavy Foot</td><td>Unarmoured</td><td>Average</td><td>-</td><td>Pikemen</td><td>Pikemen</td><td>5</td><td>2</td></tr>
</table>

The list fully describes the bases available to the army by type, armour, quality and combat capabilities. The list also states how many bases are allowed in each battle group and how many bases there should and can be in the army.

## EXAMPLE:

The superior determined horse on the first line cost a basic 18 points for each base. Adding for impact and melee pistols capability makes a total of 21 points each. They must be in battle groups of 4 bases, costing 84 points each. Any combination of superior or average battle groups of determined horse can be chosen, but the army must have between 8 and 32 bases of them in total.

## COMMANDERS

Each army must have a commander-in-chief and 1 to 3 subordinate or ally commanders. Ally commanders are only available for ally contingents specified by the army lists in our companion army list books, drawn either from the same or more commonly from other lists. An ally commander can only affect battle groups of his own contingent and these can only be affected by him.

## BATTLE GROUP COMPOSITION

All troops are organized into battle groups.

Battle groups must comply with the following restrictions:

- If using our companion army list books the number of bases in a battle group must correspond to the range specified in the list.
- Each battle group must initially comprise an even number of bases (not counting regimental gun markers), with the following exceptions. If using our companion army list books, these can only be used if specified by the list:
  - A battle group can only initially have 3 bases if this is explicitly stated in the list. e.g. If the battle group size is specified in the form "2,3,4", and not if specified in the form "2-4".
  - A battle group can only initially have 7 bases if it is specified in the list as a Swedish brigade formation.
  - A battle group can only initially have 9 bases if this is explicitly stated in the list. e.g. If the battle group size is specified in the form "6,9,12", and not if specified in the form "6-12".
- If using our army lists, a battle group can only include troops from one line in a list, unless the list specifies a mixed formation by indicating the battle group to be of types from more than one line. e.g. 4 musketeers & 2 pikemen – as in the New Model Army list above.
- All troops in a battle group must be of the same quality. Where a choice of quality is given in a list, this allows battle groups to differ from each other. It does not override the above rule for each battle group.
- All troops in a battle group with the same troop type and combat capabilities must be of the same armour class. Where a choice of armour class is given in a list, this allows battle groups to differ from each other. It does not override the above rule for each battle group.
- Elephants can only be in battle groups of 2 bases each.

*King's Life Guards*

# APPENDIX 6: CHOOSING AND USING YOUR ARMY

*How do you choose* your army? The best answer is to pick an army that really interests you, as you will find it much easier to research and paint. The complete set of companion army list books that accompany *Field of Glory Renaissance* contain over 130 different armies. They all have their own strengths and weaknesses, so which you choose is largely a matter of personal preference.

If you prefer to fight against historical opponents, you will find that the armies in our companion army list books are designed to give relatively balanced battles, allowing a reasonable chance of victory for most armies. If your group of friends prefer to fight only within historical and geographical sub-periods, you will be well advised to choose from armies that fought against several of your available opponents. In most sub-periods this should still allow you plenty of choice.

If your main interest is the mainstream of European warfare, pick a conflict that interests you (and your friends) and collect an army (or armies) from that period. If your interest is in the wider world, pick an army from further afield.

This will present its own challenges, particularly if it has to fight an up-to-date European army. Ottoman armies comprising horse archers and firearm infantry without pikes were historically a major threat to Christian Europe and can be successful on the table. You might even fancy trying out some of the more exotic armies, such as Moghuls, with elephants, rocketeers and grenade throwers as well as massed bow or lance-armed cavalry, or Aztecs, following up a barrage of atlatl-propelled darts with a fierce charge with obsidian-bladed wooden swords, hoping to capture prisoners for sacrifice on top of the great pyramid of Tenochtitlan. The choice is yours.

The rules are designed for balance between historical opponents, but also accommodate "what if" battles between non-historical opponents (common in tournaments). European technological advantages are largely offset by the points system, but there remains added challenge in some match-ups.

Another important factor when picking a first army is the potential to use some troops in a variety of different armies. Uniforms were uncommon until the mid 17th century, and pike and shot were often armed, equipped and dressed in similar fashion in different national armies – in fact many were mercenaries with careers in several armies. Similarly, most European mounted types resembled each other. It is therefore possible to use these types in a wide selection of armies.

The flip side to interchangeability is that there is no finer sight on the wargames table than an

*English Civil War "Be ye for King or Parliament"*

accurately presented and painted army, with the correct historical flags and (where applicable) uniforms. You will identify with your army more closely if all the figures are correct and you have researched the flags, uniforms and commanders' names. To field the army of one of history's great generals such as Gonzalvo de Cordova, Gustavus Adolphus, Turenne or Montecuccoli certainly boosts a player's morale. It can also save you from endless alchemical attempts to produce an invincible army by juggling the army lists instead of by perfecting your tactical skills.

Before buying, think about the weaknesses that the army may have against likely opponents. An all-mounted army might look good on paper and be effective on an open table, but may have difficulty fighting around heavy terrain. Choose an army whose character and tactical approach mesh well with your temperament and playing style and enable you to enjoy the battle even if fate turns against you.

Eventually, having chosen which army you intend to field, think about its strengths and weaknesses and try to design an order of battle that will maximise its strengths. Most armies have a set of core troops that will to a large extent dictate your battlefield tactics and fighting doctrine. Structure your army in such a way that the battle groups will support each other. Try to imagine how the army will look when it is deployed, how it will manoeuvre and attack, and how it will effectively deploy or counter firepower, an increasingly important element of battle over our period.

Finally, make sure you have the right commanders to suit your play style. Remember that commanders can be used to control the troops from a distance, but can also be used to lead a head-on charge to victory.

## TACTICAL ADVICE FOR BEGINNERS

The most important lesson that a beginner has to learn is that he should have a plan. Almost any plan is better than no plan at all. A good plan, however, is the first step to victory. It should take into account the layout of the battlefield, the relative strengths and weaknesses of the opposing forces and the enemy's likely actions. If you misjudge, you will find it difficult to change your plan or redeploy, so best get it right first time if possible.

Ask yourself how your army differs from that of the enemy. Who has the best infantry? Does one side have foot with advantages in an assault while the other's foot prefers to keep the enemy at shooting distance? Usually one side will benefit from a strong attack based on its foot, while the other will prefer to avoid or delay contact. Who has the best horse? If you do, you may be able to carry out sweeping manoeuvres on his flanks, but if he does, or if his army greatly outnumbers yours, you will need to avoid being outflanked yourself. Your infantry will not perform well if they feel threatened by enemy horse, so you need to counter them with horse of your own, or secure your flanks on terrain.

*Ottoman Artillery*

Does the enemy have any troops that are certain to give you problems? Can you counter them by slowing or distracting them with light troops or a forlorn hope? Can you use terrain to counter their advantage? Can you support your horse with commanded shot to even the odds against superior enemy horse? Can you rely on firepower to disrupt the enemy as they advance?

Skilfully placed medium or heavy artillery can reduce your opponent's options. If ignored, it will cause a trickle of base losses which will eventually cripple or destroy battle groups. It may force your opponent to attack or to avoid the field of fire of the artillery. Similarly, enemy artillery can ruin your day. If possible, deploy troops out of enemy artillery range if you do not plan to immediately advance. Artillery is very vulnerable to capture unless supported by foot battle troops.

It is not always necessary to attack immediately, but if you adopt a defensive position, don't rely on your opponent attacking where you want him to. Few opponents will co-operate by making a suicidal attack on an impregnable position. If you adopt a passive defence, a clever opponent will concentrate his main attack on your weakest point while demonstrating against the rest of your battle line to keep it occupied. He may concentrate shooting on part of your line until its cohesion fragments before charging your demoralised troops. A defensive stance followed by a pre-planned counter-attack can be more effective.

It is often effective to attack on one wing while skirmishing or defending on the other. Obviously the attacking wing should contain strong battle troops and the refused wing should contain troops capable of skirmishing or be in a secure defensive position. If your refused wing appears endangered, do not be tempted to bolster it by draining troops from your attack – which may then peter out. In a large game with several players per side, make sure to give control of the refused wing to a defensively minded player. Some players are unable to restrain themselves from attacking whatever the situation, often with disastrous results. Similarly, avoid giving command of your attacking wing to an over-cautious player.

You should try to keep your plan and your deployment as simple as possible, with most of your troops deployed in divisions under the control of your commanders. This will allow you to make double or triple moves in the early part of the game and prevent your troops from being attacked in flank. Battle troops in the second line of a division can provide support as well as tactical flexibility.

If you plan a wide, on-table, outflanking move, this should be led by a commander. Or you might try an off-table outflanking march, as these can be very effective. The danger is that it may arrive too late or not at all. Ambushes can be effective, but do not ambush just because you can. Such stratagems need to fit your overall plan.

Troops held back behind the front line can give support to the front line troops and can act as reserves to plug a hole or exploit an opportunity. A chequer-board divisional formation can advance quickly, give the front line support in the approach, then close up into a solid line at the point of crisis. A further interrupted line of battle groups behind the main line will give additional support, and is a good place to put lower quality troops unfit for the front line. A central reserve of good quality mobile troops can be used to achieve a crucial advantage

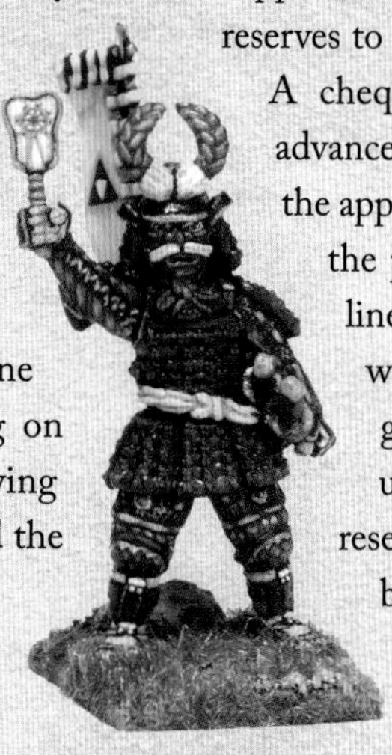

*Samurai Commander*

at the point of decision if employed in the right place at the right time.

An army with strong reserves will obviously occupy less frontage than an army deployed in less depth, creating a risk that you might be outflanked. However, terrain can be used to secure flanks, and failing this your flank reserves should be suitably positioned to counter any enemy outflanking manoeuvre. This flexibility and ability to deal with all eventualities can be contrasted with the rigidity of the army deployed thinly on too wide a front, which has no counter to an enemy breakthrough and will find it difficult to compensate for deficiencies in its original plan.

An exception to the above general rule might be armies based around horse archers, who cannot expect to win a frontal contest and must therefore attempt to outflank the enemy on one or both wings. They may still benefit from keeping a strong reserve; even if this leave gaps in their line, the enemy will find it difficult to exploit this without breaking up their own formation, which in turn may present opportunities for the horse archers to concentrate their shooting or to attack flanks.

A good tactic to delay the enemy is to rush forward with your light troops (light horse, light foot or dragoons) to obstruct his path and prevent him making second and third moves. They can then fall back slowly in front of the enemy, evading if charged. Remember, however, that light foot and dragoons are vulnerable to mounted troops in the open and may be caught when they try to evade. They may be better able to divert or delay the enemy if deployed in terrain on the flanks of the enemy advance.

Flank attacks, especially by battle troops, can be overwhelming, so you must avoid enemy getting behind the flanks of your battle groups unless you have troops ready to intercept them if they charge. Conversely, if you can manage to outflank the enemy the battle should be all but won. Early Tercios are resistant to flank or rear attacks, so can afford to be more aggressive even when lacking mounted support.

A commander fighting in the front rank of a battle group will greatly improve the odds in close combat, but there is a risk of losing the commander. On balance, the benefit usually outweighs the risk if the combat is otherwise at least equal, or if the result of the combat is critical. However, once committed, the commander cannot be used to rally other troops or influence their cohesion tests or complex move tests until the close combat and pursuit is over. It is usually unwise to hazard a great commander in combat – though this was a risk often taken historically, sometimes with fatal results. Do you feel lucky?

# APPENDIX 7: EXAMPLES OF UNUSUAL SITUATIONS

*The rules already cover* what to do in different situations but for ease of reference we include here diagrams and descriptions for a number of reasonably common and apparently complicated situations. You will also find explanations and details, along with scoring ideas for competition organisers and much more at www.fieldofglory.com .

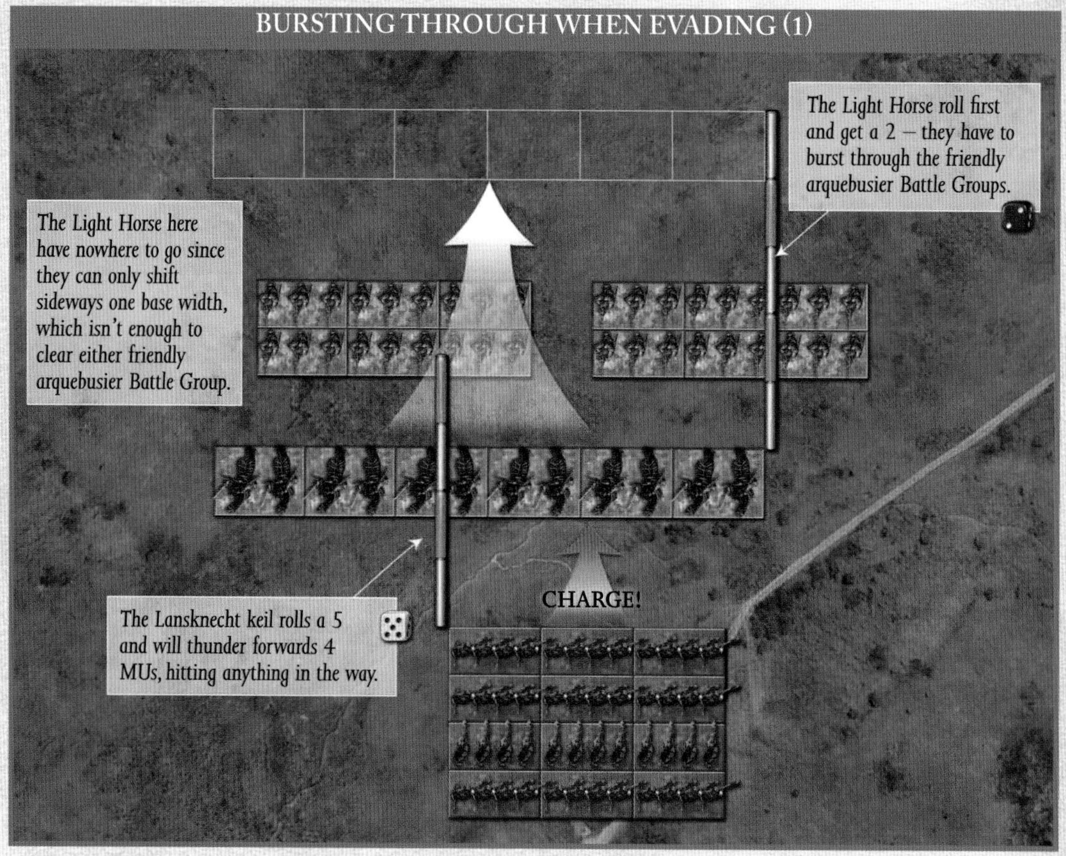

## BURSTING THROUGH WHEN EVADING (2)

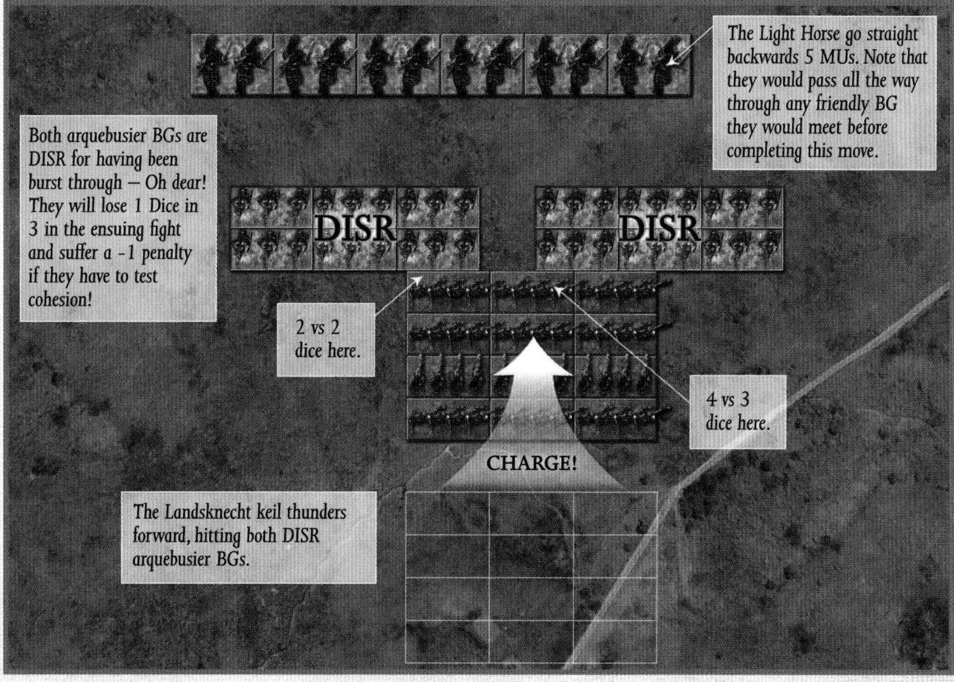


## CONTRACTING DURING AN EVADE (1)

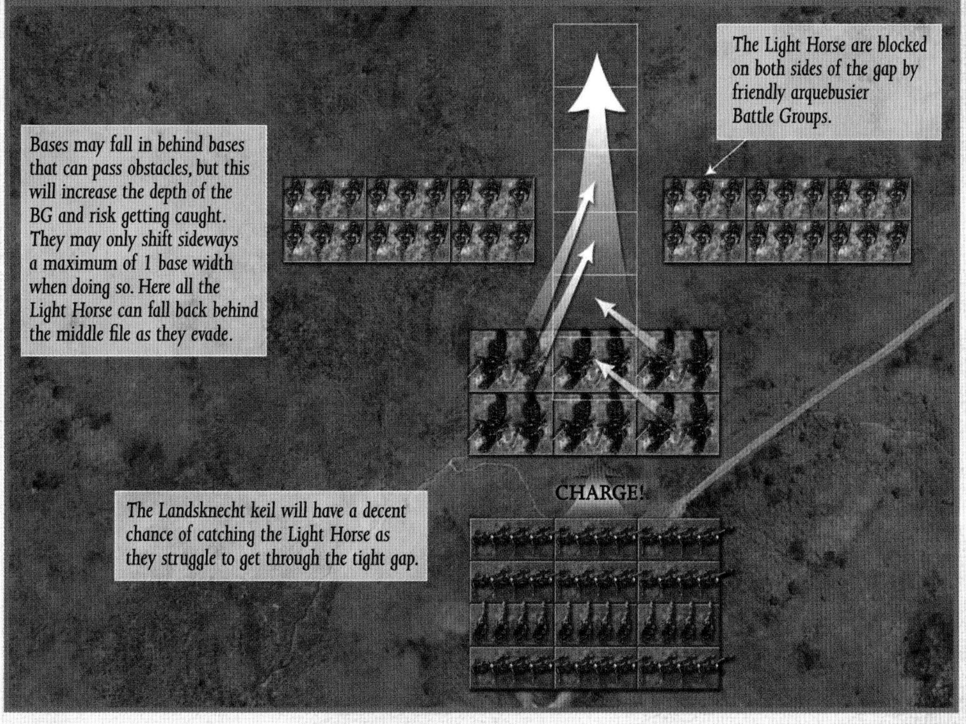

## CONTRACTING DURING AN EVADE (2)

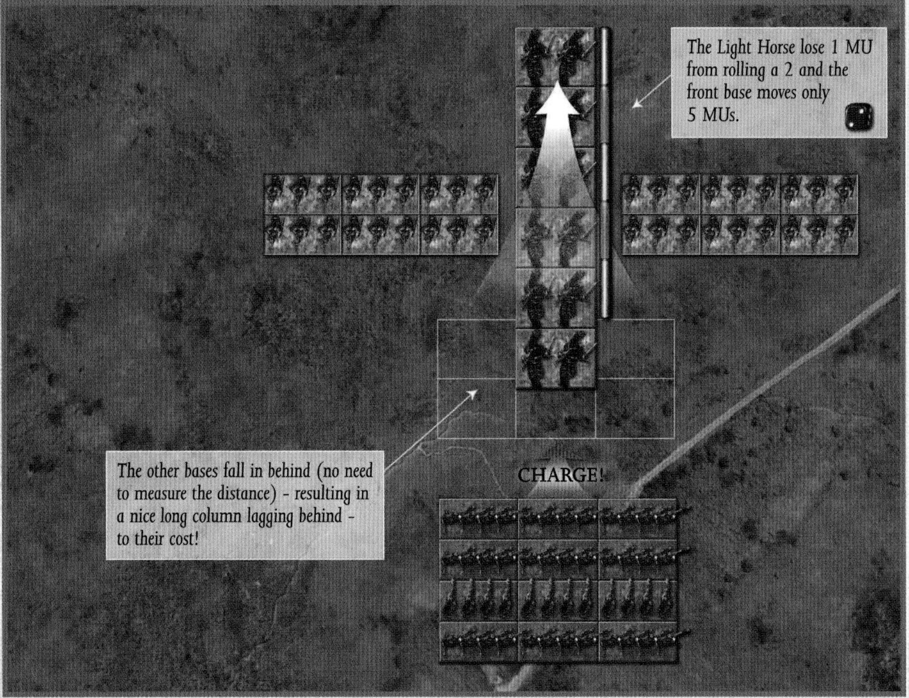


## CONTRACTING DURING AN EVADE (3)

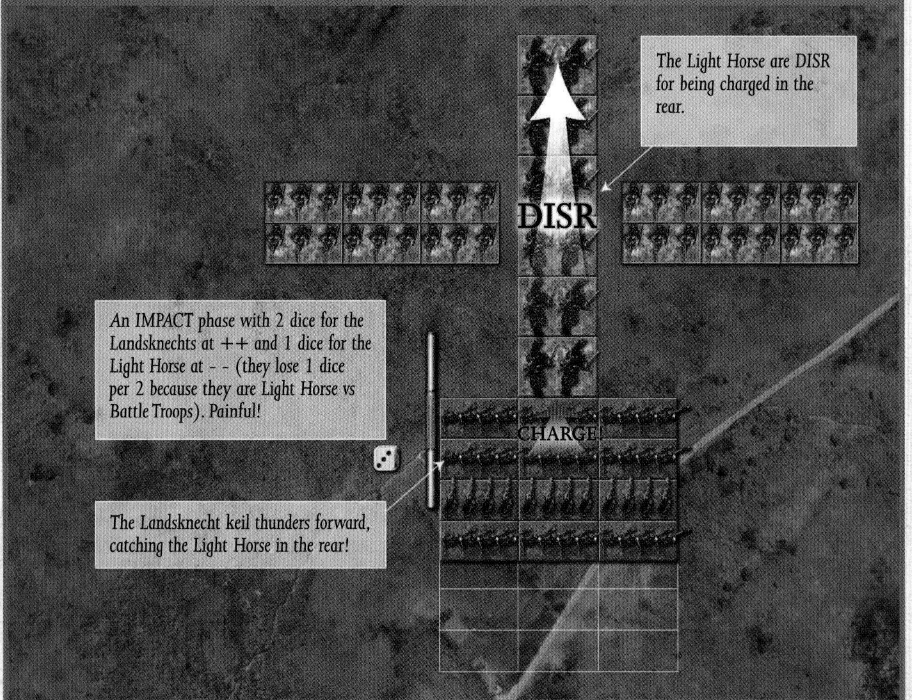

## COMPLEX EVADE (1)

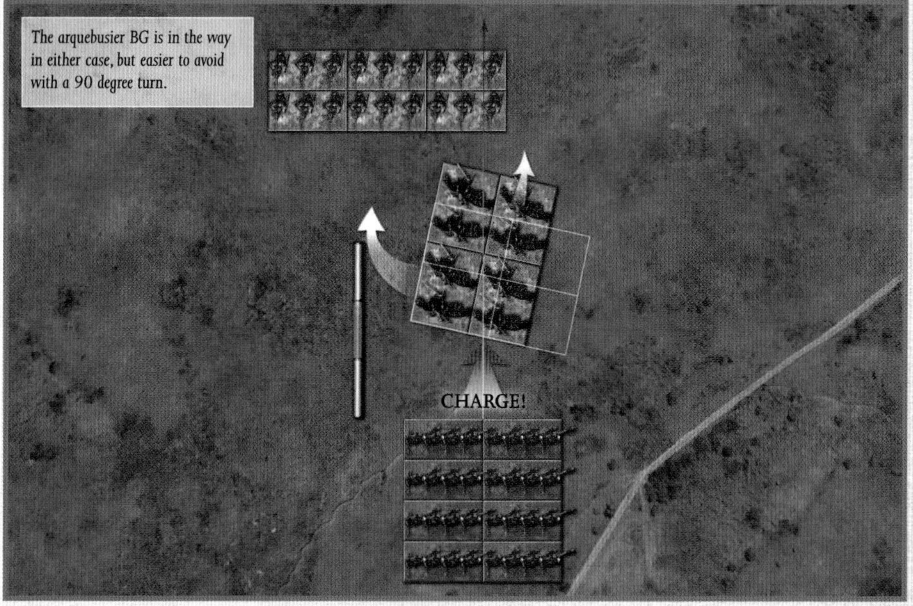


## COMPLEX EVADE (2)

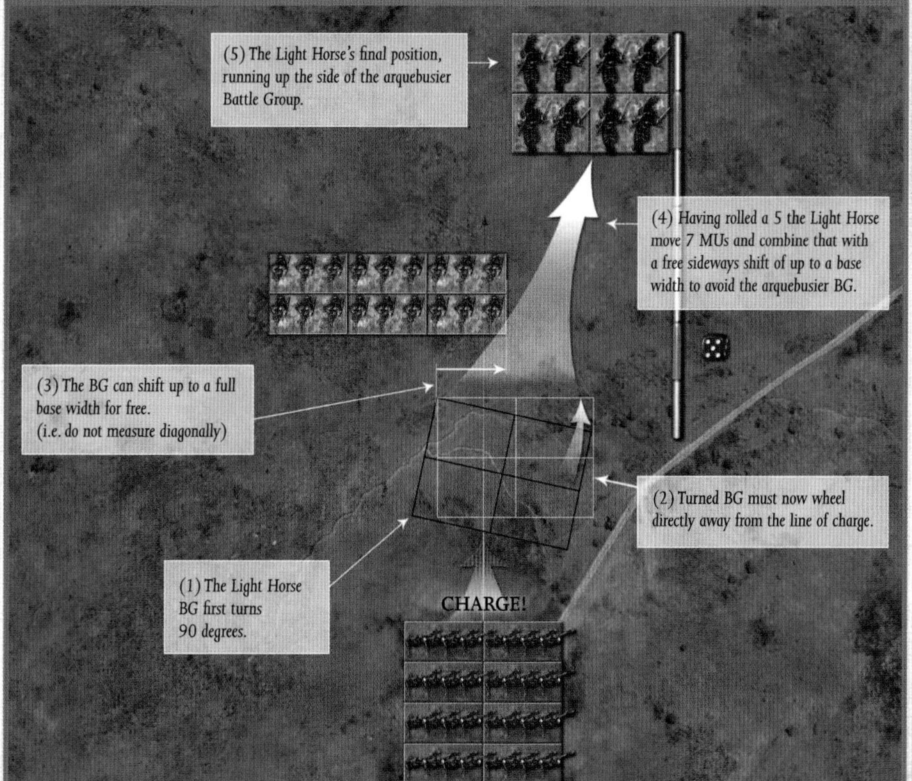

# APPENDIX 8: READY RECKONER

## SHOOTING DICE

**The following table shows how many dice you get when shooting with 1 dice per 2 bases or 1 dice per 3 bases:**

The principle is that you get one shooting dice for each full set of 2 or 3 bases respectively.

| Shooting Dice | | |
|---|---|---|
| Bases Shooting | Shooting Dice @ 1 per 2 | Shooting Dice @ 1 per 3 |
| 1 | 0 | 0 |
| 2 | 1 | 0 |
| 3 | 1 | 1 |
| 4 | 2 | 1 |
| 5 | 2 | 1 |
| 6 | 3 | 2 |
| 7 | 3 | 2 |
| 8 | 4 | 2 |

## REDUCING COMBAT DICE FOR DISRUPTION ETC.

**The following table shows the number of dice you must drop if losing 1 dice per 3 (e.g. if Disrupted) or 1 dice per 2 (e.g. if Fragmented):**

The principle is to take the dice you have and if losing 1 per 3 remove every 3rd one that you have. For example, if you have 5 dice – remove the 3rd one. There isn't a 6th one, so you only lose 1 dice. If you have 7 lose 2, if 9 lose 3.

Note that, for example, light horse in close combat against any troops other than light horse or light foot must first lose 1 dice per 2 for that, then if disrupted must lose 1 dice per 3 from the dice they have left.

If there were 6 bases in the battle group, in two ranks, then they would start with 6 dice. They would drop 3 dice for fighting troops other than light horse or light foot, leaving 3. They would then drop 1 more dice for disruption, leaving 2 to throw.

If there were 4 bases in the battle group, in 2 ranks, then they would start with 4 dice. They would drop 2 dice for fighting troops other than light horse or light foot, leaving 2. They would not drop any dice for disruption because they do not have 3 dice left, so once again they are left with 2 to throw.

| Reduction in dice for DISR/FRG or Terrain | | |
|---|---|---|
| Dice initially | Dropped Dice @ 1 per 3 | Dropped Dice @ 1 per 2 |
| 1 | 0 | 0 |
| 2 | 0 | 1 |
| 3 | 1 | 1 |
| 4 | 1 | 2 |
| 5 | 1 | 2 |
| 6 | 2 | 3 |
| 7 | 2 | 3 |
| 8 | 2 | 4 |
| 9 | 3 | 4 |
| 10 | 3 | 5 |
| 11 | 3 | 5 |
| 12 | 4 | 6 |

## CALCULATING 1 HP3B AND 1 HP2B

**For normal troops, the following table shows the number of hits required to score 1 HP3B:**

| 1 Hit per 3 Bases | |
|---|---|
| Bases in first 3 ranks of battle group | Number of hits required |
| 1, 2 or 3 | 1 |
| 4, 5 or 6 | 2 |
| 7, 8 or 9 | 3 |
| 10, 11 or 12 | 4 |

**For normal troops, the following table shows the number of hits required to score 1 HP2B:**

| 1 Hit per 2 Bases | |
|---|---|
| Bases in first 3 ranks of battle group | Number of hits required |
| 1 or 2 | 1 |
| 3 or 4 | 2 |
| 5 or 6 | 3 |
| 7 or 8 | 4 |
| 9 or 10 | 5 |
| 11 or 12 | 6 |

# APPENDIX 9: FULL TURN SEQUENCE

*The detailed order of play* in each turn is shown below. The rules treat all events in one box as happening before those in the next box. We recommend that in your first few games you work through them systematically box by box. However, once you become more familiar with the game, it usually makes sense to run through several steps at one time in areas where both players judge that these won't affect events elsewhere. Do not move to a new phase without completing the previous phase. The active player chooses which side goes first within a step if it matters but is not specified otherwise in the rules.

| FULL TURN SEQUENCE |
|---|
| 1) IMPACT PHASE |
| Roll for arrival of outflanking marches and straggling |
| **Declare all charges** (designating at least one charge target for each). |
| CMT for any troops requiring a CMT to charge. Any that fail have their charge cancelled. |
| Mark wheel direction (if any) for each charge for which evasion or interception might be possible. |
| Resolve CTs for FRAGMENTED troops being charged. If they break: Resolve CTs for seeing them break. Make their initial rout move. |
| Declare and move all **interception charges.** (If it counts as a legal flank or rear charge it cancels the enemy charge.) |
| CMT (if required) for light troops not wishing to evade battle troops. |
| Make all **evade** moves. |
| Resolve CTs for FRAGMENTED troops being charged as a result of intervening friends evading. If they break: Resolve CTs for seeing them break. Make their initial rout move. |
| Make all **charge moves** in any order. Wheel direction can be changed if all targets evaded out of the original charge path. Troops contacted by a charge counting as a flank or rear charge (except battle troops by light troops) drop 1 cohesion level. |
| **Resolve impact combats.** |
| For each BG in turn, resolve post-combat CT (if it lost), then death roll, then roll to inflict commander losses. |
| After the above is completed for all combats, resolve CTs for seeing friends break or commanders lost. |
| Make initial rout moves for troops broken this phase (other than FRAGMENTED troops that broke when charged). Make initial pursuits and remove a base for each pursuing BG remaining in contact at the end of its initial pursuit move. Roll to inflict commander losses. Resolve CTs for seeing commanders lost. |
| 2) MANOEUVRE PHASE |
| Reform BGs and active player conforms his troops in close combat to enemy if possible. |
| Feed additional bases into existing melees. Active player expands or shifts first. |
| Make normal movement (first taking a CMT if required) for each BG or division individually and move commanders. |

| |
|---|
| **3) SHOOTING PHASE.** |
| Resolve all shooting – both sides shoot. Resolve post-shooting CTs, then death rolls. |
| After the above is completed for all shooting, resolve CTs for seeing friends break. |
| Make all initial rout moves for troops broken this phase. Make all initial pursuits and remove a base for each pursuing BG remaining in contact at the end of its initial pursuit move. Roll to inflict commander losses. Resolve CTs for seeing commanders lost. |
| **4) MELEE PHASE** |
| Resolve all melee combats. |
| For each BG in turn, resolve post-combat CT (if it lost), then death roll, then roll to inflict commander losses. |
| Roll for assaults on a fortified camp. |
| After the above is completed for all combats, resolve CTs for seeing friends break or commanders lost. |
| Make all initial rout moves for troops broken this phase. Make all initial pursuits and remove a base for each pursuing BG remaining in contact at the end of its initial pursuit move. Roll to inflict commander losses. Resolve CTs for seeing commanders lost. |
| **5) JOINT ACTION PHASE. BOTH SIDES** |
| Make break-offs, active player first. |
| CMT to stop pursuing or looting. |
| Move commanders. |
| Commanders attempt to bolster or rally BGs but only those whose cohesion level did not drop this turn. |
| Move routers & pursuers. Remove a base for each pursuing BG remaining in contact at the end of its pursuit move. Roll to inflict commander losses. Resolve CTs for seeing commanders lost. |
| Remove any BGs that are autobroken and no longer pursued or are reduced to 1 base. |

# INDEX

# MOVEMENT

| MOVE DISTANCES & TERRAIN DISORDER | | | | |
|---|---|---|---|---|
| Troop type | Open | Uneven | Rough | Difficult |
| Light foot | 4 | 4 | 4 | 3 |
| Warriors | 4 | 4 | 4 | 3 |
| Medium foot, mob | 3 | 3 | 3 | 2 |
| Determined foot | 4 | 4 | 3 | 2 |
| Heavy foot | 3 | 2 | 2 | 1 |
| Light horse and commanders | 6 | 6 | 5 | 3 |
| Gendarmes (if not fully armoured), cavaliers, horse, determined horse, cavalry and camelry | 5 | 4 | 3 | 1 |
| Fully armoured gendarmes | 4 | 3 | 2 | 1 |
| Elephants | 4 | 4 | 3 | 1 |
| Dragoons | 5 | 5 | 4 | 3 |
| Battle wagons | 3 | 2 | 1 | N/A |
| Light artillery | 2 | 1 | 1 | 1* |
| Limbered artillery | 2 | 1 | 1 | N/A |
| Unlimbered medium artillery | 1* | 1* | 1* | N/A |
| Unlimbered heavy artillery | 1* | N/A | N/A | N/A |
| * Pivot only on either front corner of battle group | | | | |

| NO EFFECT | DISORDER | SEVERE DISORDER |
|---|---|---|

| SIMPLE AND COMPLEX MOVES | | Troop Type | |
|---|---|---|---|
| Type of move | Move to be made (advance means a move from the Advance section below) | Light Troops | Others |
| **Charge** | Any charge move | simple | simple |
| **Advance** | Any other forward move with no more than a single wheel | simple | simple |
| **Double Wheel** | A forward move including 2 wheels | simple | impossible* |
| **Pivot light or medium artillery** | Pivot forwards up to 1 MU on one front corner of the battle group | n/a | simple |
| **Pivot heavy artillery** | Pivot forwards up to 1 MU on one front corner of the battle group | n/a | complex |
| **Unlimber** | Unlimber medium or heavy artillery | n/a | complex |
| **2nd move** | *Advance* by a single battle group or division if all requirements for a 2nd move are met. | simple | simple |
| **3rd move** | *Advance* by a single battle group of mounted troops or dragoons or a division entirely of mounted troops and/or dragoons if all requirements for a 3rd move are met. | simple | simple |
| **Expansion** | Expand frontage by 1 or 2 bases while stationary | simple | complex |
| | Expand frontage by 1 or 2 bases followed by an *advance* | simple | impossible |
| **Contraction** | Contract frontage by 1 or 2 bases with an advance of at least 3 MUs before or after | simple | simple |
| | Contract frontage by 1 or 2 bases while stationary or with an advance of less than 3 MUs before or after | simple | complex |
| **Formation change** | Any of the following (singly or in combination): Turn a tercio or keil 90 degrees. Form square. Move bases around in the battle group, without changing its facing or the position of its front corners (except to turn a tercio or keil 90 degrees or form square). | n/a | complex** |
| **90 degree turns (not tercios or keils)** | Turn 90 degrees while stationary | simple | simple |
| | Turn 90 degrees with an *advance* before or after – only possible for light troops and mounted troops | simple | complex |
| **180 degree turns** | Turn 180 degrees while stationary | simple | simple*** |
| | Turn 180 degrees with an advance before or after – only possible for light troops | simple | impossible |
| | Turn 180 degrees, move up to 3 MUs in an *advance* and turn back again – only possible for light troops | complex | impossible |

* Simple for a 1 base wide column moving entirely along a road

** Formation changes permitted or required in the impact phase do not require a CMT.

*** Complex if turning captured or recaptured artillery 180 degrees.

| COMPLEX MOVE TEST | |
|---|---|
| **Roll two dice, apply quality re-rolls, and add the scores. Apply the following modifiers.** | |
| +1 if a commander in *line of command* is in *command range* | |
| +1 if this same commander is with the battle group testing | |
| +1 if this same commander is a great commander | |
| -1 if testing to stop pursuing or looting | |
| -1 if any of the bases are DISRUPTED or DISORDERED, or are warriors | Count the worst of these two, but never both. |
| -2 if any of the bases are FRAGMENTED or SEVERELY DISORDERED | |
| **Score to pass** | **8** |

# COMBAT

| SHOOTING DICE | | |
|---|---|---|
| Artillery (except when on battle wagons) | 1 dice per base at short or long range | |
| Regimental gun | 1 dice per marker at short or long range | |
| Dragoons | 1 dice per front rank base at short range | |
| | 1 dice per 2 front rank bases at long range | |
| Foot battle troops with musket* or mounted battle troops with carbine, bow or crossbow | 1 dice per base of 1st shooting rank at short range | |
| | 1 dice per 2 bases of 2nd shooting rank or at long range | |
| Horse with pistol | 1 dice per base of 1st shooting rank | |
| | 1 dice per 2 bases of 2nd and 3rd shooting ranks | |
| Foot with salvo capability | 1 dice per 2 bases at short or long range | |
| Other foot battle troops with arquebus, musket, bow or crossbow | 1 dice per base at short range | |
| | 1 dice per 2 bases at long range | |
| Battle wagons | 1 dice per base width from long edge only at short or long range | |
| Foot or mounted with other shooting capability (including any troops with bombs, bow*, javelins or slings and light foot or light horse with musket, arquebus, carbine, bow or crossbow) | 1 dice per 2 bases at short range | |
| | 1 dice per 3 bases at long range | |
| DISRUPTED or DISORDERED | Lose 1 dice per 3* | Dice loss for Disruption, Fragmentation, Disorder or Severe Disorder is not cumulative, but whichever is worst applies.<br>*including dice for regimental guns |
| FRAGMENTED or SEVERELY DISORDERED | Lose 1 dice per 2* | |

| IMPACT PHASE DICE | | |
|---|---|---|
| Battle wagons | 2 dice per front rank base width | |
| Other troops | 2 dice per front rank base | |
| Regimental guns | 1 dice | |
| REDUCTIONS | | |
| Light foot or light horse | Lose 1 dice per 2 unless:<br>• Light Foot fighting against Light Foot.<br>• Light Horse fighting against Light Horse or Light Foot.<br>• Any fighting FRAGMENTED enemy. | |
| THEN | | |
| DISRUPTED or DISORDERED | Lose 1 dice per 3* | Dice loss for Disruption, Fragmentation, Disorder or Severe Disorder is not cumulative, but whichever is worst applies.<br>*including dice for regimental guns |
| FRAGMENTED or SEVERELY DISORDERED | Lose 1 dice per 2* | |

| MELEE PHASE DICE | | |
|---|---|---|
| Elephants, gendarmes, cavaliers or determined horse | 2 dice per front rank base. No dice for rear rank bases of any type. | |
| Battle wagons | 2 dice per front rank base width. No dice for rear rank bases of any type. | |
| Other troops | 1 dice per base in first 2 ranks. | |
| Troops in overlap | 1 dice per overlapping file (irrespective of the number of ranks). | |
| REDUCTIONS | | |
| Light foot or light horse | Lose 1 dice per 2 unless:<br>• Light Foot fighting against Light Foot.<br>• Light Horse fighting against Light Horse or Light Foot.<br>• Any fighting against FRAGMENTED enemy. | |
| THEN | | |
| DISRUPTED or DISORDERED | Lose 1 dice per 3 | Dice loss for Disruption, Fragmentation, Disorder or Severe Disorder is not cumulative, but whichever is worst applies. |
| FRAGMENTED or SEVERELY DISORDERED | Lose 1 dice per 2 | |

| SHOOTING RANGES (MUS) | Short | Long |
|---|---|---|
| Musket, musket* and salvo | 3 | 6 |
| Foot bow, bow* and crossbow | 4 | 6 |
| Sling and mounted bow, bow* and crossbow | 4 | - |
| Arquebus and carbine | 3 | - |
| Bombs, pistols and javelins | 2 | - |
| Heavy artillery | 3 | 36 |
| Medium artillery | 3 | 24 |
| Light artillery | 3 | 8 |

## SHOOTING ROLLS TO HIT:
(Quality re-rolls apply.)

| ADVANTAGE | PoA | Minimum score to hit |
|---|---|---|
| Big advantage | ++ | 2 |
| Advantage | + | 3 |
| No advantage | No PoA | 4 |
| Disadvantage | - | 5 |
| Big disadvantage | - - | 6 |

## CLOSE COMBAT ROLLS TO HIT:
(Quality re-rolls apply.)

| ADVANTAGE | PoA | Minimum score to hit |
|---|---|---|
| Big advantage | ++ | 3 |
| Advantage | + | 4 |
| No advantage | No PoA | 4 |
| Disadvantage | - | 5 |
| Big disadvantage | - - | 5 |

## SHOOTING POAS

| Nearest rank of target is: | | | If shooting with: |
|---|---|---|---|
| Any one of | Unarmoured mounted battle troops unless entirely 1 base deep | + | Bow, bow*, sling or javelins |
| | Fully armoured gendarmes | - | Bow, bow*, sling or javelins |
| | Any mounted troops | - | Musket, musket*, salvo, arquebus, carbine, pistol |
| | Elephants | + | Any except bow, bow* or sling |
| | Battle wagons | - | Any except bombs or artillery |
| | Artillery | -- | Artillery |
| | Fully armoured foot | -- | Bow, bow*, sling, or javelins |
| | | - | Artillery, carbine, pistol or crossbow |
| | | | Any of the following at long range: musket, musket* or salvo |
| | Armoured or heavily armoured foot | - | Artillery, carbine, pistol, crossbow, bow, bow*, sling, or javelins |
| | | | Any of the following at long range: musket, musket* or salvo |
| | Unarmoured foot | - | Artillery, carbine, pistol or crossbow |
| | Any target | 0 | Regimental guns |
| Any one of | Any | - | Any, if shooting at a battle group in close combat other than as an overlap only |
| | Any | | Any, if shooting by a battle group which is in close combat other than as an overlap only |
| | Any | | Any, if shooting to rear (Light Horse with bow only) |
| | Any | | Captured or recaptured artillery |
| | Any foot | | Foot battle troops with ***threatened flank*** (see ***glossary***) |
| Battle troops which<br>• have any file of their battle group in 3 or more ranks (unless this is the 3 deep pike file of a Swedish brigade formation), or<br>• are a tercio, or<br>• are mob, or<br>• are in ***square***, or<br>• are shot at from ***enfilade*** (see ***glossary***) | | + | Artillery |
| In cover or behind field fortifications or an obstacle | | - | Any except heavy or medium artillery |

## MELEE POAS

| | | | |
|---|---|---|---|
| Any one of… | Pike or protected shot, unless FRAGMENTED or SEVERELY DISORDERED | + | against any mounted |
| | Pistol | + | against any except:<br>• elephants<br>• STEADY foot who are any of pike, protected shot or foot with bayonet<br>• mounted swordsmen if the pistoliers are not STEADY |
| | Swordsmen | + | against any except elephants, STEADY pistols, or STEADY foot who are any of spearmen, pike, protected shot or foot with bayonet |
| | Spearmen in 2 or more ranks, unless FRAGMENTED or SEVERELY DISORDERED | + | against any except pike in 3 or more ranks, protected pike, protected shot or foot with bayonet |
| | Heavy Weapon | + | against any except pike in 3 or more ranks, protected pike, protected shot or foot with bayonet.<br>Also cancels enemy 'better armour' POA if any. |
| | Elephants | + | against any |
| Pike in 4 or more ranks, unless FRAGMENTED or SEVERELY DISORDERED | | + | against any |
| Protected cavaliers, protected horse or protected determined horse | | + | If they are at an overall disadvantage against any mounted after all other POAs of both sides have been totalled and netted out (raising - to 0, worse to -) |
| Better Armour (front rank) | | + | against any except shot, heavy weapon, elephants or battle wagons |
| Fighting enemy in two directions | | - | unless early tercio, or later tercio/keil not in contact to its rear |
| *Uphill* or foot defending field fortifications, an obstacle or a riverbank | | + | |
| If fighting as an overlap - foot with swordsmen or heavy weapon capability or warriors | | ++ | **Final overall POA regardless of all other factors** |

## IMPACT POAS

| | | | | |
|---|---|---|---|---|
| Any one of | Foot using salvo. Pike in the same battle group as foot using salvo | | ++ | against any foot |
| Any one of | Impact foot. Pike in the same battle group as impact foot. | | + | against any foot |
| Any one of | Pike or protected shot, if not charging and not FRAGMENTED or SEVERELY DISORDERED | | + | against any mounted |
| Any one of | Spearmen in 2 or more ranks, if not charging and not FRAGMENTED or SEVERELY DISORDERED | | + | against any mounted |
| Any one of | Spearmen in 2 or more ranks, if not FRAGMENTED or SEVERELY DISORDERED | | + | against any foot except pike in 3 or more ranks, protected pike, protected shot, foot with bayonet or impact foot |
| Any one of | Heavy weapon | | + | against any foot except pike in 3 or more ranks, protected pike, protected shot, foot with bayonet or impact foot |
| Any one of | Foot with light spear unless they are charging mounted shock troops | | + | against any except pike in 3 or more ranks, protected pike, protected shot, foot with bayonet or impact foot |
| Any one of | Regimental guns | | 0 | against any |
| Any one of | Elephants | | + | against any |
| Any one of | Battle wagons | | + | against any mounted |
| Any one of | Pistol | | + | against any except elephants, battle wagons, impact mounted or non-charging STEADY foot who are any of pike, protected shot or foot with bayonet |
| Any one of | Heavy lancers | Only in open terrain (see *glossary*) | + | against any except elephants, battle wagons, pistol or non-charging STEADY foot who are any of spearmen, pike, protected shot or foot with bayonet |
| Any one of | Light lancers | Only in open terrain (see *glossary*) | + | against any except elephants, battle wagons, heavy lancers, pistol or non-charging STEADY foot who are any of spearmen, pike, protected shot or foot with bayonet |
| Any one of | Impact mounted | Only in open terrain (see *glossary*) | + | against any except elephants, battle wagons, heavy lancers or non-charging STEADY foot who are any of spearmen, pike, protected shot or foot with bayonet |
| Pike in 4 or more ranks whether charging or not, unless FRAGMENTED or SEVERELY DISORDERED | | Only in open terrain (see *glossary*) | + | against any |
| Any mounted | | Only in open terrain (see *glossary*) | + | against any light foot, dragoons, warriors or unprotected medium foot without bayonet |
| Protected cavaliers, protected horse or protected determined horse | | | + | If they are at an overall disadvantage against any mounted after all other POAs of both sides have been totalled and netted out (raising - to 0, worse to -) |
| *Uphill* or foot defending field fortifications, an obstacle or a riverbank | | | + | |
| Charge counting as on flank or rear | | | ++ | **Final overall POA regardless of all other factors** |

## DEATH ROLL

| |
|---|
| Roll 1 dice for the battle group. (**No re-rolls**). |
| • Add +1 to the dice score if the battle group started the battle with only 2 bases |
| • Add +2 to the dice score if the battle group won/drew a close combat or the hits suffered were from shooting (unless the *majority* of the shooting dice - whether they scored hits or not - were attributable to any combination of artillery, regimental guns and firearms). |
| If the score does not exceed the number of hits, remove a base. |
| If a base was removed, and there were more than 6 hits, deduct 6 from the hits and roll again for the remainder. (Use the same modifiers.) |

| AUTOBREAK | | | | |
|---|---|---|---|---|
| Initial BG size | Bases remaining to trigger autobreak | | | |
| | elite | superior | average | poor |
| 2 | 1 | 1 | 1 | 1 |
| 3 | 1 | 1 | 1 | 2 |
| 4 | 1 | 1 | 2 | 2 |
| 6 | 2 | 2 | 3 | 4 |
| 7 | 2 | 3 | 4 | 4 |
| 8 | 3 | 3 | 4 | 5 |
| 9 | 3 | 4 | 5 | 6 |
| 10 | 3 | 4 | 5 | 6 |
| 12 | 4 | 5 | 7 | 8 |
| 14 | 5 | 6 | 8 | 9 |
| 16 | 6 | 7 | 9 | 11 |

| ATTRITION POINTS | |
|---|---|
| Each grand battle group currently BROKEN, routed off table or destroyed | 4 |
| Each grand battle group currently FRAGMENTED | 2 |
| Each grand battle group straggling off table | 2 |
| Each other battle group currently BROKEN, captured, routed off table or destroyed | 2 |
| Each other battle group currently FRAGMENTED | 1 |
| Each other battle group straggling or evaded off table | 1 |
| Camp sacked by enemy | 2 |

# COHESION

| REASONS TO TEST | |
|---|---|
| **Immediately** | **At the end of the current phase** |
| | A BG breaks etc. within 3 MUs - battle troops ignore light troops |
| A battle group charged by other than light foot when FRG | Artillery is captured for the first time within 3 MUs |
| Losing a close combat | A commander in line of command is lost within 3 MUs |
| Suffering 1 hit per 3 bases from shooting and/or warriors taking 2 hits from shooting by arty | **Joint Action Phase (JAP)** |
| | To bolster or rally a BG with a commander |

| COHESION TEST | | | | |
|---|---|---|---|---|
| **Throw 2 dice (Quality re-rolls apply). Score 7 to pass.** | | | | |
| MODIFIERS | | | | |
| Battle group suffered at least 1 HP2B from shooting* | | -1 | Commander in *line of command* (see *glossary*) in *command range* if battle group is not in close combat, or with the battle group if it is in close combat | +1 |
| Battle group suffered at least 1 HP3B from close combat** | | -1 | Extra if he is a great commander | +1 |
| At least 2 more hits received than inflicted in close combat** | | -1 | Battle group counts as *supported* (see *glossary*) | +1 |
| Battle group has lost at least 25% of its original bases | | -1 | Current Cohesion State | |
| Foot battle troops with *threatened flank* (see *glossary*) | | -1 | Disrupted or Severely Disordered | -1 |
| More than 1 reason to test | | -1 | Fragmented | -2 |
| | | | Broken | -3 |
| Any one of… | Any troops shot at by artillery*<br>OR<br>Elephants, cavalry, camelry or light horse shot at by firearms*<br>OR<br>Any troops testing for having lost close combat even partly against elephants**<br>OR<br>Medium foot, warriors or dragoons testing for having lost close combat even partly against mounted troops or heavy or determined foot in *open terrain*** (see *glossary*)<br>OR<br>Any troops testing for having lost impact phase combat even partly against lancers, impact mounted or foot using salvo**<br>OR<br>Foot testing for having lost impact phase combat even partly against impact foot** | -1 | * Only applies when testing as a result of shooting hits. The modifier for being shot at by artillery or firearms applies whether or not they scored the hits.<br>** Only applies when testing as a result of losing a close combat. The modifier for fighting specific enemy troop types applies whether or not these inflicted more hits on the battle group than it inflicted on them.<br>Other tests do not use these modifiers even if they occur in the same phase. | |

| RESULT | |
|---|---|
| **If the final score is:** | |
| 7 or more | • Rise one cohesion level if testing to bolster or rally the battle group.<br>• Otherwise no change in cohesion level. |
| 3, 4, 5 or 6 | • Drop one cohesion level (ignore if testing to bolster or rally the battle group). |
| 2 or less | • Drop two cohesion levels if:<br>  • Testing for losing a close combat in which the battle group received at least 2 more hits than it inflicted.<br>  • Testing for seeing friends break or commander lost.<br>• Otherwise drop one cohesion level (ignore if testing to bolster or rally the battle group). |

| Variable Movement Distance (VMD) | |
|---|---|
| Roll 1d6 | |
| 1 | -2 MUs |
| 2 | -1 MU |
| 3 or 4 | Normal distance |
| 5 | +1 MU |
| 6 | +2 MUs |
| **Quality re-rolls do not apply** | |

| QUALITY RE-ROLLS | |
|---|---|
| ELITE | Reroll 1's & 2's. Cannot go lower |
| SUPERIOR | Reroll 1's. |
| POOR | Reroll 6's. |

# GAME SET UP

| GAME SETUP PROCEDURE | |
|---|---|
| 1 | Roll for Initiative - The player gaining the initiative chooses the territory type. |
| **Selecting Terrain** | |
| 1 | Player with initiative selects his compulsory terrain piece from the priority pieces. |
| 2 | The other player selects his compulsory piece from the priority pieces. |
| 3 | The player with initiative selects 2-4 selections of available terrain. He cannot choose both a coast and a river. |
| 4 | The other player select 2-4 selections of remaining available terrain. He cannot choose a river, a coast or a village. |
| **Placing Terrain** | |
| 1 | Player with initiative places a river or coast if any. |
| 2 | Player with initiative places a village if any (including any integral hill). |
| 3 | Player with initiative places his compulsory item. |
| 4 | The other player places his compulsory item. |
| 5 | Player with initiative places his open spaces if any. |
| 6 | The other player places his open spaces. |
| 7 | Player with initiative places the rest of his terrain except roads. |
| 8 | The other player places the rest of his terrain except roads. |
| 9 | Player with initiative places roads if any. |
| 10 | The other player places roads if any. |
| 11 | Remove all open spaces. |
| **Army Deployment** | **For each number, each player in turn, starting with the player without initiative:** |
| 1 | Places his camp <= 10 MUs from his rear table edge.<br>Places FF markers <= 15 MUs from rear table edge, > 12 MUs from side table edges (leaving sufficient room to deploy the FF within those bounds). |
| 2 | Detaches any shot |
| 3 | Places any ambush markers in the 2 outer thirds of the table, <= 18 MUs from rear edge if without initiative, up to half-way across table if with initiative. Only ambush markers representing mounted troops, commanded shot or light troops (or dummy markers) can be placed within 12 MUs of a side table edge. |
| 4 | Records outflanking marches - commander, BGs and which flank. |
| 5 | Deploys BGs in alternate 25% batches. (See main rules). Light troops, artillery and forlorn hope <= 15 MUs from rear edge, other troops <= 10 MUs from rear edge. Only mounted troops, commanded shot and light troops can be deployed within 12 MUs of a side table edge. |
| 6 | Deploys FF on the FF markers <= 15 MUs from rear table edge, > 12 MUs from side tables edges.<br>Deploys the net difference in naval units if he has more than the other player. |
| 7 | Commits to dismounting if any. |
| 8 | Deploys commanders <= 15 MUs from rear table edge. |

## PRE-BATTLE INITIATIVE MODIFIERS

| | |
|---|---|
| +2 | C-in-C is a great commander |
| +1 | C-in-C is a field commander |
| +1 | The army has 10-24 bases of horse, determined horse, cavaliers, cavalry, light horse, camelry or dragoons, excluding commanders |
| +2 | The army has more than 24 bases of horse, determined horse, cavaliers, cavalry, light horse, camelry or dragoons, excluding commanders |

## TERRAIN SELECTION

| TERRAIN SELECTION | | | | | | | | | Maximum (priority) | | | | | | | | |
|---|---|---|---|---|---|---|---|---|---|---|---|---|---|---|---|---|---|
| **TERRITORY TYPE** | Open | BG | B | EF | P | G | F | V | M | SS | SH | Vg | I | GH | Ob | Rd | Rv/C |
| AGRICULTURAL | 2 | 3(2) | | 4(2) | 2 | | | 2 | | | 1 | 1 | | 2 | 2 | 2 | 1 |
| HILLY | | 3 | 3(1) | | 1 | 1 | 2 | | 1 | | 3(2) | 1 | 1 | 3 | 1 | 1 | 1 |
| WOODLANDS | | | 2 | | 2 | 1 | 4(2) | | 2 | | 1 | 1 | | 2 | 1 | 1 | 1 |
| STEPPES | 4(2) | 4 | 2 | | | 1 | | | | | | | | 1 | | | |
| MOUNTAINS | | | 2 | | 1 | 1 | 1 | | 1 | | 4(2) | 1 | 2 | | | 1 | 1 |
| TROPICAL | | | 2 | | | | 4(2) | | 2 | | 1 | 1 | 1 | 1 | | 1 | 1 |
| DESERT | 2 | 2 | 2 | | | 1 | | | | 4(2) | 1 | | 1 | 1 | | 1 | |
| **COLOUR KEY** | Open | Uneven | Rough | | | | Difficult | | | | | | Impassable | Special | | | |

## TERRAIN PLACEMENT

| DICE ROLL | Placement | DICE ROLL | Placement |
|---|---|---|---|
| 1 | Touching opponent's long edge | 2 | Touching your own long edge |
| 3 | Touching side edge or coast in opponent's half | 4 | Touching side edge or coast in your own half |
| 5 | In opponent's half > 8 MUs from any edge | 6 | In your own half > 8 MUs from any edge |
| Terrain Adjustment Dice | | | |
| 0-2 | No change permitted | 3-4 | Slide up to 6 MUs |
| 5 | Slide up to 12 MUs or pivot | 6+ | Can remove piece entirely |
| -1 on adjustment dice score for compulsory terrain. | | +1 on adj. dice score for impassable terrain, river or coast | |
| No piece can be placed (prior to adjustment) closer than 4 MUs to any other piece except: | | | |
| • Any piece can be placed closer than 4 MUs to a coast, river or road. | | | |
| • A road can be placed closer than 4 MUs to any piece, but not through it unless a village. | | | |
| • A road must pass through or touch a village if there is one. | | | |
| A river or a coast counts as 1 piece but 2 selections. A road counts as 1 piece and 1 selection. | | | |
| Rivers and coasts can be removed, but not slid or pivoted. | | | |

## AMBUSHES

The player with pre-battle initiative can place ambushes up to half way across the table from his side's rear table edge, in the two outer thirds of the table's width. The other player can place ambushes up to 18 MUs forward from his side's rear table edge, in the two outer thirds of the table's width. Only ambush markers representing mounted troops, commanded shot or light troops (or dummy markers) can be placed within 12 MUs of a side table edge.

Ambushes must not be visible from any part of the enemy deployment area for light troops (even if the enemy have no light troops).
Battle wagons and artillery cannot ambush.

## OUTFLANKING MARCH ARRIVAL TEST

| **roll two dice for each outflanking march (no re-rolls)** | |
|---|---|
| **modifier** | |
| +1 | If the flank march is led by a field commander |
| -1 | If the flank march includes foot other than light troops |
| **score** | **result** |
| 9 or less | Roll again next turn |
| 10 or more | Success – see below |

## STRAGGLING TEST

| On the turn when the outflanking march should arrive, roll two dice for each battle group to see if it is straggling. Straggling battle groups will not arrive in time for the battle. | |
|---|---|
| **modifier** | |
| +1 | Gendarmes, cavaliers, horse, determined horse, cavalry, camelry and light troops |
| -1 | Elephants, battle wagons and artillery |
| **A battle group is straggling (and will not arrive) if it scores less than 5. Quality re-rolls apply** | |